Note to the Student

Dear Student,

If you winced when you learned the price of this textbook, you are experiencing what is known as "sticker shock" in today's economy. Yes, textbooks are expensive, and we don't like it any more than you do. Many of us here at PWS-KENT have sons and daughters of our own attending college, or we are attending school part-time ourselves. However, the prices of our books are dictated by cost factors involved in producing them. The costs of typesetting, paper, printing, and binding have risen significantly each year along with everything else in our economy.

The prices of college textbooks have increased less than most other items over the past fifteen years. Compare your texts sometime to a general trade book, i.e., a novel or nonfiction book, and you will easily see substantial differences in the quality of design, paper, and binding. These quality features of college textbooks cost money.

Textbooks should not be considered only as an expense. Other than your professors, your textbooks are your most important source for what you learn in college. What's more, the textbooks you keep can be valuable resources in your future career and life. They are the foundation of your professional library. Like your education, your textbooks are one of your most important investments.

We are concerned, and we care. We pledge to do everything in our power to keep our textbook prices under control, while maintaining the same high standards of quality you and your professors require.

Wayne A. Barcomb
President
PWS-KENT Publishing Company

THE KENT SERIES IN BUSINESS EDUCATION

Word/Information Processing: Concepts, Procedures, and Systems, Second Edition *Arntson*
MS/PC DOS on the IBM PC and Compatibles: Concepts, Exercises, and Applications *Arntson and Auvil*
Word/Information Processing: Exercises, Applications, and Procedures *Arntson and Todesco*
Modern Business English: A Systems Approach *Carbone*
HOW 5: A Handbook for Office Workers, Fifth Edition *Clark and Clark*
Universal Transcription *Clark and Clark*
Business English, Third Edition *Guffey*
Essentials of Business Communication *Guffey*
Business Communications: Principles and Methods, Eighth Edition *Himstreet and Baty*
Automated Office Systems for Managers and Professionals *Kupsh and Rhodes*
Self-Paced Business Math, Third Edition *Lee*
Records Management in the Computer Age *Lundgren and Lundgren*
Business Mathematics, Fifth Edition *McCready*
Office Machines: Electronic Calculators, Seventh Edition *McCready*
Business Math Basics, Third Edition *Swindle*
Communications in Business, Fifth Edition *Wells*

RECORDS MANAGEMENT
IN THE COMPUTER AGE

TERRY D. LUNDGREN
CAROL A. LUNDGREN
Utah State University

Acquisitions Editor: Read Wickham
Production Editor/Cover Designer: Susan Krikorian
Compositor: G&S Typesetters, Inc.
Text Designer: Jean Coulombre
Interior Illustrator: Debra Doherty
Manufacturing Coordinator: Marcia Locke
Cover Printer: John P. Pow Company
Text Printer/Binder: Maple-Vail Book Manufacturing Group

Cover photo courtesy of Clayton J. Price. Reprinted with permission.

PWS-KENT Publishing Company is a division of Wadsworth, Inc.

Printed in the United States of America

1 2 3 4 5 6 7 8 9—93 92 91 90 89

Library of Congress Cataloging-in-Publication Data

Lundgren, Terry D.
Records management in the computer age.

Includes index.
1. Records—Management. 2. Information resources management.
I. Lundgren, Carol A. II. Title.
HF5736.L88 1989 651.5 88-29134
ISBN 0-534-91873-5

Preface

The efficient storage and retrieval of information is essential to the successful operation of businesses, organizations, governments, and societies. Most individuals also can profit from a careful plan of information storage and retrieval for their personal records. However, the operations and procedures for a productive information system do not automatically spring into existence. Indeed, because records management skills must be acquired through study and thoughtful application, businesses sometimes overlook this necessity and "reinvent the wheel" to deal with their information resources. Fortunately, information increasingly is being recognized as a valuable business resource that must be efficiently managed. Also increasingly, the field of records management is called upon to provide the knowledge and skills for effective information management. This text is designed to meet these crucial needs.

Records Management in the Computer Age is for the practitioner, the student, and the teacher who want state-of-the-art information on the management of records. Therefore, the text is suitable for an introductory records management course at the postsecondary level, as well as for a reference guide to records management on the job. The text includes a wealth of practical examples from the latest ideas in manual paper systems to the exciting interface of records management with computer database management systems. In fact, the last three chapters are written specifically to help the reader integrate records management and database management.

This book contains sixteen chapters divided into two major parts. The first part, "Records Management Procedures and Equipment," provides a framework for understanding all aspects of the field of records management. The second part, "Records Management Applications in Business and Government," provides specific examples of records management in the real world. If this book is used as the primary text for a class in records management on the semester system, we recommend that the chapters be read in sequence, approximately one chapter per week. On a quarter system, the teacher may wish to assign the first ten chapters during the first eight weeks and use selected chapters from the second part of the textbook for discussion during the last two weeks of the quarter.

Each chapter begins with a set of learning goals that define the scope of the chapter. Then the body of the chapter material is organized by major heading and subheading. The chapters conclude with a summary, a list of terms, discussion questions that review the material, activities that require application of the concepts through directed projects, and references for further reading. A highlight that helps clarify a particular concept or situation follows several chapters. The appendices include information on standard filing rules, publications in the field, and alphabetic divisions. The glossary lists important terms and their definitions in alphabetical order. Finally, an index to the subjects discussed in the text is provided.

The teacher's manual that accompanies this textbook provides an outline for each chapter, answers to discussion questions, notes on the activities, definitions of terms, teaching suggestions, exercises, transparency masters, and test questions.

We wish to express our gratitude to the many professionals in the field who contributed their time and knowledge. Those who made significant contributions include Cindy Wheeler, Records Clerk in The Budge Clinic; Susan Lewis, Office Manager for the Logan City Police Department; Gwen Moore, ARMA International; William Testerman, Corporate Manager for Hughes Aircraft Company; and Dawn Jackson, Reservations Supervisor for the Salt Lake City Marriott Hotel. Also, we would like to thank the equipment manufacturers who provided photographs and the reviewers who guided us with their expert opinions throughout this endeavor.

We are indebted to the staff of PWS-KENT, who gave us this opportunity to share our ideas and knowledge. We wish to thank our acquisitions editor, Read Wickham, whose insights were especially helpful in the early stages.

Finally, we encourage users of this text to write us at any time with comments or suggestions.

Terry and Carol Lundgren

Contents

Part

1

Records Management Procedures and Equipment

Chapter 1 The State of Business Records Management

Learning Goals

1. To understand the meaning of records management.
2. To know why records management is important.
3. To become familiar with some methods and equipment used in the past to manage records.
4. To consider the effects of computer technology on records management.
5. To see the relationship between records management and information management.
6. To recognize an organizational records management cycle.

Introduction

What is a record and what is records management? Anyone who plans to handle records efficiently needs to understand these terms. He or she also needs some ideas about the past and the future of records management. Chapter 1 provides this introductory information. In addition, we have tried to impress on the reader the importance of records management and set the stage for future chapters. Finally, we hope that you, the reader, will begin to view records management as both an essential *and* an interesting aspcct of business activity. Toward that end, our perspective of records management throughout this text is based on our business experience, case studies, articles about records management, and research in the records management field.

The Meaning of Records Management

Records management is a complex term that requires careful definition. One reason is because there is no universal definition of a record. In fact, any information that is recorded in some way can be a record depending on who is doing the defining. Therefore, we must start with a common understanding of what we mean by a record.

What Is a Record?

A *record* is evidence of an event that is in a tangible format that allows it to be retrieved. Let's consider each part of this definition.

First, a record is evidence of an event, but it must be evidence to more than one person. Another way of saying this is that a record should contain data that are meaningful in a social sense. *Data* are usually defined as evidence that serves as a basis for decision making, measuring, calculating, or discussion (McLeod, 1986: 15). Processed data or data that have been made more meaningful to someone is the definition of *information*. Whether an item is data or information depends on the context in which it is used. For example, a person who maintains a client mailing list would view each entry on the list as information. A person who accesses the mailing list to determine how many clients live in a particular location would view the entries as data that provide information about clients.

Second, for an item to be a record, it must be stored in some tangible form. The three major forms in which records appear are paper, film, and magnetic media. A *paper record* is data, pictures, or text stored on anything composed of the chemical composition of paper, regardless of the size, color, or weight of the paper. A *film record* is data, pictures, or text stored on film—sometimes a particular type of film, such as microfilm. *Magnetic media* are data, pictures, or text stored and retrieved through magnetic encoding and are typically associated with computers. Floppy disks, tapes, and fixed or hard disks are examples of magnetic media. But other tangible forms for records also exist. Climatological data, as captured in the rings of a cross-section of a tree trunk, are evidence meaningful to climatologists (Williams, 1986: 88); although such records may be of no use to a business, they are nevertheless records as far as climatologists are concerned. In the following chapters, however, we will be concerned with those records that are stored in paper, film, or magnetic media form.

The third condition for an item to be a record is that it must be retrievable. Each of the three forms named above (paper, film, and magnetic media) is retrievable because it can be stored and brought out again later.

A *nonrecord* is any information that does not exist in a tangible form, or that cannot be stored or retrieved. One example of a nonrecord is data obtained through ordinary conversation; but this nonrecord can become a record under certain circumstances. For example, conversation may be accepted in a court of law as "hearsay evidence." When the court accepts this evidence, it becomes a record. At that time, the evidence also is converted to one of the previously described forms (paper, film, or magnetic media) and it becomes retrievable.

In summary, an item is a record if (1) it is evidence of an event or has societal meaning, (2) it is stored in a tangible form, and (3) it can be retrieved.

What Is Management?

Management is the planning, staffing, organizing, directing, and controlling of a business activity. *Planning* means establishing objectives and the methods to achieve them. Planning can involve establishing policies as well as procedures. *Staffing* is selecting the personnel to do the activity. *Organizing* is arranging the tasks, people, and resources to accomplish the objectives set in the planning stage. *Directing* is the training, supervision, and motivation of personnel. *Controlling* is measuring how well the objectives have been met and, if they have not been accomplished, making adjustments.

Records management, then, is the planning, staffing, organizing, directing, and controlling of records and those processes associated with records. Records management is organized around the life cycle of a record, which begins with the creation or acquisition of a record and ends with the permanent storage or destruction of the record. (The stages in the life cycle of a record are discussed in detail in Chapter 5, "The Records Information System.")

The Importance of Records Management

In an industrial society, most records are business records. These records are identification and evidence of business transactions. Their primary use is to accurately identify location, quantity, and quality at a specific time. The records identify people, services, and goods in the recording of economic transactions.

In the modern industrial world, records are indispensable for daily operations and activities. Accurate and reliable information is essential for nearly every transaction. Word of mouth, personal identification, and memory are often insufficient to provide accurate information in our society. Just consider what is involved when a person contacts a company to verify a statement of account—place yourself in that person's position. First, the business needs to locate a record of your statement. Then previous records that verify the information on that statement must be located—probably by you as well as by the business representative. Finally, you and the business representative must agree that you are referring to the same records and that the information is accurate.

Maintaining accurate records that can be retrieved is essential to the continuation of every business. Fast retrieval of records has become so important that it is a major concern in business today. For example, through automated processes, the United States Department of State now has the capability to process and retrieve passport records more rapidly than ever before. The department uses a combination of bar coding technology, high-speed microfilming, and computer-assisted retrieval to provide passport customers with the fastest possible response to requests for information. (Each of these automated processes is discussed in later chapters.)

For information that does not require a high level of accuracy over time, and that is not likely ever to be required in another physical location, records are probably not as important. For example, small groups such as neighborhood committees usually do not require much in the way of records. Most decisions and matters of importance to the group can be remembered by the members. Small business owners sometimes think that the same is true for them. Consequently, the small business owner may decide to keep only a few records that seem to be particularly important—other records are not kept or may not be kept safely. The result could be disastrous if the owner died or the business was destroyed. If a business loses your records, you undoubtedly would be concerned not only about how the business manages its records, but also about how it manages all of its operations!

Even when records are managed well, a disaster makes one realize just how important records are. Examples of business disasters like the following one abound. At 2:45 A.M., a truck driver noticed smoke coming from the roof vents of the Pender County Farm Bureau Insurance office. When firemen arrived, they discovered that the fire was in the attic of the one-story building. Firemen could not get to the fire's source due to a double roof system that had been created during recent remodeling. As the fire raged out of control, the agency manager realized that the building was doomed. The office had had 8,500 letter-size files consisting primarily of casualty and life policies for customers in the area; all but 1,000 of these files had been housed in open-shelf filing equipment. The manager requested that firemen hose down the open-shelf filing equipment since it contained records that had not been backed up in another location. When the fire was completely out, the building had been gutted and the heat had melted most of the plastic equipment such as telephones and computer terminals. Ten percent of the 8,500 files had been totally destroyed; another 50 percent had been at least partially charred; the remaining 40 percent were still intact but had been water damaged. Fortunately, the office was able to restore many of its records through disaster recovery procedures. (Methods for restoring records are discussed in Chapters 10 and 12.)

Of course, mismanagement can be as hazardous for a business as a disaster. The inability to find a necessary document, the misplacement of orders, or the misfiling of important documents all will lead to a waste of time and money, as well as customer dissatisfaction. Many businesses that fail have had a records management problem. Certainly, records are necessary, and this need has been recognized practically since the caveman era.

Past Attempts to Manage Records

The history of records could, without exaggeration, be called the history of the world. People have kept records in some form since the beginning of human society. However, simply recording information or having records is not the same as managing records. People have recorded information on clay tablets, walls of caves, parchment, and papyrus. Very little, if any, management of those records was done (or needed) because the volume of information did not require it.

The world's earliest known written records are inscriptions on clay tablets. These inscriptions were written in the fourth millennium B.C., and are records of accounts and receipts (Friberg, 1984: 110–11). The need for accurate records was a catalyst in the development of writing and numeric systems. Similarly, the development of paper was encouraged by the need to solve problems in the storage and retrieval of cumbersome materials, such as clay tablets.

The *spindle file* was one of the earliest methods of storing paper records, designed in the sixteenth century. This file, which is still in use today, is simply a thin upright spike on which papers are impaled. Although a modest invention, the spindle concept was revolutionary. Paper documents could be stored on spindles; they did not take up much space and the records stayed put! Today the spindle file is still used to store notes, bills, and similar small records.

In the seventeenth century, documents were handwritten by clerks. So much time was required to make a record of a business transaction that merchants often kept only mental notes. Other documents, such as court records, were kept quite well. There are over 500 existing records of the Salem witchcraft trials—documents that were prepared by court reporters while sitting in the

Figure 1.1 More records? Just use a bigger spindle!

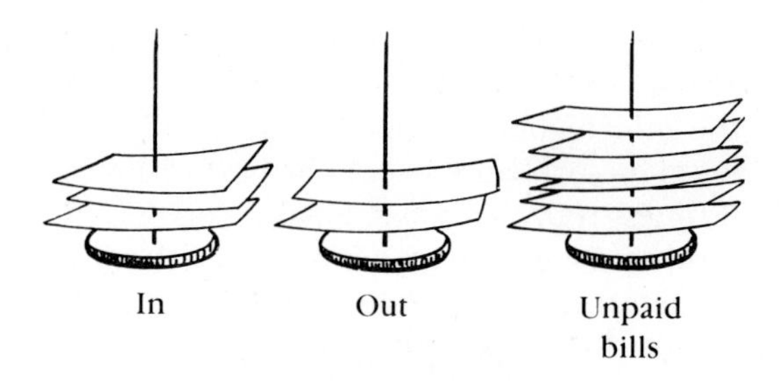

courtroom writing with quill pens and ink on parchment (Coltan, 1988: 34). As the population increased and geographical boundaries expanded, the scope of business activities increased. The population became industrialized and records moved from written to printed form. The need to keep even more records and to manage them more efficiently became apparent.

Throughout history, innovations and inventions have affected how records are managed. On the one hand, the need for better records management encouraged innovation; on the other hand, innovative thinking and the resulting inventions have altered the ways in which records are managed. Sometimes it is difficult to determine which came first—the need for better records management or the inventions that made better records management possible. For example, the typewriter improved the speed at which we could create records (accelerating the number of records that could be produced) and thus spurred the need for better records management. Typewritten documents were easier to read and arrange than handwritten ones—making better records management possible.

Vertical filing is a particularly important records management method inspired by the need for better retrieval. This system, in which papers stand on end between supporting guides, came into popular use in the 1800s and continues to be an effective method for records storage today. Paper records were originally stored flat in drawers; as the quantity of records increased, the record drawers were alphabetized. Nevertheless, retrieving documents from stacks of records was slow and inefficient. With increased volume came more drawers and more stacks; the storage and retrieval problems became greater and greater. Vertical filing made organization and retrieval of records much easier and faster.

Some inventions had little to do with records management initially but they did inspire new methods of records management. Two such inventions are the camera and the computer.

Figure 1.2 Early Storage in Flat Files

The invention of the camera made filming records possible. Today many records are stored in film form, which has several advantages over paper storage, including space savings and better accessibility. In fact, film storage is a major component of records management. (Chapter 8 provides a detailed discussion of the processes and equipment used to store records on film.)

The invention of the computer was motivated by the need to process large amounts of data very rapidly. The forerunner of computer technology, the punched card, was used to tabulate census data as early as 1890. Because a computer can complete standardized operations quickly and access large amounts of data, it proved very useful for processing records. Today the computer is performing all of the traditional functions of records management—and managing records in ways that were not feasible before the computer age. (Chapters 15 and 16 focus on the computerization of records management.)

A New Direction for Records Management?

Computer technology is revolutionizing the field of records management. It is adding to and expanding the field as well as replacing some of the existing functions. Records management by computer has raised several questions: Will magnetic media replace paper in the office? Where does records management fit into information processing? What is the difference between records management and database management?

Records Management and the Paperless Office

Whether paper will eventually disappear is a current topic of controversy. Some office experts believe that paper records will continue to increase indefinitely and be stored and retrieved in the tried-and-true filing cabinet (Minicucci, 1986: 30). Others contend that paper records will become unnecessary and all information will be stored on film or magnetic media or in computer memory (the "paperless office" idea). Which view is correct? Are we moving toward the paperless office or the "less-paper" office? Or will paper records continue to increase at current rates?

Paper is one of the most expensive, least transportable, and most cumbersome storage media available today (Mahmarian, 1984: 35). Yet it is the most familiar media; it is easily processed by people; and a substantial amount of information is presently stored on paper. An examination of paper production and consumption in the United States shows that paper use continues to increase, though the *rate* of increase has slowed slightly (Bureau of the Census, 1987). Some offices are, in fact, paperless and others are moving toward the less-paper office. However, it seems likely that storage and retrieval of paper records will continue to be an important records management function.

Records Management, Information Processing, and Database Management

When records are organized via computer, people can ask the computer questions about those records and the computer will search for information. In addition to providing efficient storage and retrieval, the computer allows users to obtain information about the records as a group. This is called the *database function*—an accepted subset of information processing but a new aspect of records management (Tellefsen, 1984: 65–74). To understand where records management fits in with respect to information processing and database management, we must re-examine the meaning of a record.

A record can be either data or information, depending on the context of its use. For example, suppose you want to know if an insurance company has any policyholders younger than fifteen years of age. The insurance records are paper documents stored in vertical files. As evidence of the policy, the records are data. If you search the records and determine that there are two policyholders younger than fifteen years, then those records are information. The process of searching for and retrieving data has created information. *Information processing* is defined as processing that transforms data into information (O'Brien, 1985). Records management is concerned with the *methods* of storage and retrieval of that information. Information processing includes database management. *Database management* is the planning, controlling, and organizing of a database. A *database* is any body of coherent data; for example, the names and addresses of customers, or all of the journals that deal with psychology. Therefore, database management is closely related to records management because information retrieval is a necessary activity in database management.

Information retrieval means getting information from wherever it is stored. A person performs one step in information retrieval when he recalls information stored in his brain cells; for example, where to find telephone numbers. That person performs another step in information retrieval when he looks up a particular telephone number in a telephone book. The first step requires no records management by itself, but the second step requires that the information be stored in some retrievable format with which the user is familiar.

Records management is indeed moving in new directions, and businesses must try to manage their records within a continually changing environment. As businesses change and grow over time, and incorporate new technologies, they must pass through a series of stages collectively known as the organizational records management cycle.

The Organizational Records Management Cycle

The organizational *records management cycle* is the sequence of events that societies, organizations, small businesses, and even individuals go through over a period of several years or decades in their attempts to manage records. This cycle (not to be confused with the records cycle discussed in Chapter 5) actually begins *after* records are created and stored.

A typical scenario begins with Stage I, the *maintenance stage*, in which the new or existing business is operating successfully. In this stage, there are no serious records management problems. Whatever system of records management the business has is considered adequate. If the business alters its characteristics or increases in size, or both, then it will enter Stage II, the *growth stage.* The requirements for records management increase as the volume of records and the variety of types of records increase. At some point, the business may enter Stage III, the *problem stage.* In this stage one or more of the following symptoms is evident:

- There are no guidelines for organizing records.
- The need to "get organized" is apparent although little or no time seems to be available to do so.
- Few or no provisions exist for the maintenance and updating of records.
- Increasing numbers of records cannot be located.
- Retrieval time of more and more records is unacceptably slow.
- No system exists for disposal of records.

Finally, the situation becomes intolerable, often as the result of a crisis. The business has entered Stage IV, the *disaster stage.* The crisis may occur when a specific record is needed and cannot be located, whereupon heads roll and a crash program for better records management is instituted.

If short-term remedies are instituted, the business finds itself back in Stage III—the problem stage—faced with its original problems. However, if a significant investment in procedures, equipment, and people is made and the new system functions well, problems disappear or are reduced to manageable levels and the business returns to Stage I, the maintenance level.

The disaster stage is the end of the line. Either the business deals successfully with the situation and returns to an earlier stage or the business continues to deal with repeating disasters until it runs out of resources.

This organizational records management sequence is a repeating cycle. Although the time a business spends in a particular phase is determined by many factors, the most important include the changes and

Figure 1.3 Rise in Excess Costs Due to Poor Records Management

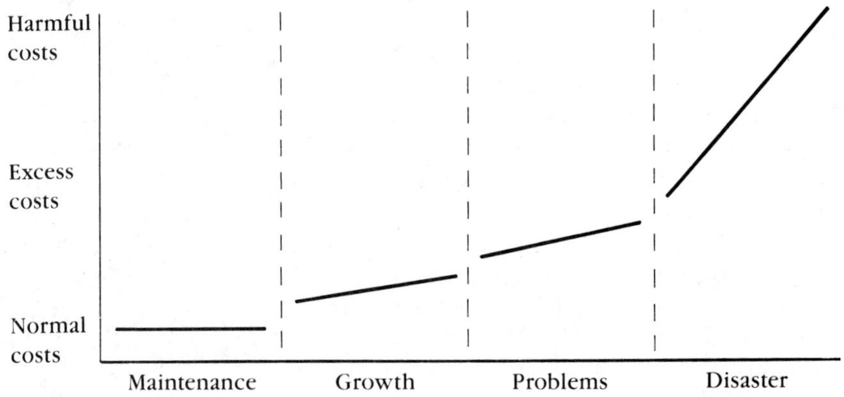

growth of the business as well as the changes and growth of the surrounding society.

Excess costs or resources that accompany the stages of an organizational records management cycle can grow at an alarming rate. *Excess costs* are those costs that occur as a result of a poor records management system. A poor system incurs needless costs in wasted time and duplication of effort. One of the largest elements of excess cost in a business is the time spent waiting for the retrieval of records. Figure 1.3 illustrates this rise in excess costs.

A business can effectively remain in Stages I and II (maintenance and growth) through systematic evaluation and updating of its records management program. Similarly, a business with slow growth and the ability to absorb continuing excess costs can remain in Stage III (problem) for a long time. Most businesses, however, cycle through these stages, spending most of their time in some part of the problem stage. In reality, the first three stages of the organizational cycle are an accepted part of business activity. With good records management, however, a business can avoid the disaster stage.

Summary

Records management involves the planning, organizing, staffing, controlling, and communicating of the procedures needed for records—evidence with a social value that is stored in a retrievable format. Business records are essential in modern society to track business transactions accurately. The expanding scope of business activities and the increase in records have created a need for more efficient records management.

Inventions have resulted from the need for better records management and have contributed to its efficiency. The spindle file and the vertical method of filing paper records are examples of inventions that resulted from the need for better records management. The camera and the computer, too, are examples of inventions that have influenced records management.

Records management is concerned with the methods of storage and retrieval, whereas information processing involves methods that transform data into information. One aspect of information processing, database management, is closely related to records management. Records management currently involves the management of both paper and computer records.

An organization typically goes through four stages in its cycle of records management: maintenance, growth, problem, and disaster. The time a business spends in each stage depends on the changes in and growth of the business. With good records management, the business can avoid the disaster stage.

List of Terms

records management
record
data
information
paper record
film record
magnetic media
nonrecord
management
planning
staffing
organizing
directing
controlling
spindle file
vertical filing
database function
information processing
database management
database
information retrieval
organizational records management cycle
maintenance stage
problem stage
growth stage
disaster stage
excess costs

Discussion Questions

1. What are the requirements for something to be considered a "record"?
2. Is it possible to accurately define the term "records management"? Why or why not?
3. What is the difference between data and information?
4. What is meant by "information processing"?
5. What is the relationship between inventions, such as the camera and the computer, and records management methods?
6. Name and explain two historical methods of records management.
7. What is the relationship between records management and database management?
8. What factors support a trend toward the "paperless" office?
9. What is the typical sequence of events in an organization's records management cycle?
10. How are excess costs related to the records management cycle?

Activities

1. List your personal records. (Be careful. Not everything you store is a record!)

2. Management is sometimes difficult to define in terms of what is actually happening. Interview a manager to determine what managers do. Can you fit your results into the text definition?
3. Some early societies used to use a person as the official "records keeper" to keep business accounts. What problems would a business encounter today with this approach?
4. A library is a "paper-intensive" system. Describe a library of the future that would not use paper.
5. Using the popular news (magazines, newspapers, TV, or radio), give a documented example of an organization at each stage of the records management cycle.
6. Go to an office supply store that sells spindle files. How much do they cost? Are there different kinds? Who uses them and what are they used for?

References

Bureau of the Census. *Statistical Abstract of the United States, 1987*, 107th ed. (Washington, D.C.: U.S. Government Printing Office, 1987).

Colton, Norah. "Court Reporting at the Salem Witchcraft Trials." *National Shorthand Reporter* 49, no. 6 (April 1988): 34–35.

Dixon, Debra. "Information Salvage: The Tobacco Connection." *Records Management Quarterly* 22, no. 1 (January 1988): 15–17, 132.

Friberg, Joran. "Numbers and Measures in the Earliest Written Records." *Scientific American* 250 (February 1984): 110–18.

McLeod, Raymond, Jr. *Management Information Systems*, 3rd ed. (Chicago: Science Research Associates, 1986).

Mahmarian, Richard E. "Information Transfer Technology Evolves from New COM Developments." *Information Management* 18 (June 1984): 35.

Minicucci, Rick. "Managing a Melange of Media." *Today's Office* 21 (August 1986): 29–34.

O'Brien, James A. *Computers in Business Management*, 4th ed. (Homewood, Ill.: Richard D. Irwin, 1985).

Tellefsen, Gerald. "No Requiem for Records Management." *Modern Office Technology* 29 (October 1984): 65–74.

Williams, George E. "The Solar Cycle in Precambrian Time." *Scientific American* 255 (August 1986): 88–89.

Chapter 1 Highlight

The Cycle of Business Records for the Individual

The cycle of business records, from the maintenance stage through the disaster stage, applies to individuals as well as organizations. All records that will be stored, retrieved, and updated are subject to the cycle, regardless of whether those records are in a large or small system. Discussing the cycle on a personal level may enable you to conceptualize the stages more easily. Also, a records manager whose personal records are well organized probably will be more committed to good records management in a business setting. Finally, good records management at the individual level has the same payoff as good records management at the business level—increased productivity.

Most individuals, like most businesses, are in the problem stage of records management. As we go through life, our personal records expand both in volume and in scope. Again, like most businesses, our personal records expansion is slow and unspectacular. The volume of personal records—from photographs to tax returns—steadily grows and new records series are added as we expand our obligations and careers. People start collections and inventories: they save vehicle titles, old tax information, souvenirs, and personal memorabilia. Because we rarely monitor our personal records efficiency, it is easy to slip into the problem stage.

In the problem stage, excessive time is spent attempting to locate important documents; some records cannot be found, and others that accumulate should be purged. Now we are candidates for the disaster stage. Just as in organizations, the disaster stage is unanticipated and often the result of a significant event. For the individual, it could be a routine police patrol stop and subsequent request for automobile registration—which can't be found! Or the mail may bring your federal income tax forms and you will have to search for the necessary records. Sales of small file cabinets, folders, and other records equipment increase around tax time; merchandisers recognize this as a high probability time for an individual's disaster stage, or the individual's recognition of the problem stage characterized by the "I've got to get organized" syndrome.

The steady sales of "personal business management systems" such as small notebooks, calendars, and scheduling materials also prove that individuals often feel a need to organize their personal work records. Similar to personal records, these are records people use in their jobs for work-related activities and they are usually located around the workplace (for example, a desk). Included here might be the floppy disks and documentation used on a microcomputer. Too often, these records are at the problem stage, continually bumping into the disaster stage. How often have we heard the phrase "I've got to get organized" in the workplace!

Remember, good records management starts at the individual level. (How much time have you wasted looking in vain for a record that "should be around here"?) As you read this text, you will gain ideas for increasing the efficiency of your personal records management. For now we suggest that the following procedures be considered for productive personal records management:

1. Don't go crazy when the "get organized" feeling comes over you. Categorizing and storing seldom-used records by a complex scheme will not likely be remembered at a later date. A practical method is to organize the items physically by subject. Keep these items in this box and those items in that container.
2. Keep things organized. Don't pile the record items up intending to "get to them later." If you have specific locations for the record items, place them there immediately; if a record item does not have a location, make one. Put the "I don't know what to do with this" items in a specific location and evaluate the entire pile at least once a week.
3. Don't wait until your records are needed (such as at tax time) to organize them. As a rule of thumb, inspect and organize each type of personal records at least twice a year. (Yes, this includes your wallet and/or purse.) Go through all of the items and throw away any that are now unrecognizable.

Chapter 2 Legislation Affecting Records Management

Learning Goals

1. To understand the effect of federal legislation on the development of records management methods.
2. To become familiar with legislation affecting records management: Paperwork Reduction Act, Freedom of Information Act, Privacy Act, and Copyright Act.
3. To understand the legal requirements for managing employee records to protect individual privacy.
4. To become familiar with the concept of "fair use" in copyright law as it pertains to paper records and magnetic media.

Introduction

There are thousands of federal, state, county, and local laws that regulate different types of records. There are laws that specify what information a record should contain, how it should be displayed, who can access the record, if copies can be made of the record, and how long the record must be retained. Basically, legal considerations generate three major concerns for records management: retention scheduling, standardization, and records security.

Retention scheduling involves determining how long records should be retained and the method of their disposal. Most records are retained for legal reasons and the legislation regarding time limitations are clear. A *Fortune* 500 company may have hundreds of laws regulating its business records. (The relationship of regulations to the retention schedule is discussed in Chapter 5, The Record Information System.)

The most important economic impact of legislation occurs from *standardization*, that is, uniformity in records management practices and equipment. Encouraging this practice can result in a national annual savings of millions of dollars! Consider the savings for a single large business if standardization saved just five cents for every record created and accessed. However, significant costs are incurred by government and industry in meeting some requirements of legislation.

The final concern of legislation is *records security*—controlling the access of records. Security of records can ensure an individual's privacy as well as protect the rights of the record's owner to remuneration. Numerous pieces of legislation passed in the last few decades have affected how records security is defined and implemented.

This chapter looks at legislation that deals with these major concerns for records management and begins with an historical overview of federal legislation that has profoundly affected records management.

Federal Paperwork Management

On the recommendation of the first *Hoover Commission* (1947–1949), Congress established the General Services Administration (GSA). In 1950, the Federal Records Act gave that agency the responsibility for managing government records. This was the beginning of records management as an activity that involved more than the mere storing of records. Since 1950, other federal laws have influenced the dissemination of information and, consequently, the type, form, and distribution of federal records. The *Paperwork Management Task Forces* of 1949 and 1955, set up under the Hoover Commission, plus federal legislation enacted since 1955, have affected records management both in the federal government and in private industry.

Federal Task Forces

In 1946, President Harry Truman established a commission, chaired by former President Herbert Hoover, to study the organization of the executive branch of the federal government. A special task force was formed to focus on one particular aspect of that organization—the management of federal records. The results of its findings were published in 1949. The chairman of the 1947–1949 task force, *Emmett J. Leahy*, had served as Director of Office Methods for the United States Navy during World War II. Leahy had also headed his own management consulting firm. Due to the importance of Leahy's role in this first attempt to review and recommend changes in federal records management, he is considered the father of records management.

The recommendations of the Paperwork Management Task Force to the 1949 Hoover Commission led to the establishment of the General Services Administration and the passage of the *Federal Records Act* in 1950. This act dealt principally with that portion of the recommendations to the commission relating to retention, disposal, and storage of records (U.S. Congress, 1955). Subsequently, the commission reported that significant savings in these areas had been achieved, but a more thorough examination of records management problems in government was needed. Therefore, the Paperwork Management Task Force continued its work under a second commission organized in 1953. Emmett Leahy also chaired this task force.

The specific objectives of the 1953–1955 task force were:

1. To measure the costs and dimension of government paperwork activity.
2. To identify areas of potential savings.
3. To suggest appropriate organizational

changes to improve government paperwork management.

The task force found that federal offices produced more than a billion letters a year at a cost of about $1 billion. The task force also found that the government used 18 billion printed or mimeographed forms and required over 125,000 different reports internally or from its field offices. Over $100 million a year was being spent for management directives and instructions. In excess of $20 million was being spent for technical manuals in the Navy Department alone—millions of dollars were being spent for the purchase and rental of typewriters and "giant mechanical brains" to process paperwork! To alleviate these problems, the task force made several recommendations:

1. To centralize paperwork management in the General Services Administration.
2. To establish standards for retention of government documents.
3. To control costs of equipment operation and repair.
4. To continue studying and seeking solutions to paperwork management problems.

The report of the 1953–1955 task force described the quantities and costs of paper used in government operations for technical manuals, pamphlets, periodicals, forms, and reports. The report also emphasized the need to control not only the volume of paperwork but the accompanying personnel, supplies, operating space, and equipment needed to manage it. The task force highlighted the major problem that has plagued, and continues to plague, every organization that has records—the burden imposed on management by the growing volume of paperwork. Today, paperwork is still a burden on management and has been increased rather than decreased by computer technology.

Project ELF

One recommendation of the 1953–1955 Paperwork Management Task Force concerned the use of legal-size documents in government agencies:

> *All agencies of government should survey their actual requirements for legal-size file cabinets and the actual need for documents of this size. The results of this survey should be closely related to plans of each agency to procure or keep legal-size file cabinets. In addition to more discriminating use, investigation will have to be made of the need for legal-size paper, including review of pertinent laws, Executive orders, and regulations which specify its use. (U.S. Congress, 1955: 21)*

Over the years since this recommendation was made, an interesting observance has come to light. In many cases, as much as 95 percent of the documents found in legal-size cabinets are letter-size!

In 1980, the Association of Records Managers and Administrators (ARMA) introduced *Project ELF*, a program to *e*liminate *l*egal-size *f*iles in government and industry and to establish letter-size paper—8½-×-11-inch—as the standard for records and correspondence. This standard has been adopted for all federal courts, by some departments and agencies of the federal government, and by over half of the state court systems. Today ARMA continues to promote Project ELF by setting up ELF commissions to aid city, county, and state governments and court systems, and major corporations in converting from legal-size to letter-size records.

The Paperwork Reduction Act of 1980

Over the past thirty years, the federal government has continued to review how paperwork is managed in the federal government. It has also attempted to centralize responsibility for the management of federal records and information resources. Under the *Paperwork Reduction Act* of 1980

(Public Law Number 96-511), many formerly segregated activities, such as records management, telecommunications, and operations of the Federal Information Center and Consumer Information Center, were combined in the formation of the Office of Information Resources Management.

The Paperwork Reduction Act of 1980 changed the concept of information from a "free good" to a "management resource" to be managed as any other resource. The objectives of the act covered a wide range of information resource management activities, going well beyond reduction of paperwork in the federal government. Some of the objectives were essentially the same as earlier ones of federal paperwork management, with one major difference. The Paperwork Reduction Act of 1980 tried to create a more effective and efficient use of computer technology for managing information, and included the following objectives to meet that goal:

1. Reduce the information burden imposed on the public by the federal government.
2. Reduce the cost of collecting, managing, and disseminating information by federal agencies.
3. Ensure that federal agencies collect only as much information as needed and can be used effectively.
4. Eliminate inconsistencies among federal information policies by ensuring uniformity wherever possible.
5. Improve the efficiency of government programs and reduce the public burden through the effective use of telecommunications.
6. Ensure that the legitimate privacy and confidentiality concern of individuals and enterprises are safeguarded.

The underlying thrust of the Paperwork Reduction Act is to reduce the amount of paperwork that continually overwhelms government operations and also to reduce the paperwork that businesses must produce in order to satisfy government regulations. A continual complaint of businesspeople is the vast quantity of paperwork required by government legislation.

The act requires many government agencies that deal with the public to clearly specify why information is needed and to indicate whether the public must furnish the information. For example, the Internal Revenue Service (IRS) carries the following on its forms:

> **Paperwork Reduction Act Notice**
> *We ask for this information to carry out the Internal Revenue laws of the United States. We need it to ensure that taxpayers are complying with these laws and to allow us to figure and collect the right amount of tax. You are required to give us this information.*

The Paperwork Reduction Act of 1980 also established the Office of Information and Regulatory Affairs as the agency responsible for information policy. The mandate of that office was to improve the use of information technology. For example, two of its tasks under the act were (1) to develop a program to enforce federal information processing standards, particularly software language standards; and (2) to develop, with the General Services Administration, a five-year plan for meeting the automated data processing and telecommunications needs of the federal government.

The Freedom of Information Act

The *Freedom of Information Act*, enacted in 1966, applies to virtually all records compiled by agencies of the federal government. However, this act does not govern records in the possession of Congress, the courts, or the executive office of the president. The act requires federal agencies to release information upon request by any person, institution, association, or corporate entity unless that information meets certain exemptions from disclosure. Those exemptions include:

1. classified national security information
2. internal information of no concern to the general public or that would jeopardize any agency's ability to fulfill its statutory obligations
3. information protected by another federal statute or information that another statute permits an agency to withhold at its discretion, such as federal income tax returns
4. commercial or financial information submitted to the federal government by businesses or individuals when the disclosure of that information might cause competitive harm to the submitter
5. legally privileged information, such as documents that would violate attorney–client confidences
6. information that would result in invasion of personal privacy
7. investigatory records compiled for law enforcement purposes
8. information regarding bank audits by federal officials
9. geological and geophysical information and data. (McIntyre, 1986: 14)

The disclosure of information in a federal agency must be carefully evaluated by the records manager. The evaluation must consider not only information that can be disclosed legally, but also information that should not be given to third parties. Records that should be withheld must be protected; yet, if the requester believes that information to which he or she is legally entitled is being withheld, such as when the requester or third party is referred to in records kept by the federal government, a lawsuit may result. Because this "third-party" condition can be encountered in other disclosure situations, many businesses have set a definitive policy for disclosing information to third parties.

The Privacy Act of 1974

The *Privacy Act* of 1974 was passed to protect the rights of individuals regarding the personal information collected and disseminated about them by federal agencies. The act provides the following safeguards:

1. Individuals are permitted to determine what records about them are being maintained and to have access to those records, copy them, and correct them.
2. Individuals are permitted to know who has access to information about them and to prevent that information from being disseminated without their consent under certain circumstances.
3. Federal agencies are required to collect, maintain, use, or disseminate any record of identifiable personal information in a manner that assures that such action is for a necessary and lawful purpose, that the information is current and accurate for its intended use, and that adequate safeguards are provided to prevent misuse of such information.
4. Violators, unless exempted from the provisions of the act by some other statute, are subject to civil suit. (King, 1979: 28–29)

Records management dilemmas abound in the interpretation of what constitutes privacy. For example, naive records clerks may keep individuals from seeing records that they have a legal right to access, including personal medical information held by a federal agency. The disclosure issue arises because physicians within the medical community do not uniformly provide medical records to their patients. Some physicians fear the emotional trauma that could result from a patient's misinterpretation of medical records—a valid concern that must be weighed along with the requirements of the Privacy Act before medical information is disclosed.

Two other significant privacy problems are (1) protecting an individual's records from access by third parties who do not have a legal right to see them; and (2) accounting for the disclosures of information that are made. In other words, if an individual wishes to know who has received information about him or her, the records management system must have some means of providing this information and some means of identifying *what* information was provided—a service that can be very costly.

The ramifications of the Privacy Act are not limited to records management in federal agencies. Many states have proposed and/or enacted privacy legislation that includes businesses. Both large and small businesses often maintain medical, employment, financial, and other personal information about their employees. Maintaining the privacy of employee records while permitting access by authorized persons is a constant and costly records management dilemma.

The availability of employee information to unauthorized people is a major concern in business. Therefore, such groups as the Business Roundtable and the federal Privacy Protection Study Commission have encouraged industry to take the initiative in controlling access to employee records. In some states, such as California and Michigan, laws have been enacted to regulate access to and dissemination of employee information. Generally, however, businesses have established their own policies for dealing with this sensitive area. According to a survey conducted by *Personnel* magazine in 1981, only a small percentage of companies put their policies in writing and distribute them to management (Levine, 1981: 4–11). The businesses that responded to the survey also stated that they had two significant problems: (1) limiting what is kept in employee files; and (2) controlling the release of information to people both within and outside the organization.

Limiting Information in Employee Files

Vast amounts of personal information on employees are stored in corporation computers, and there may be no limit on the length of time the information is kept. Businesses keep both compliments and reprimands in employee personnel files. Employee files may also contain performance appraisals, salary information, attendance records, references, results of application tests, and education records. Some businesses that require extensive investigation of employees before they are hired hold even more sensitive information. In these organizations, one method of safeguarding employee privacy is to keep investigation records separate from personnel records. Another safeguard in many businesses is to allow employees to view and make corrections to their files.

Controlling Access to Employee Records

In many businesses, only members of the personnel staff and various levels of management have authorized access to employee records, and the employees themselves may see their own records. Internal access by any employee within the organization is difficult to control. Without a significant resource commitment to security, the business will have difficulty preventing unauthorized access.

External access to employee records is usually more carefully controlled due to the legal liability imposed by federal or state laws. A business can require written authorization from the external party before releasing information. For example, a written authorization may be needed before the business will acknowledge a particular person's employment and the length of that person's service. In compliance with federal and state laws, businesses will require authorization for releasing salary or other financial information.

Both the Freedom of Information Act and the Privacy Act were influenced significantly by public opinion and concern. These acts were implemented at a time when the public's confidence in government was shaken by misuse of information. The Freedom of Information Act is intended to provide public admission to information. The Privacy Act limits admission to information that directly touches the requesting individual. The price paid for agencies to meet the requirements of the acts is high; it includes the costs to provide and protect information (over $12 million annually for the Federal Bureau of Investigation). Satisfying government regulations also reduces the efficiency of federal law enforcement agencies such as the Federal Bureau of Investigation and the Secret Service (Riggin, 1984).

The Copyright Act of 1976

Records personnel not only store and protect records but also copy records for some purposes. In copying records, they may become subject to the copyright law. *The Copyright Act* of 1976 defines the current law. A *copyright* gives the original producer the exclusive rights to publish, produce, or sell the rights to an original work for the duration of the copyright. Copyright works can include books, articles, musical compositions, dramas, motion pictures, sound recordings, computer programs, and other literary and artistic efforts. To copyright a work, the author need only put the notice of copyright on all visually perceivable copies. The notice consists of the copyright symbol, ©, or the word "Copyright," or the abbreviation "Copr." with the year of first publication, and the name of the owner; for example:

Copr. 1988 MARY DOE.

Registration with the U.S. Copyright Office, Library of Congress, is not a condition of copyright, but would be extremely useful if there were an infringement suit.

The intent of a copyright is to protect the owner's creative investment. It may take a musician years to write and perfect a song; yet once it is published, anyone can make a copy in seconds or perform it publicly. The Copyright Act of 1976 guarantees that the owner of a copyright has the exclusive right to reproduce the work for public distribution and to grant permission to others wishing to perform or reproduce the work if they are paid or compensated in any way. This means that only the owner can give permission to copy the work.

The Copyright Act also prohibits the copying of certain documents such as paper money, government securities, and military badges or identification cards. When records being copied are protected by the Copyright Act, violation of its provisions may result in a lawsuit.

Under certain conditions, though, copyright materials are allowed to be reproduced. For example, the owner of the copyright may give legal permission to copy the work. The act also specifies, for the first time, legal exceptions to the copyright law under the judicial doctrine of "fair use." The provision of the act regarding "fair use" is of particular importance to records personnel.

Fair Use

In lay terms, the Copyright Act provides that a copyrighted work (such as a book, magazine, song, or poem) may be copied if the intended use of that copy is "fair," presumably to the author or holder of the copyright. The courts have relied on two factors in determining fair use: (1) the user's purpose and (2) the economic effect on the copyrighted work. The *fair use* portion of the act allows duplication of a copyrighted work for scientific, educational, research, or news reporting purposes if not for monetary gain. Other factors considered are:

- □ how large a portion of the copyrighted work was used
- □ the nature of the copyrighted material (such as whether it was a directory of names or a poem)
- □ the purpose of the use (for example, if it was used for advertising) and the potential damage to the marketability of the work.

Public Domain

When records are classified as being in the *public domain*, this means that a copyright never existed or the copyright has expired. By law, a work cannot be copyrighted if it consists "preponderantly" of materials created by the United States government and, hence, is considered in the public domain.

In 1978, a major revision of the Copyright Act changed the rules regarding copyright expiration. Prior to 1978, a copyright expired after twenty-eight years but could be renewed for another twenty-eight years. Now, any work created after January 1, 1978, holds a copyright good for the life of the author plus fifty years; if no author is specified, the duration is one hundred years from creation or seventy-five years from first publication, whichever is shorter. A work becomes copyrighted at the moment of creation, provided that the notice of copyright is included. In other words, a work may be placed in the public domain simply by making it available without the copyright notice. Public domain records will usually include all government publications, archival materials, and items clearly indicating that they are public domain. If there is any doubt about the copyright status of a record, one should assume that the materials are *not* in the public domain.

Copying Paper Documents

It is difficult to control what is copied in a large business. Often a business cannot guarantee that copies will not be used for illegal purposes. Therefore, some organizations (such as libraries) have equipped their copying machines to print a statement on each document reproduced that usually includes a notice that the copying may be in violation of the Copyright Act and the user should be aware of a possible violation.

What can and cannot be copied? If the material has a copyright notice and "fair use" does not clearly apply, then don't copy it. If appropriate, you can contact the copyright owner and obtain written permission to make copies for a specific use. Generally, if records personnel believe that they may be held liable for something that is being copied, management should be informed. An attorney or the company's legal department can provide guidelines for duplicating company records. (Additional information on copyright requirements regarding reprographics is given in Chapter 9.) Also, *Document R1, The Nuts and Bolts of Copyrights*, can be obtained from the Copyright Office, Library of Congress, Washington, D.C. 20559.

Copying Software

With more and more records being stored on magnetic media, another question concerning fair use has arisen. Is it legal for a business to copy its magnetic media? What if the magnetic media include proprietary (owned) programs? Generally, "fair use" allows copying of magnetic media if there is no intent to profit from that use. For example, a business could make copies of all its software to provide for accidental loss. The same business could make 100 copies of all its software for the same proposed reason, but it is likely that a court would view that many as an unreasonable number of backup copies and suspect a profit motive.

It is simple and inexpensive to copy the magnetic media used with microcomputers. A business that has purchased a $395 word-processing program may be strongly tempted to make more than backup copies. Software protected by copyright means that backup copies are legal and that the software should not be used by two different people in two different places at the same time. In other words, the software should be treated "like a book." Violating the principle of making only necessary backup copies is called *software piracy*. The popular microcomputer press regularly expresses software manufacturers' concerns with piracy.

The leading microcomputer software manufacturers estimate that their software is pirated at the rate of one illegal copy to every three-to-five legal copies. Some manufacturers have resorted to elaborate schemes to prevent their software from being copied, but often these schemes make it difficult for the buyer to produce legal copies for backup or transfer to a fixed disk. Software buyers have exerted considerable pressure on manufacturers to stop the copy protection schemes. At present, the trend has been for manufacturers to eliminate copy protection and to rely on the buyer's ethics.

In a large business or organization with many microcomputers, it is a generally accepted practice to use the same software for many applications. This promotes uniformity, reduces training costs, and allows easy exchange of information. In these cases, the software manufacturer may give the organization a *site license,* which allows the organization to copy the software freely as long as its use is restricted to a specific site. For example, a business may purchase a site license for thirty microcomputers for a word-processing package. This would allow the business to simultaneously use the package on all of its microcomputers. The business would pay less for a site license than if it purchased thirty copies of the software, and the software manufacturer is assured that its copyright is protected.

Summary

Several attempts have been made to improve the management of federal paperwork, beginning with the 1947–1949 Paperwork Management Task Force headed by Emmett Leahy. The federal government has continued to monitor paperwork management and has incorporated the need for total information resource management (including computer technology) into recent legislation. The Paperwork Reduction Act of 1980 reflects this focus. An attempt to standardize records is reflected in Project ELF, a program sponsored by the Association of Records Managers and Administrators (ARMA) to eliminate legal-size files in government and industry.

Legislation that protects the rights of individuals includes the Freedom of Information Act of 1966, which allows individuals to review information held by federal agencies, and the Privacy Act of 1974, which prohibits unauthorized access to certain information. The Privacy Act also protects the rights of individuals regarding information collected and disseminated about them by federal agencies, and allows those individuals to review and correct that information. Both the Freedom of Information Act and the Privacy Act are of particular importance to records personnel in industry because employee records are often affected by these acts either directly or indirectly.

Finally, the Copyright Act of 1976 and its amendments protect the rights of owners of original works by requiring the owner's permission for duplication of the work except under certain circumstances. Understanding the concept of "fair use" and determining if a record is in the public domain are important to avoid violation of the copyright law. Software piracy is a recent concern. Records personnel should seek legal advice concerning what may be copied and avoid possible violations of copyright for both paper and magnetic media.

List of Terms

retention scheduling
standardization
records security
Hoover Commission
Paperwork Management Task Force
Emmett J. Leahy
Federal Records Act
Project ELF
Paperwork Reduction Act
Freedom of Information Act
Privacy Act
Copyright Act
copyright
fair use
software piracy
site license
public domain

Discussion Questions

1. What were the major objectives of the task forces of 1949 and 1955?
2. What are the objectives of Project ELF?
3. What were the goals of the Paperwork Reduction Act of 1980?
4. What agencies or entities are *not* affected by the Freedom of Information Act?
5. What are some differences between the Privacy Act of 1974 and the Freedom of Information Act?
6. Why do private businesses need to be aware of the requirements of the Privacy Act?
7. Why is the legislation that protects an individual's privacy costly to businesses?
8. What are the two major problems that businesses encounter in attempting to comply with privacy requirements?
9. In lay terms, what does a "copyright" consist of?
10. Define "fair use" as it pertains to the duplication of software.
11. Explain when a software program is or could become a public domain program.

Activities

1. Contact a government office in your community and find out what, if any, records have been affected by Project ELF. Also, prepare a list of the legal-size records that were eliminated. If legal-size records are still being kept, find out why this is the case.
2. Interview at least two people who handle records in small businesses

or in public offices and ask them to explain their understanding of the Privacy Act. Write a short report on your findings.

3. A goal of the Paperwork Reduction Act is to reduce redundant or irrelevant information. Obtain a form from a business or organization and suggest what parts of it could be eliminated.
4. Contact your local credit bureau and determine what information it collects. Find out if the bureau is aware of the provisions of the Freedom of Information Act and what procedures the bureau follows in obtaining and disclosing information.
5. Some people feel that the establishment of a national information system that would consolidate business, bank, local, state, and federal agency information about all individuals would really increase records efficiency. What do you think? Prepare a dialogue between two people discussing the pros and cons of this situation and present it to your class.
6. One objective of the copyright law is to encourage creative genius by assuring that creative works receive just monetary reward. Do you think this is a valid argument? Explain why or why not.
7. Attempts to restrict copying of media have led to the development of an industry devoted to breaking copy protection schemes. There are ways to copy microcomputer disks, audio cassette tapes, and paper. Research the situation in regard to phonograph records and compact disks (CDs) and write a report of your findings.

References

Association of Records Managers and Administrators. *Project ELF* (Prairie Village, Kan.: ARMA International, July 1985).

Fenwick, William A. "Privacy." *Data Management* 13 (May 1975): 18–21.

Jackson, Carolyn. "Information Resources Management." *The Air Force Comptroller* 15 (July 1981): 20–21.

King, Jessie Kitts. "Privacy Act Implementation." *ARMA Quarterly* (January 1979): 28–32.

Levine, Hermine Zagat. "Consensus: Privacy of Employee Records." *Personnel* 58 (May/June 1981): 4–11.

McIntyre, Thomas J. "The Freedom of Information Act." *FBI Law Enforcement Bulletin* 55, no. 8 (August 1986): 13–18.

"The Privacy Act of 1974." *Data Management* 13 (June 1975): 36–43.

"Respecting Employee Privacy." *Business Week* (January 11, 1982): 130–32.

Riggin, Stephen P. "U.S. Information Access Laws." *FBI Law Enforcement Bulletin* 53, no. 7 (July 1984): 13–19.

Ringer, Barbara. "Finding Your Way Around in the New Copyright Law." *Publishers Weekly* 210 (December 13, 1976): 38–41.

Rinzler, Carol E. "What's Fair About 'Fair Use'?" *Publishers Weekly* 223 (April 8, 1983): 26–28.

"Rules Regarding Access to and Review of Personal Information in Systems of Records." *Federal Reserve Bulletin* 61 (October 1975): 666–70.

U.S. Congress. *Paperwork Management, Part I in the United States Government.* A Report to the Congress by the Commission on Organization of the Executive Branch of the Government. January 1955.

U.S. Congress. House. Subcommittee of the Committee on Government Operation. *Paperwork Reduction Act Amendments of 1983 (H.R. 2718) and Catalog of Federal Domestic Assistance (H.R. 2592).* 98th Cong., 1983.

Walsh, Frank. "The New Copyright Law: Stronger and More Specific." *Public Relations Journal* 33 (August 1977): 6–7.

Chapter 2 Highlight

The Software Wars

With the introduction and widespread use of the microcomputer, excellent software applications have become available. These programs include games, word processing, spreadsheets, databases, and many other areas for which there is a demand for microcomputer applications. The superior programs often have retail prices in the $300 range, and sometimes go as high as $500, $600, and even $1,000. The microcomputer itself—the hardware—usually costs in the neighborhood of $1,000. The microcomputer and a couple of $1.00 disks, however, can be used to copy a $300 program.

In a typical scenario, a business might buy a $300 software program to handle some business function. The program works well and is copied and distributed to others for use in their jobs at the company. Some people copy the program to use at home. According to the copyright laws, all of these copies are illegal. Such illegal copying is so widespread that major software producers estimate that for every purchased copy of their program, there is at least one illegal copy. This is not only costly to the software producer but, when the user of an illegal copy calls the producer for help, it is a bitter pill to have to swallow.

In order to deal with this situation, software producers have tried "copy protection" for their software. The idea of copy protection is to prevent a purchaser from making copies with standard microcomputer hardware and software. The immediate response to copy protection was the development of "copy unprotection," software that allows a purchaser to make a copy of protected software. With each new type and version of copy protection, a new type and version of copy unprotection appeared. The war was on. During the years 1983 to 1987, copy unprotection programs were selling millions of copies and updates per month! Each new announcement of an improved copy protection scheme was met by the announcement that the new unprotection software could "break" the latest scheme.

The copy protectors and unprotectors enjoyed a popular demand for their products. The turning point in the war occurred in 1985 when it was reported in computer publications that major software companies were considering a killer version of copy protection. If an owner tried to copy their software with a special unprotection program, the killer version would sense this attempt and not only stop the copy but also damage the program and perhaps the microcomputer itself. Software users and the popular microcomputer media were outraged. The articles, letters, and editorials against copy protection schemes reached global coverage in the first months of 1986.

Like most conflicts, the software copy protection wars benefited primarily the weapon/armorer groups while the producers and users paid the prices. The copy protection schemes did not stop users from making copies. The schemes were costly for software producers to install and damaged their reputations, casting them as greedy and unresponsive to their users. Users paid through the loss of time (and even data) when a problem occurred and they were unable to use a backup copy of the program. As a result, copy protection was slowly dropped. By the middle of 1988, every major software producer had removed copy protection from its products.

Is copy protection gone? Not by a long shot. The basic motivation of software producers to protect their investments remains, but so do users' feelings that they have a right to make a backup copy of any software.

Buyer's responses to past protection schemes suggest that only the producers of higher-priced software without significant competition can afford to protect their software. Their methods usually involve a hardware "key" that is sold with the software. The key is plugged into the computer and is required for the program to run. Although copies of the software can be made, they will run only with the special key. We would not be surprised to start to see advertisements for "unkeys" that allow the software to be run without the key—and the war continues.

Chapter 3 Organization of the Records Management Function

Learning Goals

1. To understand the relationship between the goals of records management and how businesses define the scope of the records management function.

2. To become familiar with the operations that are considered a part of records management.

3. To understand how the size of a business affects the records management function.

4. To become acquainted with the difference between the traditional and the integrated approaches to organizing the records management function in corporations.

5. To know the options for handling the records management function in the small business.

6. To understand how an audit can measure the effectiveness of the records management function.

Introduction

The records management function includes those activities that a business defines as falling within the scope of management of business records. Because each business also defines that scope, the activities included in the records management area differ from industry to industry and among individual businesses.

In this chapter, we will discuss the scope of the records management function and the activities that can be logically included within that scope. We will then discuss how these operations are organized in large corporations and how a hypothetical records management department could be configured. Next, we will present options for handling the records management function in the small business. Finally, we will describe how an audit can be an effective tool to evaluate the performance of the records management function.

The Scope of the Records Management Function

The scope of the records management function is determined to a large extent by the goals a records management system is expected to achieve. Those goals are not always stated clearly by the business itself, but in the records management profession, specific goals for records management have been identified (Diamond, 1987). The goals of any records management system, regardless of size, should be:

1. the efficient organization, storage, retrieval, and management of active records
2. a vital records program to protect essential documents
3. an economical and efficient method of storing and retrieving inactive records
4. a records retention schedule (a listing of records and the length of time they are kept).

Each of these goals is explained fully in later chapters. At this point, they provide a basis for understanding why certain operations are considered records management operations and why businesses organize the records management function in different ways.

Records Management Operations

Records management can encompass a number of operational areas. While records management, narrowly defined, is the management of business records, the range of activities that are necessary to efficiently manage the many types of records goes far beyond merely filing and retrieving paper records. The records management function may include the following activities, each of which is considered a *records management operation.*

Active files management: Storage and retrieval of active records is the largest segment of records management in most businesses.

Vital records management: This includes the identification, maintenance, and protection of those records that are considered vital to the operation of the business.

Inactive files management: This includes the records center for older records that are not in regular use; and archives management, which pertains to storing and preserving records for historical or scholarly purposes.

Micrographics management: This includes converting paper documents to microfilm, microfiche, or some other similar medium, as well as editing, cataloging, and maintaining microfilm files.

Reprographics management: Sometimes called *copy management*, this area includes the equipment, personnel, and procedures involved in printing and duplicating documents, as well as the electronic transmission of documents.

Forms management: Three out of every four records are forms, and businesses often design and print their own. This area includes design, construction, and control of forms.

Reports management: Millions of reports are generated by businesses annually to meet internal and external reporting requirements. Some types of reports are progress, financial, and status. Reports are the most expensive type of record to produce. This area includes creation, control, and distribution of reports.

Correspondence management: Correspondence is second in volume to forms and includes both internal and external documents. Management of correspondence involves efficient creation of internal documents and distribution of both internal and external documents. Therefore, distribution often includes mail services.

Word processing: Because the primary role of word processing is document creation, this area has the equipment and personnel associated with the creation of business documents.

Data processing or electronic data processing (EDP): This area is concerned with the regular, computer-based transaction processing of an organization, including regular report activities to clients, billing, and other repetitive tasks that process large amounts of data.

The Records Management Function in the Large Corporation

The large corporation may include all of the records management operations in one division called, for example, information resource management. Here, the scope of a particular operation will be sufficient to warrant its own department; the following operations are typically departmental with their own manager or supervisor: data processing, word processing, the records center, micrographics, and central files.

To illustrate the functional organization of an information resource management division, consider a word processing (WP) department. Word processing usually implies an organizationwide function, a computer basis, and links to records management operations. The WP department produces virtually all of the business's text documents (the data documents, for example, client notices, are produced by data processing) using computer-based operations and equipment. Although most of the documents are original, many can be produced from earlier documents with some editing. The earlier documents may be in WP's internal records, as well as in a central file or even in a data processing department. Thus, efficient WP operations require coordination with other departments.

Traditional Organization

Traditionally, records management that is departmentalized is placed organizationally with other support operations such as mail services and building security. In this arrangement (Figure 3.1), the division that includes records management and the other support operations is called administrative services, and it does not include data processing. All of the divisions under the administrative services umbrella operate relatively separately from each other.

The general functions of the administrative services division are defined as services that support the primary functions of the business, such as dealing with the business mail, telephones, cleaning, office supplies, distribution of equipment, and taking

Figure 3.1 Old Style, or Traditional, Records Management in the Organization

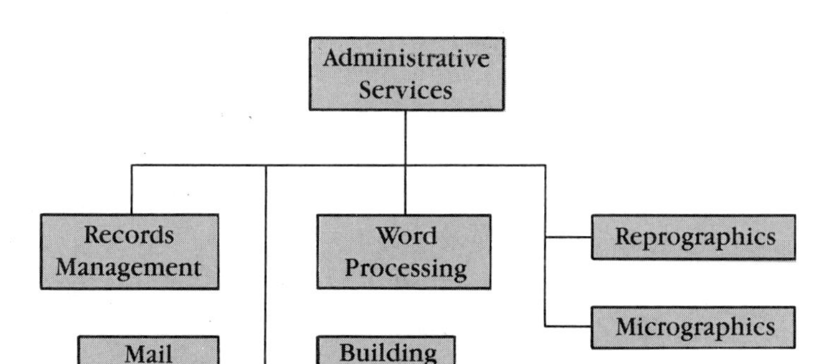

Figure 3.2 New Style, or Integrated, Records Management in the Organization

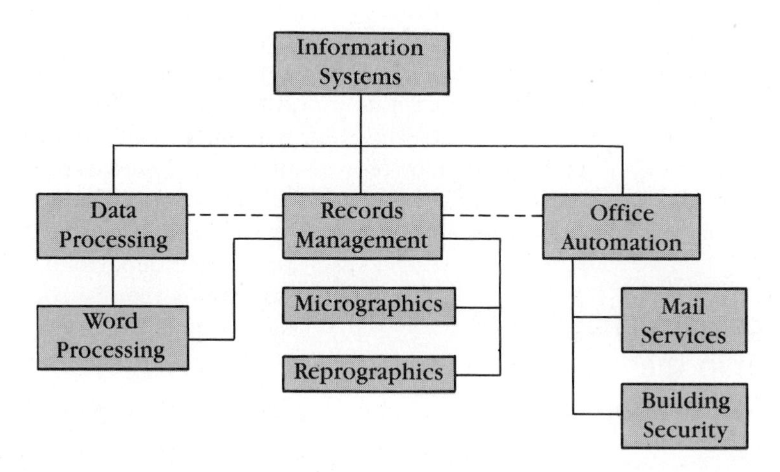

care of the heating/cooling. Although they are useful, and even *essential* activities, they are not directly related to the primary function of a business. Therefore, these operations/functions when organized in the traditional (old style) configuration, are treated as separate operations, related only by the fact that each provides support to the business. Data processing is considered more closely related to the primary function of the business than the other records management operations. (In fact, traditionally, data processing has had no relationship to records management.)

Integrated Organization

With the increasing impact of the computer into word processing, data processing, micrographics, mail services, and the other records management operations, the recent trend has been to integrate these operations with others, especially data processing. As a result, a new organizational style has emerged in which related operations are included in a single, larger division called information systems, under the management of a vice president. Figure 3.2 shows a sample organization chart of this integrated arrangement (new style).

In this configuration, data processing is related to records management and all of the operations are linked to each other. Administrative services has been slightly altered in emphasis and renamed office automation. Word processing is doubly linked to data processing and records management due to the influence of the computer. Similarly, micrographics and reprographics are integrated, via computer technology, with records management. The dotted lines indicate that data processing and office automation work closely with the records management department to achieve a total integration of all records management operations. Also, building security is still included here because many of its activities are automated.

The organization charts shown in Figures 3.1 and 3.2 are intended to be representative. Probably no business would have an organization chart exactly like either of the ones shown. The point is that the general scheme of organizing records management operations has been affected by the changes that are occurring due to the influence of technology. Previously related or loosely related functions can now interact more easily, often share resources and banks of information, and, therefore, need to be organizationally linked.

The Organization of the Records Management Department

Although each organization defines its departments somewhat differently, the records management department may include several or all of the operations associated with managing records; or it may handle only one operation (for example, active files management) while other operations are in other departments. The records management department in a corporation or in the branch office of an international organization typically can have the following operational areas and staff positions. (The positions associated with these areas are included in this discussion to illustrate job descriptions found in business today.)

Central Files: This is the major active records function. The largest number of personnel, equipment, and records are usually in this area.

Vital Records: The dual functional goals of vital records management are to identify the records essential to the operation of the business and to guarantee adequate safeguards of those vital records.

Records Center: The primary function of the records center is the storage and retrieval of inactive records.

Micrographics: The function of micrographics is to provide reduced-size images of records for efficient storage and retrieval.

Reprographics: In a large organization today, this area may include any type of reproduction function, from the control of company copy machines to a full-featured printing shop.

The following positions are occupied by records personnel in the typical records management department.

Records Manager: He or she is the overall manager of the department, responsible for all activities and personnel within the department.

Records Analyst: The function of a records analyst is to determine the appropriate characteristics of records and assess the value of information. This may involve anything from record creation to drafting retention schedules.

Figure 3.3 Records Management Organization Chart

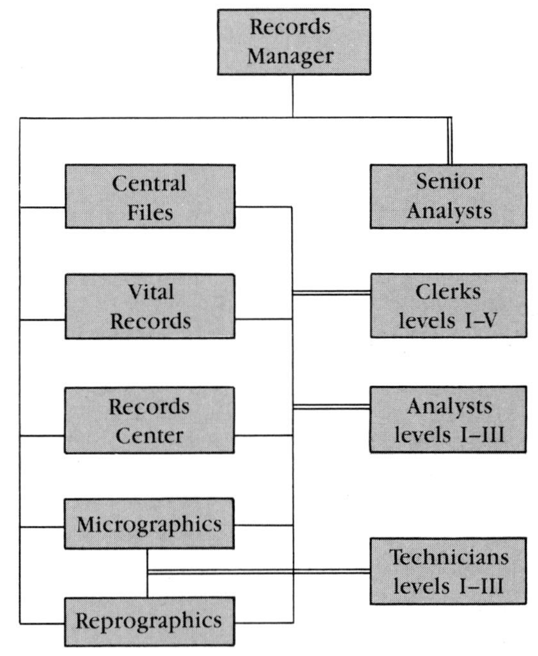

The double lines indicate multiple positions are available for the indicated function.

Records Clerk: The primary duty of a records clerk is to file and retrieve records. This position has different levels that indicate the degree of knowledge about the system and associated skills.

Records Technician: Technicians have specific skills related to a particular area, such as micrographics. These skills are usually associated with the operation of different types of equipment. This position also has levels that reflect the degree of expertise.

Figure 3.3 shows how a records management department in a large organization might be organized. The single-line connections indicate the lines of authority and connections between functional areas. The double lines connecting the areas to the clerks, analysts, and technicians indicate that each functional area may have its own clerks, analysts, and technicians. In this configuration, the responsibility for forms, reports, and correspondence management would be part of the records manager's job description.

Most large organizations will include all of the functional areas shown in Figure 3.3 and may even have others, such as word processing and mail services, as well. They may not have the same relationship to each other and, in some cases, an organization may choose to have some operations handled by an outside company rather than internally. For example, there are many *service centers* that provide micrographics services to the large organization that does not need internal integration of this function. Similarly, many commercial records centers exist to provide efficient, inactive records storage and retrieval to businesses. (The use of service centers is described later in this chapter, and Chapter 10 provides detailed information on the operations of corporate and commercial records centers.)

Records Management in the International Corporation

An international corporation is one that has offices in different countries. In some international organizations, the records management function is defined by the home office, but the specific arrangement of records management operations and the degree of integration among them is decided by each branch office. In other words, a general records management policy is established, but exactly how it is implemented varies from branch to branch.

Because the international organization has a common business focus, the management of its records creates an additional problem in coordinating the addition, editing, and deleting of records during storage and retrieval. Any business that has offices in different physical locations will encounter the problem of records coordination. However, technology affects the organization of the records management function in an international corporation somewhat differently than in the corporation whose offices are in one location. For example, it may not be feasible to centralize all the records in the international organization.

One solution to centralizing records is to make sufficient duplicates in order to have a complete set of records at all locations. This solution, however, is not only costly, it involves severe problems in maintaining records correlation. For example, suppose that Acme Corporation has locations throughout the world; when a client file is updated, that update is sent to a central location for storage, but is not sent to all of the corporation's locations. While this approach may have been, in the past, the only practical one, new technology has provided alternative solutions; that is, the combination of telecommunications with virtual central records. *Virtual central records* means that although records may not be physically present at a particular location, they are accessible via some telecommunications technology.

Telecommunications in records management usually means the transmission and reception of records in a digital format. For example, a home office may keep its client records on optical disks in a digital format. If a regional office in another city needed a client file, the digital records could be telecommunicated over ordinary telephone equipment. Anywhere that a telephone connection exists, it is possible to telecommunicate with the proper hardware and software. As you can imagine, there is an immense potential for records telecommunications.

Other similar coordination problems can be resolved by telecommunications. Rather than keep multiple copies of records in various locations, a single master file is kept, and other locations access the master file using telecommunications. In this way, the integration of records management operations occurs. The general process of integrating the records management of physically distinct locations is called *distributed records management.* An example of such an operation is provided in Chapter 13. Particularly for the internationial business with its geographically dispersed offices, telecommunications is the records management technology of the future.

The Records Management Function in the Small Business

We define small businesses as those with as few as two full-time employees or as many as fifty—for example, a family-owned business. Small businesses have consistently made up about 27 percent of all businesses in the United States; in 1984, there were 21,171,000 of them, each a separate business with a need for records management (Bureau of the Census, 1986).

The small business has its own unique problems because the same person typically handles all of the records management functions in a restricted physical location. Equipment and supplies usually are not coordinated and the concept of several operational areas under a unified records management function is often economically impractical.

Probably the greatest problem of the small business is correct recognition of the level of organization needed for efficient records management. The typical approach to the records management function in a small business is to assign records management tasks to internal employees as subordinate chores. Because no records management policies exist, records management functions are accomplished by whomever is available at the time. This approach results in one person handling the records management functions as secondary to other duties. Without an overall plan, and with records management seen as an inferior activity, the inevitable result is a slow deterioration of the functions. Following the example in Chapter 1, the small business treads the trail of the problem stage of the systems life cycle. Yet other approaches are possible and desirable.

Option 1: Small businesses may use service organizations to provide certain records management functions such as archival storage, microfilming, computer transactions, accounting services, bookkeeping services, etc. At the most comprehensive level, a small business may contract with a professional records management firm to provide all of its records functions. A professional firm may be expected to maintain the archival records, deal with all aspects of active and inactive records, and be available for questions and problems as they arise. These contractual relations can provide cost-effective alternatives to internal solutions. The problem for the small organization is deciding when contractual arrangements are appropriate and estimating their cost-effectiveness at regular intervals. Also, many small businesses are located in areas where such professional services are not available.

Option 2: The small organization may find that the need for records management activity is cyclical. The need for efficient staff can be satisfied through services that provide temporary records management specialists. One drawback is that the specialists leave with their knowledge and the result is a lack of uniformity, control, and continuity in the operations of the records management functions.

Option 3: A third alternative for the small business is to hire temporary consultants to identify, plan, and implement critical records management functions. Vendors may serve in this role and provide, for example, a complete system for records storage and retrieval. The system might include equipment, color coding supplies, and the procedural manuals needed to use the supplies. Consultants may also be used periodically to provide continuing services such as training and evaluation.

Option 4: An option not often considered to achieve a professional level of records management by the small organization is shared expertise (Hayes, 1987). *Shared expertise* means the hiring of one records management expert by two or more cooperating organizations. This solution requires that the desired expertise be available and that the firms cooperate in dividing that expertise. This solution is probably best initiated by one small business who enlists another business with similar records management needs. Together, they would advertise for and hire the services of the appropriate individual. Problems may occur in the areas of supervision, reporting, and renewal or termination of the records management individual's contract.

Option 5: The preceding options emphasize the use of service organizations and consultants to provide the necessary records management skills. For a small business with long-term employees, it may be desirable to develop potential and skills through *in-service training*; on-site programs, college courses, seminars, and other alternatives can have immediate and long-term benefits for the employee and the business.

The major problem with this option concerns the tenure of the employees. One possible solution is to require a specific length of service in return for the training opportunities. For example, a business might pay an employee's costs of a college course and give the person release time to attend the course in return for a promise to stay for at least six months after completion of the course.

Auditing the Records Management Function

An *audit* is a regular examination designed to verify that an activity is being carried out according to established procedures and policies. For the records management function, the purpose of the audit must be specified because its purpose will determine the criteria to be used to evaluate performance. Then, the audit must specify what is to be examined, who will do the audit, and when the audit should be performed. Let us examine each of these points in turn.

The purpose of the audit can be operational or administrative. An operational audit looks at the system's effectiveness: "Is the system performing its function efficiently?" The essence of an operational audit is retrieval efficiency: "Are records requests satisfied within acceptable time limits?" Alternately, an administrative audit is concerned with cost effectiveness: "Is the system functioning at the lowest possible cost?" The administrative audit will focus the criteria on the productive efficiency of the entire operation. Could a system pass an operational audit but fail an administrative audit? This is possible, for example, if the operational efficiency is due to excess staff working very hard with inefficient equipment.

What is to be examined in an audit? A good audit requires that comparisons be made, usually between audits made over time at the same business, or between comparable businesses. Audits generally measure activity, accuracy, retrieval, personnel, space, and costs. (Each of these terms, with a suggested measure and a range of possible values, is shown in Figure 3.4.) The actual method of measurement and the outcome value of each measure depends on the environment of the records system. The method chosen should be standardized for future comparisons.

In addition to the measures shown in Figure 3.4, an audit may also determine the legal compliance of the system. Legal compliance is measured through verification that legal statutes are observed. The relevant statutes (described in Chapter 2) deal with the Freedom of Information Act, the Privacy Act, and the Copyright Act. In addition, compliance may include satisfying federal, state, and local laws governing records retention, a topic that will be discussed in Chapter 5.

Who will do the audit? Because of the importance of the audit and the serious con-

Figure 3.4 Audit Measures for Records Management

Measure	*Example method of measurement*	*Values*
Activity	Records requested per month / Total records in system	.1–.2
Accuracy	Records located per month / Records requested per month	.97–1.0
Retrieval	Retrieval time per month / Total records retrieved	depends
Personnel	Number of employees / Total cubic feet of records	4000–7000
Space	Total cubic feet of records / Square feet of floor space	1–3
Costs	Annual total system costs / Total cubic feet of records	depends

sequences of the results, the auditor must be as qualified as the records manager of the system. Indeed, if an internal auditor is chosen, it will usually be the records manager. The major advantage in choosing an internal auditor is that the person will be familiar with the records system and its employees. Yet this familiarity may also be a major disadvantage because the auditor may not be as objective in assessing the system. An external auditor can be used to help ensure objectivity, to provide special expertise when required or when an internal auditor cannot be conveniently scheduled.

When should the audit be performed? An audit must be done on a regular basis, at least annually, to be beneficial. Exceptional audits should be done when there are significant changes to the system. The precise scheduling for the audit is important. For example, a *periodic audit* could be scheduled for the first week of March each year. The *random audit* could be scheduled for some time in the first quarter (January, February, March), with the precise time not known to the records system staff. The major advantage of the periodic audit is that time and resources can be efficiently allocated and planned. A disadvantage is that knowing when the audit is to occur may allow the records staff to divert the objectivity of the audit. The major disadvantage of the random audit is the confusion and time involved gathering the resources needed for the audit. These disadvantages can be significantly reduced with an *audit trail.* The audit trail specifies those documents and procedures that verify that the records functions are being carried out according to established procedures and policies. The specifications and procedures should appear in a records management manual, the components of which we will describe in more detail in Chapter 4.

Summary

The records management function is defined by each business, and the scope of that function is based on certain records management goals. The records management function includes operations that are related to the management of business records, which include active files management, vital records management, inactive files management, micrographics, reprographics, forms management, reports management, correspondence management, word processing, and data processing.

In large corporations, records management is usually departmentalized in a traditional or integrated configuration. The traditional approach places all support functions except data processing under the administrative services division. The areas within the division have little or no interaction. The integrated approach places all records management operations including data processing under the information systems division, and the operations work together to achieve a common goal.

In the international corporation, a major problem is records coordination. Telecommunications—the technology of distributed records management—together with virtual central records, offers a solution to this problem.

The records management department within a corporation typically includes the following activities or operations: central files, vital records, records center, reprographics, and micrographics; and the following positions: records manager, records analyst, records clerk, and records technician.

Records management in the small business often is a loosely structured function handled by one person. Other options, such as in-service training of employees and the use of service organizations, can increase the efficiency and effectiveness of records management in the small business. The use of service organizations, temporary records specialists, consultants, and shared expertise are among possible approaches to improved records management in the small business.

A records audit can verify that administrative or operational activities are being carried out according to established procedures and policies at an acceptable level of performance. An audit must specify what is to be examined, who will do the audit, and when the audit should be performed.

List of Terms

records management operation
virtual central records
telecommunications
distributed records management
central files
vital records
records center
reprographics
micrographics
records manager
records analyst
records clerk
records technician
service center
shared expertise
in-service training
audit
periodic audit
random audit
audit trail

Discussion Questions

1. What are at least two services for which a small business may have contractual arrangements?

2. What kind of business would not have all of the records management operations listed in the text?
3. What are the goals of any records management system?
4. How has technology affected the relationship between records management and other support areas in a business?
5. What is the traditional approach to the organization of the records management function?
6. What is the integrated approach to the organization of the records management function?
7. How can a small business use service organizations to fulfill its records management function?
8. What are the "typical" operations and staff positions in a records management department?
9. What activities are considered to be records management operations?
10. Which operations may be the records manager's responsibility rather than the responsibility of separate departments?
11. What is the difference between an administrative audit and an operational audit?
12. Why would a business want to have its records operation audited?
13. What effect would the size of a business have in doing an audit? What differences would you expect in the outcome of an audit by business size?
14. What factors would determine the ideal records accuracy ratio (number of files located/number of files requested) in a business?

Activities

1. Visit a small office and describe the records management system. Suggest how one or more of the options described in this chapter could be used in that office to improve records management.
2. Design a records management department for a large corporation in which five operations and at least two positions are included. Justify your design.
3. Describe the records management department in your own business/organization/school. Show the relationships between the positions defined in this chapter and the positions in your records management department.
4. Use the Yellow Pages of a telephone directory of a large city to prepare a list of businesses that provide records management services. If possible, call or write a few of the companies to obtain brochures and information on the services they provide.
5. A records analyst assesses the value of information. Choose a business or organization (for example, a school) and make up a list of criteria for assessing informational value.

References

Bureau of the Census. *Statistical Abstract of the United States, 1987*, 107th ed. (Washington, D.C.: U.S. Government Printing Office, 1987).

Diamond, Susan Z. "A Strategic Approach to Records Management." *Office Systems '87* 4, no. 6 (June 1987): 88–93.

Hayes, Kenneth V. "Are You Too Small for Records Management?" *Records Management Quarterly* 21, no. 1 (January 1987): 22–44.

"Professional Opportunities." *News, Notes and Quotes.* Newsletter of ARMA International, January to December, 1986.

Chapter 4 Responsibilities of the Records Manager

Learning Goals

1. To become aware of the scope of management responsibilities.
2. To recognize (a) the relationship between records management goals and objectives and (b) the role of the records manager.
3. To understand what the records manager does in selecting and training records personnel.
4. To become familiar with the components of correspondence, reports, and forms management.
5. To understand the purpose and uses of a records management manual.
6. To understand how performance evaluations and budgets aid the manager in the control process.

Introduction

Management of any operation requires a systematic approach to handling people, procedures, and equipment so that the business can make a profit. In many businesses, the records management department is a *cost center.* This means that it does not contribute to the profits of the business but, instead, provides necessary services for the business. Although the business could not operate effectively without these services, they are nevertheless considered expenses rather than revenue-producing functions. Managers of cost centers must constantly seek ways to cut costs and increase productivity not only in their departments but throughout the organization.

In this chapter, we will describe the five functions of management and how the records manager fulfills those functions. We will also explain correspondence, reports, and forms management as responsibilities of the records manager.

The Management Function

The five major functions of management are planning, staffing, organizing, directing, and controlling. As we discussed earlier in Chapter 1, planning involves setting goals (long-term accomplishments) and objectives (short-term accomplishments) to achieve those goals. Staffing includes identifying the skills needed for positions and selecting personnel. Organizing involves coordinating personnel, equipment, and procedures within the department. (In a broader sense, organizing also requires the manager to develop procedures to accomplish the goals of the business.) Directing includes assisting, motivating, and counseling subordinates as well as helping employees achieve departmental objectives through training. Controlling involves setting standards and measuring the degree to which those standards are met. In this chapter, two specific aspects of management control—budgeting and evaluating employee performance—will be discussed in the section on the control function of management. Methods of control as they relate to correspondence, reports, and forms management will be discussed in the section on the organizing function.

In addition to traditional management functions, managers fulfill other professional requirements, which include joining and participating in professional organizations to improve the professional status and image of the manager's particular profession. The two major professional organizations to which records managers belong are the Association of Records Managers and Administrators (*ARMA*) and the Association for Information and Image Management (*AIIM*). Both organizations encourage membership by anyone who is working in or associated with the records field.

Managers also may improve their professional image by demonstrating knowledge of their particular field by publishing in professional journals (see Appendix B, page 273) and obtaining certification. A records manager can certify expertise by becoming a Certified Records Manager (*CRM*). The CRM status requires three years of full-time experience managing records, a bachelor's degree, and successful completion of a six-part test.

In the everyday operation of the business, however, the records manager fulfills his or her management role by planning programs, staffing the department, organizing procedures, people, and equipment, directing a staff of employees, and exercising control to accomplish the goals of the business.

Planning: Setting Records Management Goals and Objectives

The reader will recall from Chapter 3 that the records management goals of an organization are:

1. the efficient organization, storage, retrieval, and management of active records
2. a vital records program to protect essential documents
3. an economical and efficient method of storing and retrieving inactive records
4. a records retention schedule.

A major problem that the records manager faces in achieving these goals is getting top management support for the necessary programs and procedures. It is difficult to justify the need for equipment and personnel and to convince top management of the eventual savings that will result from instituting detailed procedures. This has been a chronic problem in records management and a frequent topic at professional meetings. The heart of the problem is that savings obtained through efficient records management are reduced filing/retrieval times. These savings are not particularly visible and are difficult to translate into dollars. It is hard to convince anyone to spend money for elusive benefits.

A sound strategy for the records manager is to concentrate on compatibility with company goals and to work with achievable objectives. Because the major goal of any business is to make a profit, two of the records manager's goals should be to maximize productivity and minimize costs, and many records management objectives should be directed toward achieving these goals. Each manager should review top management's goals and then formulate objectives that are compatible with the resources available, the number of records personnel, and company policies. Generally, objectives should be specific, measurable, and capable of being achieved within a few weeks or months. For example, "prepare a set of filing rules to be followed by records personnel" would be a suitable objective.

Staffing: Selecting Personnel

In many businesses, the personnel department handles job advertisements, preliminary interviews, and various other staffing functions. However, the records manager is expected to specify the skills needed for various positions, to interview applicants, and to recommend, if not actually select, the person to be hired.

Preparing Job Descriptions

The records manager should be knowledgeable about all records operations and know what skills are required to perform them. Job descriptions should include the title of the position, the amount of experience and education required to perform the job, and a list of the general duties of the position. Also, a salary range is often provided. Most entry-level positions require technical skills, but the manager should consider what human relations skills the records staff needs to have. Higher positions require conceptual skills—the ability to analyze and solve problems—in addition to technical and human relations skills. Some positions require specialized skills; others require general knowledge. Because records management programs are similar but not exactly alike, the personnel should match a particular department's needs. (A detailed description of records management positions and career ladders is provided in Chapter 11.)

The components of a successful records management program must include motivation, teamwork, and persistence; unfortunately, these qualities are sometimes overlooked in selecting records management personnel (Morgan, 1986). It is easier to check for specific skills than to look for those qualities in applicants that will make them effective members of a team. For this reason, it is important that applicants be interviewed as well as tested for specific skills.

Screening Applicants

Because initial screening often is done by a personnel department, the records manager will usually interview only those applicants who are qualified for the position. Knowing that the minimal qualifications are met, the manager may be tempted to make a selection based on the attractiveness, age, or marital status of the applicant; but using these criteria for hiring purposes is inappropriate unless they relate specifically to the applicant's ability to perform the job. Affirmative Action/Equal Opportunity programs help to ensure that employment policies and practices are nondiscriminatory in terms of race, color, religion, age, national origin, sex, marital, parental, handicapped, or veteran status.

In order that ethical and legal aspects of hiring are satisfied, the records manager should obtain a list of legal interview questions and follow it in making a selection. If the business or organization has an office responsible for Affirmative Action/Equal Opportunity, the office should be consulted. In order to assess interest in the field, Dennis Morgan, past president of the South Florida Chapter Region III of ARMA, suggests that records managers ask applicants the following questions (Morgan, 1986):

- □ What, if anything, attracts you to the field of records management?
- □ What specifically do you hope to gain personally as a records management professional?
- □ How long do you expect to remain in this position if you are offered this opportunity?
- □ What element(s) of work give you the greatest satisfaction?
- □ What, if any, state-of-the-art technology intrigues you the most? the least?
- □ What, if anything, is the most boring aspect of records management?

The above questions are representative of the questions the records manager can ask to elicit information that reveals an individual's interest in and commitment to the field of records management. Not all of the questions need to be asked and these should be supplemented with other relevant questions.

Organizing: Running a Smooth Operation

To perform the organizing function, the records manager needs to understand several structural aspects of organization: (1) *chain of command*, which refers to the hierarchy of the department or business; that is, who is responsible to whom; (2) *unity of command*, which refers to the number of superiors an individual is responsible to; (3) *span of control*, which refers to the number of people supervised by a manager; and (4) *span of authority*, which refers to areas or activities over which a manager has authority. In relation to these structural aspects of organization, efficient management requires that the following principles be observed:

1. Requests for approval of programs and/or procedures are sent upward through the chain of command. This rule ensures that the organization's structure will support its objectives. It would be a serious mistake to implement a program without upper management's approval. If in doubt, obtain approval. If you like to live dangerously and do not value your career, then follow the maxim: "It is better to ask forgiveness than permission."
2. A manager may delegate responsibility but should delegate authority equal to that responsibility. If a manager does not delegate authority, then the delegation is a pretense. The manager will remain solely accountable for the quantity and quality of the work. If a manager feels that "I have to do everything myself," then this principle is probably being violated. If a manager wishes to increase the work that is efficiently completed, then he or she should give subordinates the appropriate power to carry out tasks.
3. Employees should not have more than one immediate supervisor. If such a situation cannot be avoided, then the responsibilities to each supervisor should be defined clearly. This precept is intended to avoid conflicting demands on employees.
4. Employees need a clear understanding of their jobs and a clear understanding of relationships among positions within the department and throughout the business. An organization chart, such as one shown in Chapter 3 (page 33), can help to clarify these relationships. Application of this principle increases the flow of information and employee interaction in the organization. The degree to which employees know, for example, where to go for information, or who can resolve a

problem, increases the efficiency of the organization.

5. A manager should not be responsible for more people than he or she can effectively supervise. Management research shows that, under ideal conditions in which the above principles are followed, the ideal number of employees under one manager is seven. Depending on the nature of the organization, the complexity of the jobs, and other factors, the maximum may be as many as fifteen or as few as three.

Each of the above principles applies to relationships of people within the business. Sometimes, as with the last two principles, the records manager has little choice in the decision. However, where procedures are concerned, the manager usually has more power. The following descriptions of correspondence management, reports management, forms management, and preparation of a records management manual, will help the reader understand how a records manager implements procedures.

Correspondence and Reports Management

Correspondence and reports management is concerned with coordinating the people, equipment, and procedures involved in producing written communications in the business. The records manager's major interest is in preparing procedures and monitoring the effectiveness of the program. In managing a correspondence and reports program, the records manager sets several specific objectives, such as reducing the quantity of original correspondence, and makes policies (within his or her authority), such as using preprinted forms for certain correspondence. The records manager prepares company procedures for creating written communications (for example, how to dictate), as well as develops procedures for purging documents, protecting vital records, and moving records to permanent storage.

An effective correspondence and reports program includes:

1. a commitment from top management to support the program
2. an initial survey of existing procedures and current costs, and periodic evaluation of the program thereafter
3. the refinement of existing procedures and the development of new methods to improve productivity and reduce costs
4. the involvement of staff and users in the program.

Getting Top Management Support Correspondence and reports are always generated by a business, but are sometimes overlooked as an element of records management. Also, top management is usually unaware of the costs of producing, storing, and retrieving correspondence and reports. Therefore, the first step in developing a program is to determine the volume of correspondence and reports being produced by the business and the approximate costs of production. The manager must then develop a proposal for a program to reduce costs and take the proposal to top management for approval. Usually, the reaction of top management will be tentative with a request for more information before giving approval for a full-fledged program. At this point, however, the manager has the authority to evaluate existing procedures and determine actual costs.

Initial Evaluation of Procedures and Costs The initial assessment of correspondence and reports procedures and their associated costs requires a survey of the procedures being used to create the documents. Costs to be considered include (1) the costs of the writer's time to draft the documents; (2) the cost for equipment, materials, supplies, and personnel to prepare the documents; (3) the cost of storing and retrieving copies; and

Figure 4.1 Correspondence Survey

Correspondence Survey

Instructions: Please answer the following items to the best of your ability. Return the questionnaire to the Records Management Department.

Name: ______________________ Date: __________
Department: ______________________________

1. What is the average number of the items of correspondence you produce per day? _____
2. What percent of your time per day is spent composing correspondence? _____
3. What percent of your correspondence is dictated to a secretary? _____ dictated to a machine? _____
4. What percent of your correspondence is drafted in longhand? _____
5. For what percent of your correspondence do you use form letters? _____
6. How is your correspondence reproduced for distribution?

   _____ WP equipment
   _____ typewriter
   _____ electronic mail

7. What is the average number of copies made of your correspondence? _____
8. What is the average number of pages for your memos? _____ letters? _____

(4) the cost of copying, distributing, and routing the documents. Figure 4.1 shows a survey form for assessing the cost of correspondence.

As a guide in determining correspondence costs, research shows that a single-page business letter, created and printed in separate operations, required about $10.00 in organization resources in 1988. As you might expect, the salaries of the persons involved are the largest cost element.

The assessment of existing procedures and costs for reports requires two additional items. Because reports are often lengthy, widely distributed, and generated routinely, a more detailed assessment of report cre-

Figure 4.2 Reports Inventory Form

Reports Inventory Form						
1. Group		2. Department		3. Location		
4. Date		5. Acct. No.		6. Phone		
Report Title	No. of Pages	Security Class	Orig. Dept.	Prep.*		
				M	ADP	

*M = manual; ADP = automated data processing.

Source Chuck Shiell, "Reports Control and Evaluation," *Records Management Quarterly*, July 1978.

ation and distribution is needed. A reports inventory form (see Figure 4.2) may be sent to each department to determine the scope of existing reports. In a large business, many reports are generated through the Data Processing Department. If this is the case, then data processing operations may be able to provide a complete inventory of the reports they generate, their distribution, and the costs involved. Businesses produce a variety of reports for internal use and for government agencies. Some of the most common reports are activity and production reports, forecasts, status reports, government reports required for various financial and personnel situations, and research reports concerning a particular project or problem.

The manager determines costs based on the reports inventory and, if available, information from data processing operations. Getting precise cost figures and estimating savings from proposed procedures is always difficult, but the data gathered from surveys and inventories will usually provide sufficient information for the manager to make cost estimates.

Developing Procedures to Increase Productivity The surveys and inventories of correspondence and reports procedures will help the records manager identify what procedures need to be changed and what procedures should be developed. With the data on procedures and costs from the initial estimates, the records manager plans new procedures and returns to top management for approval of a program to implement them.

For correspondence control, two approaches to increasing productivity are, first, to standardize as much correspondence as possible and, second, to encourage fast and efficient production methods. With computer-based central word processing and/or stand-alone microcomputers, there is a potential for significant efficiency increases through the application of correspondence controls. Examples of standardized correspondence and steps for efficiency can be provided in a manual for distribution throughout the company. If a correspondence manual does not already exist, one that incorporates the following items should be created:

1. *Illustrations of the letter styles used in the organization*. For computer users, the styles in use would be available as outline or format files in digital format.
2. *Examples of form letters used for various situations*. Form letters should follow a standardized design using a fill-in or checklist format. These are available from various commercial sources in notebook format or on microcomputer magnetic media.
3. *Dictation procedures designed to maximize efficiency*. For example, the procedures may suggest the use of a standard format and style.
4. *Mailing information*. This includes the use of any mailing accessories or procedures that are available to speed up operations, particularly multiple mailings.
5. *Guide paragraphs and guide letters. Guide paragraphs*, or "boilerplates," are those written for various situations; the user selects the appropriate paragraphs—usually by number—and combines them in a letter. The process is sometimes called *document assembly*. *Guide letters* are similar to form letters except that the user adapts a guide letter rather than using it verbatim. Sophisticated computer software is making the use of guides easy and practical for document assembly.
6. *Information on using the word processing center (if one exists)*. Simply announcing that centralized word processing is available may not induce employees to flock to use it. A clear, well-written correspondence manual can do wonders in encouraging the use of the word processing center.

For reports control, the two main strategies involve the quantity and quality of the reports. To control quantity, the manager can reduce the number of reports distributed by attaching a report evaluation form to all distributed reports. This form would ask the recipient to indicate:

- □ if a copy of the report is needed
- □ if the information in the report could be obtained from another source
- □ if the report format should be changed

and other questions that would help determine the value of the report to the recipient. The results of this survey will almost certainly allow for a reduction in the quantity of reports. In a severe situation, the records manager might send the report evaluation form out with instructions that if the form is not returned, the report will be automatically discontinued to that location. This may become a regular requirement when data processing is involved in the production and distribution of reports. The advantage of rapid and multiple report generation also can be a disadvantage because it is so simple to produce unnecessary reports.

The quality approach to reports control significantly aids the writing of necessary reports by the use of a reports catalog, which tells what reports have been created, what they contain, and where they are located. The manager also can improve the quality of reports and the time required to create them by illustrating standardized formats, limiting the number of pages, and providing a formula for determining readability. *Readability* refers to a reader's ability to read and understand the written material. Several formulas to determine readability have been devised; for example, the Fog Index, developed by Robert Gunning, provides a method for calculating the reading grade level at which a passage is written. Methods for determining readability can be found in most business communications textbooks.

As a rule of thumb, the grade level of written material in business should be between eight and twelve. If the reading level of the writing is too high, it will discourage the reader, encourage misinterpretations, and fail to serve its intended purpose. To lower the reading level of text, the accepted methods include shortening sentences to single ideas and replacing uncommon, difficult words with common, well-known words. Of course, attention must be paid to the overall meaning of the message when altering text.

Periodic Evaluation of the Program The manager can determine if the quantity of correspondence and reports has been reduced or if production methods have changed by conducting a follow-up survey. The questionnaires and forms used in the initial assessment are sent out again, perhaps six months or a year later, and the beginning and ending data are compared. An evaluation of the quality of the program is more difficult because the manager must make subjective judgments. Unless the manager reviews all correspondence and reports personally—and this would be impractical—the people using the procedures are in the best position to evaluate them. Simply talking to key people and recording their responses is one method of evaluating a process. Another method is to use another survey questionnaire. This approach has the advantage of keeping the respondent's identity anonymous. In either case, the manager can compile the responses and determine the attitudes of the users. A third alternative is to hire a consultant to review the program and the documents being produced. Although the consultant can provide a more objective analysis and review, the cost may not be feasible.

Involvement of Users At every step in the process of developing and evaluating a records management program, the manager should consult the people who will be using the procedures. It is tempting to tell users rather than to ask them; this temptation should be avoided if problems are to be minimized in the long run. In addition to formal information gathering, informal meetings with groups of users help the manager make satisfactory decisions and are less time-consuming than individual meetings.

Forms Management

Forms represent a considerable expense for most businesses. The estimated cost of forms shipped to corporations in 1972 was $1.4 billion; by 1986, the cost was estimated by the National Business Forms Association (NBFA) to be $8 billion. Forms are necessary, however, for several reasons; businesses use them to standardize the reporting of information, structure the type and amount of information gathered, collect information for internal decisions, and provide information to outside agencies. Poorly designed forms and uncontrolled production can result in the use of ineffective and inefficient forms, duplication of similar forms, collection of unnecessary or unusable information, maintenance of an unrealistic inventory, and, ultimately, the loss of time and money.

The traditional definition of a *form* is a printed document on which some information stays the same and other variable information is inserted. However, forms can be kept on a computer and printed *after* the variable information is inserted or not printed at all! Businesses undoubtedly will use this approach in the future, but printed forms probably will continue to be the dominant approach in many companies for several years. In any case, the elements of a good forms management program can be applied to either preprinted or computerized forms.

A typical forms management program includes three areas: analysis, design and construction, and control. Usually, the records manager has responsibility for overall management and control of the program; a forms analyst may have primary responsibility for analyzing forms, and the design and construction of forms may be in-house or relegated to a printing service.

Forms Analysis A *forms analyst* identifies the purpose of existing and proposed forms, researches similar forms within the company to avoid duplication and facilitate designing proposed forms, and determines who will use the form and how it should be routed or distributed.

Forms Design and Construction Efficient design and proper construction of forms is essential. Elements of good design include determining the best item arrangement and making the form usable and visually attractive. Item arrangement includes five basic sections:

1. title of the form and identifying number
2. routing information
3. instructions and/or introduction
4. specific items in logical groups
5. closing section, which may include signatures, approvals, and dates.

The visual attractiveness and usability of the form is achieved by providing adequate spacing between items and sections, sufficient space to insert information, clear wording, highlighted sections to capture attention, and the use of captions, check boxes, screening, and lines to emphasize items and simplify completion of the form. Figure 4.3 illustrates the various parts of a well-designed form.

Construction considerations include the type and weight of paper to use, how many copies to provide, whether to use a carbonless form, what size the form should be, and how the form should be assembled and

Figure 4.3 Forms Design and Construction

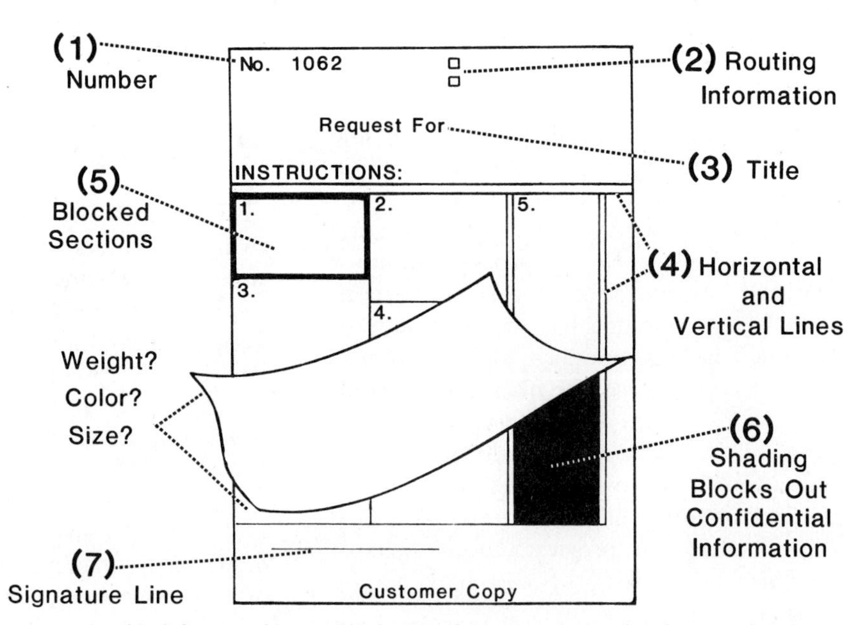

Source Carol Lundgren and Joyce Kupsh, *Records Management,* National Instructional Systems Inc., 1985. Used by permission.

bound. There are several types of form construction; a print shop can help the manager decide which style will be most compatible with the purpose of the form.

Forms Control Controlling the forms program includes providing an identification method, deciding the most cost-effective production method, using an *inventory control system,* and disposing of obsolete or unused forms.

Forms may be identified by number or subject. A numbering system has several advantages because a two-part number or a letter-number can identify a department and sequence. For example, if the personnel department is 342, a job application form can be numbered 342-4 to indicate that it is the fourth form in a personnel series. A third number can be added to indicate the last revision, such as 342-4-080687. The last number shows the month, day, and year the form was created or revised. Forms can then be filed first by the department number, then sequentially within each department, and finally by date.

A manager must choose from several methods for producing forms. If an in-house print shop exists, that method is often least expensive. Desktop publishing software can enable each department or a word processing center to prepare forms, but this method complicates the control process. A company may require a manager to go through a central purchasing office, which selects an outside printer to produce company forms. Finally, a records manager may decide to have all forms produced within the records department. In most cases, a cost comparison of the methods is a wise and necessary step.

An inventory control system for preprinted forms should show the amount and type of forms on hand, reorder information (such as reorder lead time, vendor, quantity, and form characteristics), and usage trends. This information is crucial to efficient forms control. If the reorder lead time is ignored or too many forms are ordered, the consequences can be disastrous. An inventory control system for computer forms identifies the forms that have been created, as well as access, usage, and distribution information.

The final element of forms control is to have a method for forms disposal that allows the manager to dispose of a form when it is replaced by a revised form or the need for the form has ended. One sample of the destroyed form should be kept along with a record of destroyed forms. A notebook system works well for this procedure.

A real revolution in forms management is on the horizon with the possibility of totally electronic forms. With the use of telecommunications and computers, forms can be created, filed, retrieved, altered, and destroyed—without ever being put on paper. Consider the possible advantages of computer-generated forms. The "inventory" is in digital format with virtually no space requirements or reorder points. The creation or alteration of a form is simplified and the need to "use up old stock" is eliminated. Data errors are reduced for computer entry since it is already available in the correct media. Additional sophisticated software can be used to validate data as it is entered, for example, to make sure numeric or alphabetic characters are entered in the proper locations. Finally, forms can be more easily controlled in this manner.

The Records Management Manual

A records management manual provides information on the company and records management procedures. The records manager prepares the manual primarily for use in the records management department, but it may be used throughout the company. The manual should accomplish the following objectives:

1. establish uniform procedures

2. set forth responsibility and authority for each part of the records management process
3. provide a training tool for new employees
4. keep personnel updated on organization policies and federal or agency/state retention requirements.

Ordinarily, the following items are included in a records management manual: general information (for example, a brief history of the company, a company or department organization chart, company rules and regulations), job descriptions for records personnel, filing rules, computer procedures, information on micrographic and reprographic functions and procedures, and a companywide retention schedule. The records manager should gather all the information to include in the manual. Often, items such as an organization chart and job descriptions already will be available. Charts should be used to illustrate and explain complicated procedures; a flow chart approach works well for explaining most procedures. A key objective in both designing the illustration and explaining the procedure itself should be to keep them as simple as possible. Narrative sections should be written in a clear, readable style with references to examples or other sources of information.

When a procedure is proposed, the records staff and those users who will be affected by the procedure should have the opportunity to review it and make suggestions. The same is true regarding the records management manual. Although it is not always practical to have the entire manual reviewed by every member of the records staff and every user, various parts can and should be reviewed by selected personnel before the manual is printed in final form.

Finally, the manager devises a simple updating method before the manual is printed. An unbound notebook approach with independently numbered sections has several advantages. The loose pages can be replaced easily and sections can be revised without reprinting the entire manual. Pages within sections are numbered 1-1, 1-2, 1-3, etc. Additions within a section can be numbered 1-2a, 1-2b, and so forth so that only a few pages in a section need to be changed and the rest of the section essentially can remain intact. It may be useful to use a different colored paper for changes and additions; when the manual shows a significant color change, then the entire manual should be reviewed and re-prepared in a single color again. In any case, the manual should be completely reviewed if significant changes occur in the records system, or every three to five years.

Directing: Training Records Management Personnel

Providing direction is an important part of the records manager's role. Directing is essentially a teaching function and is not synonymous with merely giving orders. A good manager will take responsibility for assisting and motivating the staff as well as meeting their training needs. You may have worked with a manager who "pitches in" to help complete a project. That person is usually available to the staff in other situations, as well.

The way in which managers direct is related to their management style. Some managers have an *authoritative style,* which means they tend to dictate orders; others have a *democratic* or *participative style,* which means they encourage staff participation in decision making. Some situations demand an authoritative approach. For example, if a decision must be made immediately, the manager must act—time for consultation is not available nor desirable. Some situations demand a combination of styles. The records manager should assess the situation and determine how to deal with it effectively. The records manager must often be a motivator, teacher, and amateur psychologist to be an effective director.

Training new employees and providing educational opportunities for staff members may be handled in some companies by a company trainer. In that case, the records manager suggests the programs needed by the staff and recommends attendees. If the company lacks a training program, the records manager can suggest other possibilities for training and even may obtain company financing (for example, tuition reimbursement) for records personnel. Finally, the records manager may choose to plan, develop, direct, and coordinate specific training sessions. This approach requires upper-management approval because of the resources necessary for implementation; significant time will be consumed in the planning and organizing of the training sessions. Although initially expensive, training generated in the records department can be flexibly tailored to specific needs, which may result in long-run benefits. Once put in place, a carefully tailored training program can be virtually self-sustaining and easily altered.

Controlling: Performance Evaluations and Budgets

To control effectively, the manager must have goals, standards, ways to measure performance to see if standards are being met, and methods for correcting deviations. Controlling also refers to keeping costs within prescribed limits. Two common methods of management control are performance evaluations and budgets.

Performance Evaluations

Performance evaluations may be subjective or objective. A subjective evaluation uses a rating system. For example, individuals may be rated as poor, average, or excellent on several technical and personal characteristics; or they may be given an overall performance rating based on the manager's perception of their performance. Criteria for an overall rating is shown in Figure 4.4. An objective evaluation of records personnel uses a formula to determine the quantity of work

Figure 4.4 Criteria for Performance Rating

Distinguished—Performance that is comparable to the best the Company has seen. It is clearly and consistently excellent, absolutely outstanding. Distinguished performance demonstrates a very high degree of expertise, far exceeding Company expectations of what is required.

Commendable—Performance that exceeds Company expectations of what is required. It is clearly and consistently effective. Commendable performance demonstrates unusual proficiency and is identifiable as being at a very high level.

Competent—Performance that is consistently satisfactory and dependable. Consistently demonstrates the level of performance expected by the Company. Fully meets and sometimes exceeds performance requirements.

Adequate—Performance that is usually but not consistently satisfactory. It comes close to fully meeting performance requirements and Company expectations, but some improvement is desirable.

Unacceptable—Performance does not meet minimum requirements of the position. Requires placing the employee on probation and establishing a plan of corrective action with specific standards and a progress review schedule.

performed compared to a preset standard. For example, a standard for performance is determined—the employee should file forty documents in thirty minutes—and records of actual performance are kept to compare to the standard. The records manager can devise formulas for measuring performance or obtain standards and performance criteria from ARMA.

Usually a combination of both subjective and objective methods are used for performance rating. Objective evaluations are made of the employee's skills and work performance. For example, the employee is measured on various skills and performance levels on a scale standardized from 0 to 100. A total is computed and combined with a subjective evaluation to arrive at an overall rating on a scale like that shown in Figure 4.4.

Regardless of the method used for performance rating, the manager should view the rating process as an opportunity to develop employees' potentials rather than as an occasion to punish them. Research evidence on this point is especially clear. Using the rating process to punish employees lowers their morale, decreases productivity, increases absenteeism, and increases vandalism. The following points emphasize a positive approach to evaluation:

1. Discuss the rating with the employee and work out a mutually acceptable strategy for the employee to improve.
2. Set clear and reasonable expectations for improvement.
3. Show that improvement will bring better ratings and consequently greater rewards.

Budgets

Simply stated, a *budget* is an estimated plan of operations for the future expressed in financial terms. Budgets are used for planning and controlling. The planning phrase is called budgeting, and the actual written plans are called budgets. In large organizations, it is often necessary to create a master budget in which all plans are summarized; the details are then itemized in various departmental and specialized budgets. Each department head is responsible for the preparation and administration of that department's budget. The responsibility for the overall budget resides with the organization's top financial officer. Most businesses use a budget period that is suited to their particular needs, which may be monthly, quarterly, or yearly.

The records management budget will include salaries, equipment, supplies, and any other items for which costs must be estimated. Periodically, the records manager compares actual expenses with those that have been estimated. The objective is to keep costs within prescribed limits and, when the costs exceed those limits, to determine why and what steps to take to correct the situation.

Summary

The five functions of management are planning, staffing, organizing, directing, and controlling. Records managers plan by setting records management goals and objectives that conform to the goals of the business, the major goal being to make a profit. Preparing job descriptions and interviewing applicants are part of the staffing function of the records manager. The organizing function is accomplished by coordinating the people, procedures, and equipment in the department. In doing so, the records manager follows organization principles concerning chain of command, span of control, unity of command, and span of authority. The management of correspondence, reports, and forms illustrates the organizing function.

Correspondence and reports management requires a systematic program, which includes getting top management support, evaluating procedures and costs, developing new procedures, and involving users in the program. Forms management also requires a systematic program, including forms analysis, design and construction, and control. The records manager uses a records management manual to facilitate organization and control of records management procedures.

The records manager directs by motivating and assisting employees. The manager's management style plus company policy determine to what extent the records manager is involved in meeting the training needs of records personnel. Control is the process of comparing performance to preset standards and correcting deviations. Two major operations over which the records manager has control are performance evaluations and budgets.

List of Terms

- cost center
- Association of Records Managers and Administrators (ARMA)
- Association for Information and Image Management (AIIM)
- Certified Records Manager (CRM)
- chain of command
- unity of command
- span of control
- span of authority
- guide paragraph
- document assembly
- guide letter
- readability
- form
- forms analysis/analyst
- inventory control system
- authoritative style
- democratic or participative style
- performance evaluation
- budget

Discussion Questions

1. What are the five management functions?
2. What structural aspects of organization should a manager know?
3. What is the principle of organization related to span of control? chain of command? unity of command?
4. Which principle of organization do you believe is most important and why?
5. What are the records manager's responsibilities in preparing job descriptions and screening applicants?
6. What steps should the records manager follow in setting up a correspondence and reports management program?
7. How can clearly written procedures increase productivity?
8. What are the three ways in which a records manager can evaluate a correspondence or reports program?
9. What are the elements of a good forms program?
10. What are the steps to consider in forms design?

11. What are the components of forms control and how is each component implemented by a records manager?
12. What are two methods of performance evaluation?
13. What is the purpose of a records management budget?
14. How does the records manager use performance evaluations to "control" productivity?

Activities

1. Consult several records management journals, such as *Records Management Quarterly* and *Inform,* and general business journals, such as *Modern Office Technology.* Write a brief report (four to five pages) on how one or more companies has/have instituted a correspondence, reports, or forms management program.
2. Design a form for use as an employment application for a position in a large records center. If possible, use a computer with forms software or word processing software.
3. Interview a records manager and determine what tasks he/she performs under each of the five functions of management (planning, staffing, organizing, directing, and controlling).
4. Visit any large business or organization and determine its criteria for performance rating. Try to interview both a supervisor (one doing the rating) and an employee who would be rated by that supervisor. Do they seem to agree on the criteria?
5. Visit an office and see if it has a records management manual or some type of manual that includes procedures for records management (for example, an office manual). Assess its organization, contents, and timeliness.
6. Interview someone with at least five years of work experience to determine the training and educational opportunities that the person has had in his or her career.
7. Consult one or more of the training and development practitioner journals and write a report that describes the information that directly relates to records management.

References

Dalton, Richard. "Paper Forms Go Electronic." *Lotus* (February 1987): 24.

Melrose, John. "Introduction to Records Management." ARMA Conference, Boston, Massachusetts, October 1980.

Morgan, Dennis F. "Personnel Selection and Interviewing: Professional and Personal Perspectives." *Records Management Quarterly* (July 1986): 20–22, 24.

Perry, Kenneth. *Accounting: An Introduction* (New York: McGraw-Hill, 1981).

Schiell, Chuck. "Reports Control and Evaluation." *Records Management Quarterly* (July 1978).

Chapter 4 Highlight

Office Planning and Layout

All large businesses experience growth and change, which is reflected in physical changes in the office environment. New divisions are added and existing departments are moved to new locations. In either case, people and equipment must be arranged in the new locations. Corporations often contract the new office planning and layout to consulting firms that specialize in this activity. Probably the second source of office planning and layout is the records management department.

The records manager can depend on regular requests for office layouts and planning. Commonly, requests come from the office that is obtaining new equipment or from personnel in the old office. They ask that a plan be devised to accommodate the new resources. Because records storage equipment is a primary component of almost all offices, the records manager is expected to know how to arrange the office.

In reality, although some knowledge and planning are essential, it rarely takes special expertise to arrange office furniture. If you have a list of the furniture, it is fairly simple to estimate the needed access space and layout. For example, vertical drawer files require at least 30 inches to pull out the drawers and another 16 inches for the person who will access them to stand. Scale layouts can be purchased with miniature cutouts of desks, files, tables, and other types of office equipment or furniture. These can be arranged to try different layouts. The problem is that just fitting equipment into a certain amount of space is seldom the whole answer to office layout.

The following practical suggestions are for records managers who are placed in the position of planning an office layout. Keep in mind that the ideal situation is to arrange new equipment in new offices for new employees. More often, the people and equipment will be in place and you will be expected to fit them to a new location.

1. If there are existing employees, be sure to obtain their input; if reasonable, cater to their requests. These employees will be the ultimate judges of the layout.
2. Measure everything carefully. For an office layout, inches are critical. For the lack of one-half inch clearance, a door will not shut! Scale models will not always work for precise planning.
3. If the head of another department is requesting office planning and rearrangement for existing personnel and equipment, be wary. This may be an effort to solve a personnel problem. You don't want to get caught in the middle of office politics. Be sure to apply Suggestion No. 1.
4. Always present at least two or three alternatives. One of the alternatives should be a replication of the standard office, which is the closest office that has been in operation for more than three months.

Chapter 5

The Records Information System

Learning Goals

1. To become familiar with the concept of the records information system.
2. To explain the processes of acquisition and creation in a records information system.
3. To be aware of the procedures and problems involved in active records maintenance.
4. To be able to differentiate between the ways of storing active versus inactive records.
5. To be knowledgeable about the final disposition phase of the records information system.

Introduction

Records management is concerned with tracking records throughout an information flow. Traditionally, this flow has been called the "records life cycle." The records life cycle is based on the hypothetical "life" of a record—creation, use, and eventual destruction or permanent storage. Records, however, seldom go through a life cycle in a straight line from beginning to end. Therefore, it is more useful to think of records as being in an information flow that consists of specific phases, with the phases related to the functions of records management. This is called the *records information system*.

In this chapter, first we will give a general description of each of the four major phases of this system and then describe each phase in detail, emphasizing important areas and trends.

The Phases of a Records Information System

Records exist in an information flow that consists of four major phases: definition, active maintenance, storage, and final disposition. These four phases are related according to the nature and types of records involved, and together they form the records information system. Figure 5.1 shows the interrelationships involved in the system. The sizes of the different rectangles roughly represent the volume of records involved in a particular area. For example, as

Figure 5.1 The Records Information System

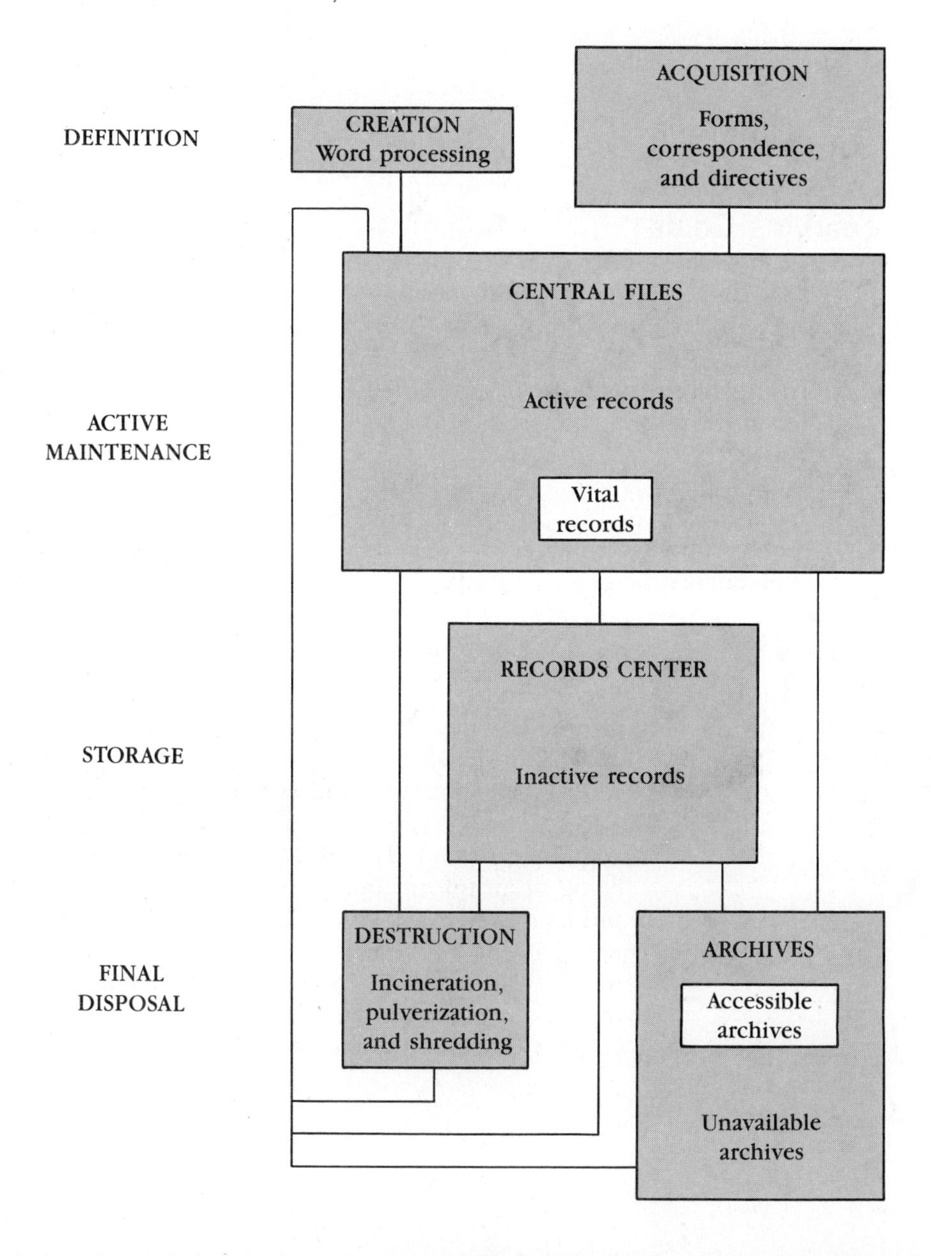

Figure 5.1 clearly indicates, central files in the active maintenance phase is the dominant activity in the entire records information system.

Definition Phase

The typical records information system begins with the definition of a record for entry into the system—the *definition phase*. In almost all businesses, more records are acquired than created. Types of records that are acquired include forms, correspondence, and directives such as manuals, instructions, notices, and other types of company documentation. The major form of records creation is through word processing. All of these sources feed into the active maintenance phase.

Active Maintenance Phase

Active maintenance essentially means the regular storage and retrieval of records. The records are called active because they are likely to be retrieved. Figure 5.1 uses the name "central files" for the active records area to indicate that these records are often filed in a centralized location. This area includes vital records that are indispensable to the operation of the business.

Storage Phase

As records age, they may be defined as inactive, obsolete, or of secondary value. Depending on their definition, they may go to the *storage phase* or to final disposal. Some records such as vital records do not effectively "age" and so are never redefined and do not leave active maintenance.

If records are defined as inactive, they will be retrieved infrequently, if at all. Inactive records are kept because there is a possibility, however small, that they might be required. Most records in this stage eventually are redefined as obsolete or of secondary value. For example, inactive client records usually are defined as obsolete after the client's death, though some may have historical (secondary) value if the client was a well-known public figure. It is possible that some records will never leave this stage; for example, many hotels keep room reservations in permanent, inactive storage as a matter of policy.

Finally, through changes in other conditions, an inactive record may return to active maintenance. For example, researchers on a new aerospace project could find that the equipment designed in an earlier project could be used again with slight alterations. Those records of the earlier project that dealt with the designated equipment would be pulled from inactive storage and returned to active status.

Final Disposition Phase

When records are defined as obsolete or of secondary value, they are destroyed or archived in the *final disposition phase*. Destruction of records through incineration, pulverization, or shredding is considered permanent removal of the record. If there is a chance, however, that the record has a secondary value—for example, a historical value—then the record may be archived. Archived records may be either accessible to the public or generally unavailable. In rare instances, an archived record may return to active maintenance.

Figure 5.1 illustrates only the general flow of records, the phases of which we have just briefly described. The following sections provide a more detailed examination of each of the major phases involved in the records information system.

Records Definition

The first phase of the records information system is the definition of items entering the system, so that they may become records. This definition of items is largely in place in any system so that the flow to the central files is quite clear. For example, in a large manufacturing business, the records are clearly defined to consist of correspondence, sales orders, purchase orders, manufacturing specifications, etc.; as these items are created or acquired, they are routinely routed to central files. Note in Figure 5.1 (on page 60) that a line runs also from the bottom areas of destruction, records center, and archives up through the definition phase into central files. This means that it is possible that some records may be redefined from the storage or final disposition stage back into active maintenance.

Creation

Many created records enter the system through *word processing* activities. The records are document, text-based records such as correspondence, reports, articles, and books. Word processing is very important because it accounts for the majority of the total paperwork costs in the business office. Efficient management of word processing will contribute significantly toward maximizing productivity in the office.

Increasingly, the word processing function is turning to the computer. Smaller offices use microcomputers, and in larger businesses the word processing function has been centralized to take advantage of the efficiencies of mini- and mainframe computer processing. With computer word processing, the paper output is routed as usual to the recipients and central files, but the electronic files remain in the word processing area and require their own records management.

Acquisitions

Most of the records that are introduced into the systems are acquired rather than created; that is, they were created in some other context and made their way into the records information system. The majority of *acquisitions* in a business occur through the mail. Other sources include customer contact, computer output, and form parts. In some businesses, forms constitute most of the paper records.

It is important to control the acquisition of records through the standardization of procedures for their entry into central files. Because of the volume of records involved, careful attention to procedures that reduce handling and routing can be very cost effective.

Active Records Maintenance

Maintaining the active records for efficient storage and retrieval is the most important phase of the records information system. This phase requires the largest investment in personnel and equipment relative to the other phases. Active records maintenance is the most visible area and often the most sensitive to user approval. If records cannot be retrieved within users' expected time frames, the entire records information system is suspect. Therefore, the single most important criteria of the entire system is the efficient retrieval of records.

In order to assess a system's retrieval efficiency, it is necessary to study and analyze the contents and procedures of the system. The first step in this type of analysis requires that a *records inventory* be taken.

Records Inventory

Retrieval efficiency is always important, so when should a records inventory be done? A number of situations may call for an inventory; for example, the records manager should institute an inventory whenever significant changes occur in the system. These changes may be obvious, as when the business acquires a large subsidiary whose records must be merged; or they may be more subtle, as when a new record series is added to the central files. Examples of external motivations for a records inventory may be demands from top management to improve efficiency, or an anticipated conversion to a computer-based system. Whatever the reason, the records inventory is directed by the records manager, who may delegate aspects to subordinates or outside consultants.

The objectives of a records inventory are:

1. To identify the types, quantities, and locations of equipment, supplies, and records.
2. To identify the purpose of the records, the users, and the frequency of use.
3. To identify the periods of storage and suggested disposition of all records.

Given the information collected from a records inventory, analysis can be performed to improve the efficiency of the system while minimizing costs. The records inventory provides the basis for:

- ☐ cost analysis
- ☐ retention scheduling
- ☐ equipment purchase decisions
- ☐ security assessment
- ☐ personnel needs.

The records inventory has two methodological approaches, the *physical inventory* and the *interview,* which may be supplemented by the *survey questionnaire*.

Figure 5.2 shows a sample records inventory form that could be used for a physical inventory. This form would be filled out by records personnel, not those who use the records. The form allows for entries that obtain the information about equipment and procedures needed to identify the system properties. The sample form is quite general and probably would be tailored to the specific business being inventoried.

While doing a physical inventory using a standard form, you should also note other information relevant to efficient records management. For example, are records piled inappropriately? Are physical materials neat? Are labels clear and legible? After the physical inventory has been taken, a review of the information almost always reveals incomplete or unclear points. A re-inventory to gather additional information that will clarify the original inventory usually is needed.

A physical inventory always should be supplemented with information gained from interviewing those persons who operate the records system. An interview schedule that includes the following questions should be prepared:

1. Who are the major users of the different types of records in the system?
2. What is the purpose and frequency of use of the different record types?
3. What are the periods of storage and suggested disposition of all records?
4. What is the most significant problem with the records information system?

The interview should involve the records manager and at least one person from each personnel category in the system. In addition, one or more representatives of the major records users should be interviewed with particular emphasis on point 4 above. In this way, a complete picture of the entire records operation can be obtained.

For records that are difficult to reach through a physical inventory because of volume or because they are in different (decentralized) locations, a survey questionnaire is appropriate. The questionnaire is a combined version of the physical records inventory and interview in a format suitable for records personnel and users to complete. A good general rule for questionnaire construction is to avoid open-ended questions that require the user to write a response. Keep the questionnaire short, concise, and with questions that only require an X in a box for a response.

In some cases, a thorough records inventory may not be necessary or feasible. The goal simply may be an appraisal of the

Figure 5.2 Records Inventory Form

Record Series/Type: ____________________

Organization: ____________________

Department/Unit Name: ____________________

Part 1st ☐ 2nd ☐ 3rd ☐ ________ of total # ________

Paper letter ☐ legal ☐ card ☐ size ________

Digital disk 8 ☐ 5.25 ☐ 3.5 ☐ online ☐
tape ☐ optical ☐ other ________

Image film ☐ fiche ☐ other ________

Frequency of use often/daily ☐ usual/weekly ☐
some/monthly ☐ rare/annually ☐

Function (users) primary ________
secondary ________

Classify alpha ☐ subject ☐ alpha/numeric ☐ num ☐
detail ________

Status active ☐ inactive ☐ vital ☐ archive ☐

Disposition status to be ________ after ________
Years from ________ to ________
Equipment vertical ☐ lateral ☐ shelf ☐
other ________

Quantity cu ft ________ inches ________ other ________

Location ________

General comments/recommendations ________

____

____

Prepared by ________ Date ____/____/____

system to determine if further analysis and information is necessary. In this case, a simpler and faster inventory may be appropriate. Figure 5.3, "The Ten-Minute Records Appraisal," shows a format for a brief records inventory. Figure 5.3 would not be completed as a survey questionnaire because the nature of the questions requires a strong background in records and information management.

A complete and thorough records inventory allows for an excellent analysis of the records information system. In addition, careful public records inventory has second-

Figure 5.3 The Ten-Minute Records Appraisal

Directions: Answer each of the following questions about the records system during a brief physical inventory and interview with records personnel.

Yes/no	*File management question*
_______	Does each record storage unit have between 10–20% free or working space available?
_______	For alphabetic files only: Are the "B", "M", or "S" sections *not* crowded?
_______	Do active files have file guides (about one guide per three inches or ten folders)?
_______	Are the records ever purged?
_______	Are all labels clearly visible and easy to read?
_______	Is there a retention schedule?
_______	Are all records in files with no loose records around (on top of, next to, etc.) the file area?
_______	Is there a checkout system?
_______	Are out guides used for removed records?
_______	Are appropriate records the only items in the files (compared to nonrecord items or "wrong" records)?
_______	Does the equipment work smoothly and easily?
_______	Is there sufficient floor space to access the equipment easily?
_______	Do all records look clean, fresh, and in reasonable condition?
_______	Is there a records manual?
_______	Are users restricted from accessing the records?

If the checklist produced two or more "NO" answers, this system is ready for a file management program.

ary benefits. A thorough records inventory will impress management and users that the records department is conscientious and concerned with efficient records management. The thorough inventory will also acquaint users with the records personnel so that future meetings will be more productive.

Records Status Assessment

One of the persistent research outcomes of studies on records inventories is that approximately 30 percent of active records should be stored in inactive, less costly areas; and from 35 to 40 percent of active records should be destroyed (Littlefield et al., 1978). A reasonable conclusion is that the single largest waste in records management results from the incorrect definition of the status of records. Specifically, consider a situation in which obsolete or seldom-used records that account for about 65 percent of central files could be destroyed, archived, or moved to inactive storage. The benefits would include:

1. *Storage space.* An increase in storage space would be made available for other activities and expansion of the active files.

Given the high cost of office space, the savings could be considerable.

2. *Equipment and supplies.* Old equipment could be recycled and the costs of new equipment and supplies would be substantially reduced.
3. *Increased storage/retrieval efficiency.* Productivity would be increased with fewer active records to maintain. The chances of losing or misfiling records would be decreased along with speedier storage and retrieval.

A major factor in a records information system's efficiency is correctly defining when an active record should be inactive, archived, or destroyed. This problem requires records retention scheduling, a topic that is considered later in this chapter. There are, however, records that never become inactive or obsolete. These vital records are so important to the business that they always remain in the active maintenance phase.

Vital Records

The records inventory should identify *vital records,* which are those records that are essential to the daily operation of a company. The traditional criteria for defining vital records is the disaster test. If a disaster occurred and destroyed central files, which records would have to be recovered to continue the business operations? These absolutely essential records are defined as "vital records."

Vital records may include accounts receivable, bylaws, copyrights, franchises, formulas, insurance policies, personnel records, and legal documents. The concept of vital records suggests that the records are irreplaceable. In fact, definitions of the importance of records are often based on the difficulty of replacement. For example, a common classification is:

Vital—cannot be replaced or can be replaced with extreme difficulty
Important—replaced with difficulty
Useful—easily replaced
Nonessential—should not be replaced

Original historical records cannot be replaced, but most records used in everyday business transactions probably could be replaced or reconstructed. Because there is always a cost involved in records replacement, both in time and money, the business question to be asked is: What are the costs for records replacement if there were a disaster and the records were destroyed? From this cost perspective, vital records need insurance and security.

The purpose of insurance is to provide protection against disaster. Based on the probability of a disaster, premiums are paid to buy the insurance. If a disaster strikes, the insurance compensates for the loss. For records, this approach is difficult to implement because the costs involved in the replacement of records is extremely difficult to estimate. Few insurance companies offer a "records replacement" policy; therefore, vital records require security and protection.

Precautions should be taken to guard vital records from a disaster. Security means providing the equipment and procedures to avoid a disaster situation, while protection refers to methods that mitigate the effects of a disaster. A *disaster* is defined as any event that removes records from normal accessibility, including theft, misplacement, insect damage, earthquake, water damage, fire, and other hazards. Both security and protection generally are achieved by similar equipment and procedures that restrict accessibility.

Because fire is the most common disaster, most pieces of equipment for vital records, such as small safes, file cabinets, and file rooms, are insulated against heat. Standards that describe how long equipment will withstand high heat are available from the Underwriter's Laboratories. For paper, the maximum acceptable temperature is 350 degrees Fahrenheit (162 degrees

Centigrade). Beyond 350 degrees, the paper will oxidize (burn) rendering it useless; if not actually burnt, the paper will be extremely brittle and very difficult to handle.

Since insurance for records is usually impractical, a generally accepted and cost-effective solution is to keep duplicates of vital records. *Dispersal* is the term used to describe the practice of making duplicates and storing them away from the originals. A common practice is to duplicate vital records on an alternate media, for example, microfilm or magnetic media, and to keep the duplicates stored off-site in a different physical location from the originals. Obviously, dispersal can be quite costly if there is a large volume of vital records that change frequently.

Records on magnetic media illustrate the problem of cost effectiveness of dispersal. For example, in a large, active organization, some files on magnetic media may be considered vital, being essential to the everyday operation of the business. Dispersal would require that the files be duplicated daily and stored off-site. To do so would require expensive computer time, equipment, storage space, and personnel on a daily basis. Additional programs that might be required if a disaster occurred would also be expensive. This cost on an annual basis might exceed the costs to replace the records from raw data should a disaster ever take place. Therefore, the business must carefully consider the tradeoff between dispersal and disaster costs. In actual practice, businesses, such as banks, create duplicate files on magnetic media on a daily basis and store those records off-site.

Classification of records as "vital," "important," and so forth is difficult to authorize; without clear direction, records personnel will tend to define almost all active records as vital. In fact, most experts agree that no more than 5 percent of an organization's records should be defined as vital. A reasonable solution is to include the definition of vital records in a retention schedule, taking care to point out the costs involved in securing and protecting them.

A relatively new concept in information management is *vital processing*. Vital processing refers to processing that is absolutely essential to the ongoing operation of the business. Examples include payroll processing, daily receipt transactions, and client billing. In the same sense as vital records, vital processing should be secured and protected. For example, arrangements should be made for off-site processing availability should a disaster prevent the processing operations. Although mainframe computer systems incorporate this eventuality and have prepared plans for possible disaster, other areas in the business may not have prepared disaster plans for records and processing.

It is a prudent business practice to have a *disaster plan*. A disaster plan is the set of policies and procedures to follow in the event of a disaster. The disaster plan specifies exactly what must be done to resume normal operations. Unfortunately, most disaster plans are formulated after the disaster. (Chapter 14 discusses the elements of a comprehensive disaster plan.)

The records information system also requires some plan for the orderly transfer of active records to inactive status and for destruction of obsolete records.

The Records Retention Schedule

The objective of a *records retention schedule* is to permit the transfer of records from active maintenance to inactive storage, destruction, or archives. Given the volume of records in a modern business, careful attention to a records retention schedule can be worth literally thousands of dollars a month in reduced storage costs, reduced equipment and supplies needs, and increased productivity in central files.

A necessary objective of the retention schedule is to ensure that legal and regulatory requirements are met. The number and scope of legal requirements is not always obvious, and the records manager often must consult the appropriate guides for this information, such as *The Guide to Record Retention Requirements in the Code of Federal Regulations* (U.S. Govt., 1988) and *Records Retention Scheduling* (Lybarger, 1980).

Figure 5.4 shows a typical records retention information form. The retention form can apply to any type of record, including paper, microfilm, magnetic media, or optical disk. The form is straightforward and the procedure is to consult the retention schedule at regular intervals to determine record status changes. If changes are noted, then appropriate arrangements are made to transfer the records. This operation is well

Figure 5.4 Records Retention Information Form

Department/Division	Page of
Section/Unit	Effective Date

Record Title/Series/Type	Code	Retention Time Active	Retention Time Inactive	Final Disposition

Retention Notes

Codes: A = active, V = vital, I = inactive, 0 = outdated.

Specify retention time in days, months, or years.

Final disposition can be: archives, destruction, or none (if none, then the corresponding retention time = 9999 years.

suited to computerization, especially on a microcomputer. (Computerization of these types of operations is explained in Chapter 14.)

Although the process of defining retention periods seems clear, in business the definition of record status is an equivocal process. In other words, clear criteria for deciding retention times rarely are available, and the business environment strongly encourages the "forever" retention period. The following hypothetical exchange between an outside records consultant and a secretary illustrates a typical occurrence:

Consultant:	When do you destroy these records?
Secretary:	Never.
Consultant:	But you really don't access these twenty-year-old records, do you?
Secretary:	I threw some records out once, and the next day my supervisor asked for them. So I'm not taking any chances.

This attitude is common. Therefore, it is important that the actual user of the records set the retention period, that the retention period be authorized by higher-level management, and that the schedule conform to statutory requirements.

Figure 5.5 is a completed records disposition request form. The records have been identified by location and function and their disposition status is requested for approval. In this example, many of the records are going to inactive status on microform media, while the original paper records will be destroyed. The inactive status of the microforms is permanent and these records will not be destroyed or archived.

When the retention schedule is a matter of policy, schedules can be published and made available to the records information system and the users. An example of a published document is shown in Figure 5.6, "Sample Retention Schedule," which shows a page of the schedule for administrative records in a county welfare department. As that example shows, the retention periods are not always specific times, but instead consist of periods of time following a particular activity. For example, ". . . destroy after being notified by the State Agency that. . . ." This condition makes it difficult to keep track of activities on the retention schedule; therefore, the retention schedule is a good candidate for computerization. The computer can tirelessly check for numerous conditions and restraints and inform records personnel when a change of status should take place.

Determining the retention requirements will involve contact with the appropriate users through meetings or a records retention authorization form. In any case, it is wise to obtain written approval from upper management for a records retention schedule. Keep in mind that a function of the records information system is to implement the retention schedule, not to dictate the scheduling.

As a practical business matter, the following steps are required for retention scheduling:

1. taking an accurate records inventory
2. analyzing the records to determine their use, status, and importance
3. suggesting a records retention schedule based on experience, existing company policy, and legal considerations
4. obtaining authorizations for the retention schedule from upper management, end users, and the legal department
5. developing procedures for implementing the transfer of records
6. publishing the schedule as official company policy.

If a business is developing a records retention program for the first time, the pre-

Figure 5.5 Records Disposition Request

R E C O R D S D I S P O S I T I O N R E Q U E S T

To:	From:
Any State Archives State Capitol Anywhere, Anystate	Office of Admissions Any State University Anywhere, Anystate

Application is hereby made under provisions of State Code Annotated, 1980 as amended 03-03-88, for the disposal of the following records in the manner recommended.

1. Location of Records:	2. Quantity:
Office of Admissions, Any State University, Anywhere, AY	10 boxes

3. Record Identity and Function:

Application Forms	5 yrs or until graduation, microfilm,destroy
General Admission Correspondence	1 year
High School Transcripts	after admission
Residency Application Forms	2 years
Dept. Eval. of Transfer Credit	5 yrs., microfilm and destroy
(continued on attached sheet)	

Beginning Date: Ending Date:

4. Statutory Retention:	5. Statutory References:
Years	

6. Recommended Disposition:

☐ Destroy for period covered by beginning and ending dates above.

☐ Destroy on a Scheduled Basis with a minimum retention period of ______ years.

☐ Microfilm and destroy records: Per SCA 10-25-80, two certified copies of the film must be on file before the records are destroyed, and one copy filed with the State Archives. An official chain of custody must be maintained.

☐ Transfer to State Archives.

☐ Other ______________________________

Date	Signature of Records Officer	Title
2/30/88		Director
Date	**Signature of Agency Head**	**Title**
2/30/88		

D I S P O S I T I O N A U T H O R I Z A T I O N

Pursuant to the provision of SCA 03-03-88, disposition of the above records is:

___ Authorized in the following manner: ___ Not authorized because:

☐ See Item ___ ☐ Must be shredded ☐ Public Data ☐ Confidential Data

☐ Private Data ☐ Public Records ☐ Privileged Records

Notes:

Figure 5.6 Sample Retention Schedule

Administrative Manual III-5750

County Welfare Department's Records Retention Schedule
Administrative Records

Item number	*Record description*	*Retention schedule*
1	*Minutes of County Welfare Board Meetings*	Disposal not recommended by this schedule
2	*Summaries of Fiscal and Statistical Reports.* These summaries are required for the identification of trends and will ordinarily show the number of applications received and approved, denied, and withdrawn.	Disposal not recommended by this schedule.
3	*Board Copies of Abstract Payments.* These are abstracts of payments for OAA, AFDC, AD, MA, general relief.	Destroy three years after payment.
4	*Paid Medical Bills.* These bills cover payments to vendors under OAA, AFDC, AB, AD, MAA, and MA.	Retain at least three years; destroy after being notified by State Agency that a federal audit has been completed for the period in which the transactions occurred.
5	*Personnel Files.* These include all Merit System applications, transaction forms, evaluation forms, correspondence, etc. The State Agency maintains a permanent master card for each employee.	Destroy five years after termination of the employee.
6	*SW Fund Receipts and Redeemed Checks*	Destroy after ten years.

ceding six steps may take as long as two years. Also, whenever possible, the benefits should be documented in dollars and cents with a cost/benefit analysis at the start of the process.

A pertinent topic related to records retention is the records purge. A purge is done to ensure that the records information system contains what the records inventory says it should contain. A *records purge* consists of checking for and removing those items, both records and nonrecords, that do not belong in the system. For example, if file equipment is used to store supplies, these nonrecords should not appear in the inventory. However, the purge is needed to remove more subtle burdens on the system's efficiency. Catalogs may be proper record items, but most catalogs are dated and are issued frequently; such frequently updated items should be purged when outdated. An annual purge is recommended for all record systems.

Finally, if retention scheduling for all records is not feasible or is not supported by top management, then the minimum retention definitions at least should include vital records. The vital records should be defined along with their methods of security and protection.

Central Files

The idealized records information system depicted back in Figure 5.1 (see page 60) showed a centralized area named "central files." Many growing organizations reach a point when their active records should be centralized. The advantages of centralized storage can be significant in terms of resources and equipment. The following information explores the advantages of *centralization*, that is, placing all the records for an organization in one location.

Centralization allows limited access to the active records. Limited access will result in better control, protection, and security. As libraries have found, even with careful checkout procedures, the system must be protected against misfiling. A misfiled record raises retrieval costs significantly.

A second advantage of centralization is that it allows for the standardization of management procedures. These procedures include a uniform classification system, checkout procedures, and standardization of filing and retrieval processes. Savings are realized in better use of equipment and supplies, as well as in minimizing the time for training and transferring of personnel. An additional benefit is the subsequent increased productivity from standardized storage and retrieval operations.

A third advantage of centralization is the reduction of duplicated records. Records system research suggests that systems that are not centralized may have at least 25 percent of the records duplicated in different locations. The costs of maintaining this duplication in space and resources can be eliminated through centralization. Centralization is not simply a matter of transferring all records to a central location, however; the process requires a careful records inventory and management plan to take advantage of the benefits of centralization. To maximize the benefits, centralization should not include every possible active record in a business. Of primary consideration is the potential use of the record.

If the users of a particular record type constitute a small, unique group, then it may not be advantageous to centralize their records. Such records should be (or should remain) decentralized, that is, kept in various different locations. The advantages of *decentralization* are:

1. more convenient and faster access
2. better control by specific users
3. increased security for confidential records.

In fact, few businesses maintain either a completely centralized or decentralized system of records storage. A combination system is often necessary.

Storage/Retrieval Systems

The objective of active maintenance is the efficient storage and retrieval of active records. In regard to active records kept in the central files, three factors that influence the efficiency of storage and retrieval are (1) the efficiency of the equipment, (2) the loss of records, and (3) insufficient retrieval information.

The first factor, efficiency of the equipment, refers to the nature of the equipment and supplies used for the records storage and retrieval. The efficiency of a records system can be optimized through careful choice of appropriate equipment. For example, for paper records that have a high access frequency, color-coded, open-shelf filing will provide excellent storage and retrieval efficiency. (A detailed discussion of records equipment is provided in Chapter 7.)

The second factor, loss of records to the system, means that records become unavailable to the records information system through misfiling and insufficient checkout control procedures. Misfiling can be minimized through attention to procedures and equipment. Again, color coding can reduce misfiling and make it easier to detect misfiles. Misfiling also can be reduced by restricting access to the files to authorized personnel. If this is not feasible, then procedures could be instituted to restrict (re)filing to specific records personnel only. For example, libraries may allow open access to their books yet request that books not be reshelved but, rather, placed in conveniently located receptacles after use for later reshelving by library personnel.

The loss of records through insufficient checkout control procedures can be controlled through the use of charge-out and follow-up procedures. When records are retrieved, a *charge-out form* should be completed that shows who has the record, when it was taken, and other pertinent information, including when the record is to be returned. The charge-out form is often made up of three parts, with one part for the person who has taken the record, the second part used to replace the record, and the third part for the tickler file. A *tickler file* is a memory aid in which items are arranged by the date—in this case, the third part of the charge-out form would be filed by the date on which a record is to be returned. When a record is returned, the second and third parts of the charge-out form are pulled. The information on those parts of the form may be accumulated and used for estimates of system activity.

Of course, not everyone who has taken a record will return it by the designated return date. At regular intervals, the tickler file should be consulted to determine if any records have passed their return due date. If so, then standardized follow-up procedures should be carried out. *Follow-up procedures* usually involve reminders to the person involved, visits, and if necessary, a "search-and-locate" mission to recover the missing records. If such a duty becomes necessary, the missing record probably will be found in close proximity to the last person who used it. Given the nature of this duty, the records manager should allocate the task to someone with a friendly personality.

No matter how carefully one selects equipment or defines procedures, though, record losses will occur. In using manual methods of controlling the records information systems, one should expect a minimal 1-percent record loss.

The third factor that influences the efficiency of storage and retrieval is insufficient retrieval information. To better understand how this factor influences efficiency, consider the following scenario of paper records filed by an alphabetic name and cross-referenced by a numeric code. The problem (and costs) in such a system occurs when there is a request for a particular record, but the correct spelling of the name is not known, nor is the numeric code fully known. This is called the *IIR* (*Incomplete Information Retrieval*) problem. In a traditional alphanumeric paper system, such problems are best handled by those records personnel with the most retrieval experience.

The IIR problem occurs in all records systems at some time. For example, suppose the correspondence that mentions XYZ Construction is requested for the last five-year period, but that the correspondence is filed by suppliers' names, and XYZ Construction is not a supplier. In a likely scenario, a best guess would be made of the supplier names and a clerk would search as many names as possible, looking in the files for the relevant information. Another common IIR problem occurs when an agent calls the home office in order to update a client's policy information, but the agent is not sure of the spelling of the client's name, does not have the policy number at hand, etc. The home office records personnel are forced to search the client files by best guess. In these situations, usually the records are eventually located, but the cost is high. If the outcome is failure to retrieve the desired records, the costs are even higher in lost time. With the introduction of computers into records management, this problem is being attacked by lexical filing systems.

One of the most significant changes in finding information in the past decade is *lexical electronic filing*. This type of system is suited for lexical or word-oriented files—for example, business correspondence. The files are entered into a computer system and are accessed as computer files, such as magnetic or optical media (Dickinson, 1985).

In a lexical computer system, the user defines what information will be included—for example, all business correspondence of a certain type, or all COBOL programs, or any type of word-oriented file. The files are scanned for all words and an internal index is built. Common and "noise" words such as *the*, *and*, *if*, etc. are ignored. This is the process of preparing the system for retrieval operations. When the system is ready for operations, a user can request the names of all files that contain a given word or combination of words. For example, one could request the names of all documents that contain the words "XYZ Construction" and then scan the listed document names to decide if a complete printed copy of some or all of the records is needed.

These systems have been developed for the entire range of computers, from the microcomputer to the mainframe. A microcomputer system can handle a few thousand files, suitable for a small office or a special project. Mainframe systems are virtually unlimited in file size. The costs range from $250 for microcomputer software to $50,000 for mainframe programs.

Although lexical electronic filing can deal with the insufficient retrieval information problem, or as we have dubbed it—the IIR problem—it may also provide capabilities and costs that are not necessary or desirable. Being able to search every word in a lexical records system is not necessary. Dealing effectively with the IIR problem may require searches on specific items only rather than all words. On the other hand, the lexical filing system is well suited for research files and library information systems.

The next step up from a lexical system is the database management system (DBMS) and its associated sophisticated storage and retrieval operations. (These computer-based systems will be discussed in detail in Chapters 15 and 16.)

Inactive Records Storage

Records that may be required less frequently than active records should be defined as *inactive records* and transferred to less costly storage. As a general practical rule, records are redefined to inactive status and transferred to a records center when their active life has effectively ended, but there are still legal reasons that may require their retrieval. (The facilities and procedures for inactive records transfer, storage, and retrieval are explained in Chapter 10.)

The transfer procedures should be well organized and allow for reasonable retrieval of the records. Theoretically, inactive records are not expected to be retrieved under normal conditions. People keep them for an exceptional or unexpected situation—for example, with client records. It is common to move client records to inactive storage when the client moves out of the service area; but a business keeps the records in case the client moves back into the service area. Or perhaps the company, in an unusual situation, previously allowed a rebate for certain policies; now finding those policies requires a search of inactive client records. Whatever the reason, if inactive records need to be retrieved, the speed of retrieval is rarely an issue. Therefore, retrieval procedures for inactive records need not stress the swiftness required of active records. For example, if it takes an average of fifteen minutes to retrieve an active record from central files, then a reasonable time to retrieve an inactive record is one or two days. Most commercial records centers can guarantee retrieval within twenty-four hours, and for special rush requests, within a few hours.

If regular retrievals of a particular series of records are made from the records center, then perhaps the retention schedule should be changed to keep that series in active records for a longer period. An analysis of the retrievals from the records center should be performed by the records manager to minimize the costs of transfers and retrievals.

Final Disposition

Final disposition means that the primary purpose of the record has become obsolete. At this point, the records can be destroyed or archived. Sometimes this decision will depend on the size and activity of the archive, sometimes on legal requirements. If the decision is made to destroy a series of records, the proper method for destruction should be identified.

Methods of Records Destruction

The objective of records destruction is to remove the record permanently from possible use after it has become obsolete and to ensure that sensitive information does not become public. For example, an executive may wish to destroy a memorandum immediately after receipt to secure its contents; or a foreign embassy in danger of being taken over by terrorists may wish to destroy some of its sensitive records.

In general, all destructive procedures should be centered in the records information system. This means that individuals should employ standard, company-approved procedures for destruction. Records that are destroyed should be listed in a log and should follow from the records retention schedule.

The primary methods of records destruction are *incineration,* or the burning of records; *shredding,* which cuts the record into thin strips or pieces; *pulverization* or disintegration, which turns records into minute particles; and *trashing,* which is a catch-all term that means simply destroying the record by ordinary trash removal processes.

Equipment is available for fast and efficient incineration, shredding, and pulverization of records. The range runs from the executive shredder, which fits on top of a waste basket and provides only minimal destruction, to the industrial pulverizer, which can turn thousands of pounds of records per hour into dust.

Guidelines for Records Destruction

Because destroyed records cannot be recalled, extra care should be taken before records actually are destroyed. Of course, federal, state, and municipal statutory regulations must be satisfied. It is also a good idea to consult popular trade guides on retention and destruction, such as the latest edition of *The Retention Book: Retention and Preservation of Records with Destruction Schedules,* published by Records Controls, Inc.

Another precaution to take before destroying records is to have the destruction authorized by a responsible party. This procedure provides additional protection for records even when they are authorized for destruction in the retention schedule. A destruction control form can be used for this purpose. The form contains a description of the records to be destroyed from the retention form, and a space for a signed authorization. With a two-part form, one part is kept by the records department and one part is sent to the authorizing person after the records are destroyed.

A final guideline in the destruction of records is security. All too often, records that contain sensitive information are not secure during the destruction process. Indeed, many small businesses and offices "destroy" records by putting them in the ordinary trash. If this is the case, the trash should be inspected during the records inventory and potential problems identified if sensitive information is found.

Archives

The *primary value* of a record is the basis of the definition of the record when it enters the records information system. When the primary purpose of a record becomes obsolete, it may still have a *secondary value*. The characteristic secondary value of a record is historical and the purpose of an *archive* is to select records with historical value for storage and retrieval.

The portrayal of the records information system back in Figure 5.1 (page 60) showed a rather large rectangle representing the archive area. If an organization has an archive, then the representation is reasonably accurate. Although some large organizations have archives, many businesses see no need to maintain one. Because of the permanence and longevity associated with archives, they are found most often in businesses and organizations that have been in existence for many years.

The archive in Figure 5.1 shows a small "accessible" section as compared to a large "inaccessible" section. Some archives display records but do not make them accessible because of security restrictions or a lack of resources. (The area of archive operation is significant enough to deserve special attention and is explained more fully in Chapter 10.)

Summary

The records information system includes four major phases: definition, active maintenance, storage, and final disposition. The definition phase includes (1) word processing, in which records are created, and (2) acquisitions, in which forms, directives, and correspondence are acquired from outside the business.

Active records maintenance begins with a records inventory, which may be a physical inventory or a survey. As a result of the inventory, vital records are identified, and security procedures for their protection are developed. Two such procedures are dispersal and disaster planning. The records retention schedule provides a time frame for maintaining active records. Active records may be kept in a central location or may be decentralized. Centralizing active records has several advantages: limited access, standardization, and reduced duplication. The problem of inefficient and inaccurate storage and retrieval of active records is being attacked by lexical electronic filing.

When active records become less active or obsolete, they are transferred to the records center for storage or to the final disposition stage in which they are destroyed or archived. The flow of records through the phases is governed by the records retention schedule.

List of Terms

records information system
definition phase
active maintenance phase
storage phase
final disposition phase
acquisitions
word processing
records inventory
physical inventory
interview
survey questionnaire
vital records
disaster
dispersal
vital processing
disaster plan
records retention schedule
records purge
centralization
decentralization
charge-out form
tickler file
follow-up procedures
incomplete information
retrieval (IIR)
lexical electronic filing
inactive records
final disposition
incineration
shredding
pulverization
trashing
primary value
secondary value
archive

Discussion Questions

1. Why is the term "records life cycle" not exactly appropriate to describe the records information system?
2. What are the phases in the records information system?
3. What are the characteristics of the two areas of records definition: acquisition and creation?
4. Who decides when a record should no longer be active? If a record is redefined, what are the criteria to determine if it will be inactive, destroyed, or archived?
5. What are the benefits of moving active records into archives or inactive status?
6. What is the correct method for conducting a records inventory?
7. What items should be included on a records retention schedule?
8. What is meant by IIR (incomplete information retrieval)?
9. What is the future of lexical electronic filing?
10. What is the preferred method for destroying records?
11. What is the purpose of a records archive?

Activities

1. Contact a large organization and obtain a copy of its retention schedule, records inventory form, and other forms relating to the operation of the records information system. Write a brief report on how the forms are used in that organization.
2. Interview the person in charge of the records of a small office. Although it is unlikely that there will be a retention schedule, try to de-

termine if there are less formal methods for removing records from the active status. Report in writing or orally on those methods.

3. Visit a library and determine the type of lexical filing system it has available (manual or electronic). Describe the system and how it is used.
4. Anthropologists have studied the garbage in urban areas for evidence of the culture of the area. In the same sense, the trash of a business could be examined as a description of its operations, particularly its records system. For this activity, study the trash of a business and write a report concerning the business's records information system. If this activity is selected, be sure to obtain authorization from your instructor.
5. Most records systems are prepared for IIR problems. Interview records personnel in a business or organization and determine what type of IIRs they most frequently encounter.
6. Visit a city or county court and describe its records information system. Draw a figure similar to Figure 5.1 (on page 60) to represent the system. Be sure to determine the court's method of storing inactive records and the retention periods.
7. As an interesting exercise to test your understanding of the concepts in this chapter, describe your personal records information system. For example, do you have any records that are vital? Do you have "archive" records (or those you intend to archive)? What method do you use for destroying records? Are any of your records confidential? How do you protect them?

References

Dickinson, John. "Lexical Electronic Filing." *PC Magazine* 4, no. 17 (August 20, 1985): 137–44.

Littlefield, C. L., et al. *Management of Office Operations* (Englewood Cliffs, N.J.: Prentice-Hall, 1978).

Lybarger, Phyllis M. *Records Retention Scheduling.* Technical Report No. 1, Association of Records Managers and Administrators, Inc., 4200 Somerset Drive, Suite 215, Prairie Village, KS 66208, 1980.

Superintendent of Documents. *Guide to Record Retention Requirements in the Code of Federal Regulations* (Washington, D.C.: U.S. Government Printing Office, 1986).

Chapter 5 Highlight

Remove Those Records!

A persistent problem in most records systems is the lack of a records purge. The result is a loss in system efficiency. Ideally, records should move through the records information system as their retention status changes. Obvious trouble points exist in both active records and inactive records.

Active records are seldom purged adequately. The purges are done too infrequently, often in response to a critical space situation rather than as a regularly scheduled activity; and it may be completed poorly, with insufficient attention to procedures. Active records are, however, usually kept reasonably operational because they are the activity heart of the system, and purges will be done even if done inconsistently or inadequately.

On the other hand, inactive records may never be purged! In some businesses, records are piled aimlessly in unmarked containers. The location for inactive records is often the room that cannot be used for office space because of its location (attics and sub-basements are prime candidates) or because of physical conditions, such as pipes and heating/cooling vents. Space is frequently shared with discarded equipment, cleaning supplies, and other scrap items.

Because the retrieval need of such inactive records is extremely low, there is little impetus to organize and purge. Sometimes purges are done only when the business quits operation. In one case, company personnel and locations had changed so frequently that the inactive records were simply lost—no one remembered where they were stored!

We offer the following possibilities for dealing with inactive records chaos. The goal is to reduce the seeming mountain of work and squeeze resources from unlikely places to deal with the problem.

1. Prepare a careful cost/benefit analysis showing that the difficulty in accessing those records is too costly to ignore. Get top management's support, establish regular procedures, and prepare a time frame for accomplishing the purge. This is the ideal solution.

2. Contact a local educational institution that offers a course in records management. Tell the teacher of that course that you have an opportunity for some students to engage in practical records management. Most schools are eager to give their students practical experience.
3. Plan one- to two-hour sessions once a week for all clerical staff to do a portion of the purging until it gets done. Have them pick the part they prefer to work on; people are often more receptive to doing tedious tasks when they have some choices. Of course, dividing the work up makes less work for everyone.

Chapter 6

Classifying Records

Learning Goals

1. To become familiar with the methods for naming paper and computer records.
2. To be able to differentiate among alphabetic, numeric, and subject classification systems.
3. To understand the straight- and terminal-digit methods for arranging records with numeric identifiers.
4. To explain the difference between classifying records and indexing records.
5. To become familiar with the procedures for indexing records for any classification system.
6. To understand how to use color coding in classification systems.

Introduction

Arranging records so that they can be retrieved easily is essential for efficient records management. The records must be physically accessible and they must have some sort of identifier that the person responsible for retrieving records will understand. Consider how you find something you have stored. You put away your clothes, food, books, etc. in appropriate physical facilities close to the location where you need them. Chances are you categorize and store similar items together. For example, most of us store our food by groups; canned goods go in one place, cereals in another, etc. In any case, you use some method of categorizing or classifying in order to find what you need with a minimum of searching. Put another way, the primary function of classification is efficient retrieval. A secondary function of classification is to allow for expansion of records with a minimum of disruption.

In this chapter, we will examine the records classification process for both paper and computer records. We will cover the naming of records, their storage arrangement, the indexing of records, and color coding.

The Classification Process

Business records require systematic management for efficient retrieval and expansion. In storing and retrieving thousands of pieces of paper and millions of bits of computer information, a business needs a more reliable and efficient method than simply storing the same type of records together. The records also need identifiers that are short, easy to read and understand, and as foolproof as possible. Letters and numbers, either alone or in combination, provide the basis for records identification and for most classification systems.

The simplest methods of arranging records are in alphabetical or numerical order. Before records can be arranged in a systematic alphabetical or numerical arrangement, however, they must be labeled—with a name or number to identify them. Problems in classifying records arise because of the many ways in which records can be named.

Naming records is the first step in the classification process; arranging the records by some standard method is the second step; and indexing the records for retrieval is an optional third step. Each of these steps usually results in some physical entity; that is, after a record is named, it is stored in a folder with a label. The folders are then arranged and stored in cabinets or some other type of equipment. (Equipment and supplies used to store records are discussed in Chapter 7.) If the record is created on a computer, it is named by the operator, but it is stored on disk or some other medium by the computer's operating system. Finally, an index of the records, which provides a directory of their location in terms of information other than the name, can be created. The index may be produced in hard copy (printed) or stored on a computer.

Although color coding is not required to classify records, methods of color coding are discussed in this chapter because they can improve significantly the efficiency of the retrieval process. Color coding may be thought of as a special type of classification process.

Naming Paper Records

The first step in the classification process is naming the record; the record is given a label by which it can be identified and later retrieved. That label may be a person's name, a company name, a number, a street address, a subject, or anything else that identifies the record in a meaningful way. For example, you may have Purchase Order No. 123 from ABC Company for 100 ballpoint pens. That purchase order may be labeled "purchase order" or "ABC Company" or "No. 123" or "office supplies." Obviously, some standardization would be necessary or the same record could be labeled differently by different people; or two different records could receive the same name. Also, naming a record is not the same as indexing a record. In records management terminology, the parts of a person's or company name are referred to as *indexing units*. However, an *index* is a listing of record names, labels, or identifiers. An index is often considered an alternate way of locating a record also. (We will explain this latter definition of indexing later in this chapter.)

Selecting a Common Identifier

How does one decide what to label a record? The first criterion is that the label or *identifier* must be something that appears on each record of the same type. However, as illustrated in our purchase order example, that still does not tell us exactly what label to use. The second criterion is that the label must be one by which the record is most likely to be referenced. It is easy to see at this point that what should be a simple matter can become quite complicated because records are referenced differently depending on how they are used. Even with these two specific criteria, there is no definite answer for how a record should be labeled. What must occur is an agreement among the parties using the record (or a particular set of records) to give it one or more identifiers. Therefore, our purchase orders could be identified first as "purchase orders" and then by their individual numbers. Using two identifiers presents the problem "which one comes first?"

Deciding How Records Will Be Labeled

In arranging parts of a record identifier or label, one rule can be applied consistently: Proceed from the most general to the most specific. In other words, take the broadest category and break it down into smaller and more specific parts. Using our purchase order example: *Purchase Order* is the general identifier; *No. 123* is the specific identifier. When the identifiers have been selected, there is a basis for arranging the records, which is the second step in the classification process.

Arranging, or Classifying, Paper Records

The ways that paper records can be arranged are referred to as *classification systems*. Because records usually are labeled with words or numbers, they can be arranged alphabetically or numerically. Many methods of alphabetic and numeric arrangement (or a combination of the two) are possible. The following explanations of classification systems will consider (1) alphabetic systems, which include geographic classification; (2) numeric systems, and (3) subject systems, which may be both alphabetic and numeric.

Alphabetic Classification

An *alphabetic classification system* uses the letters of the alphabet, A to Z, for general identifiers. The specific identifiers within the system are personal names (last names, or surnames; first names), company names, street names, or particular topics. Any classification system that arranges records by the letters of the English alphabet is an alphabetic system. The records are arranged physically starting with the As and ending with the Zs.

In an alphabetic file folder system, folders are separated by guides (heavyweight dividers) designating major alphabetic divisions. The number of divisions used is determined by the quantity of records. A miscellaneous folder, at the beginning or end of the section, is placed in each major division with the records in it also filed alphabetically. Individual names or topics appear on the file folders, and special name guides may be used for common names (those with ten or more folders).

Because people's names can have many possible variations that lead to exceptions, rules for alphabetizing names are needed. The procedure for alphabetizing names is explained in Appendix A, "Standard Filing Rules and Examples" (see page 267).

Correspondence Arrangement Figure 6.1 illustrates a typical alphabetic arrangement for correspondence. When records are arranged alphabetically in a manual (paper) filing system, arrangement of the words (or letters) on the labels (tabs) and positioning of the labels becomes important. For example, in a drawer file, all of the labels could appear on the left side. However, if the labels were arranged as shown in Figure 6.1, they could be read more easily and could help to categorize the folders. In Figure 6.1, the letters of the alphabet are on file guides that have labels (tabs) in first position (far left side). (File guides are dividers made of heavy cardboard stock.) When the labels on

Figure 6.1 Correspondence File Arrangement

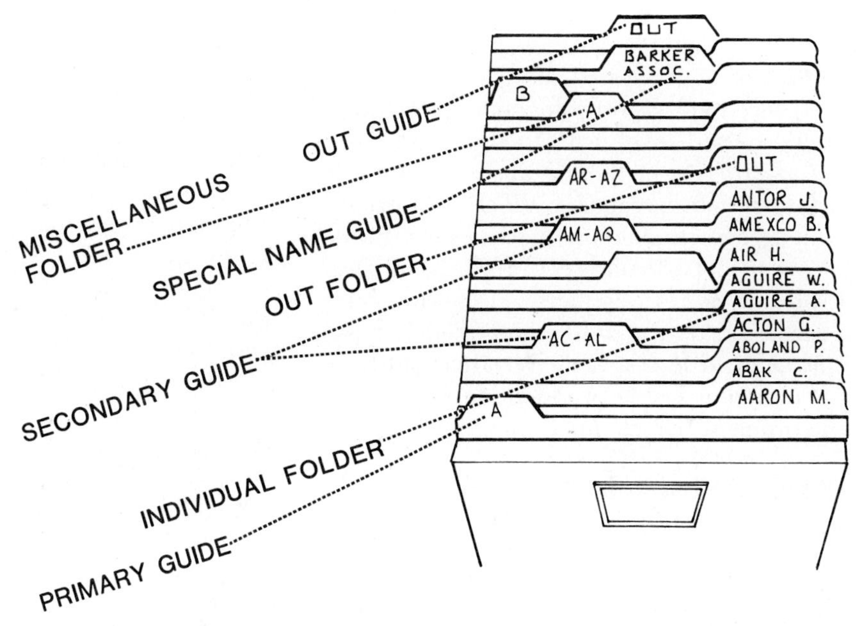

Source Joyce Kupsh and Carol Lundgren, *Records Management*, National Instructional Systems, Inc., 1985. Used by permission.

these guides are in first position and designate the major divisions of the file, they are referred to as *primary guides.* Additional divisions of the alphabet are in the next (second) position on *secondary guides.* The labels for the miscellaneous folders are also in second position. Individual names are on folders with tabs in the last two positions (far right).

A wide variety of label arrangements is possible because file guides and folders may be purchased in various "cuts" (tab widths) and positions. Generally, folders and guides are available with as many as five tab positions (referred to as fifth cut). (Chapter 7 explains the types of guides and folders that are available.)

Geographic Arrangement One type of alphabetic system is a *geographic arrangement* in which records are alphabetized by location. For example, sales records on various companies could be arranged by state and city. The state guides would be in alphabetical order and the cities within each state would also be arranged in alphabetical order. Figure 6.2 illustrates a geographic arrangement. Tabs are placed in different positions in this arrangement also. Often folders with company or individual names are alphabetized within a category, but this is not always the case. Folders could be arranged alphabetically by street and then numerically by street number. Figure 6.3 illustrates both a name and a street number arrangement.

Numeric Classification

When a number is used to identify a record, and the records are then arranged by number, the classification system is numeric. A *numeric classification system* requires two additional components: (1) a listing that shows the numbers that have been assigned, and (2) an alphabetical listing or card file that also shows the number assigned to a particular name or topic. The latter alphabetical

Figure 6.2 Geographic File Arrangement

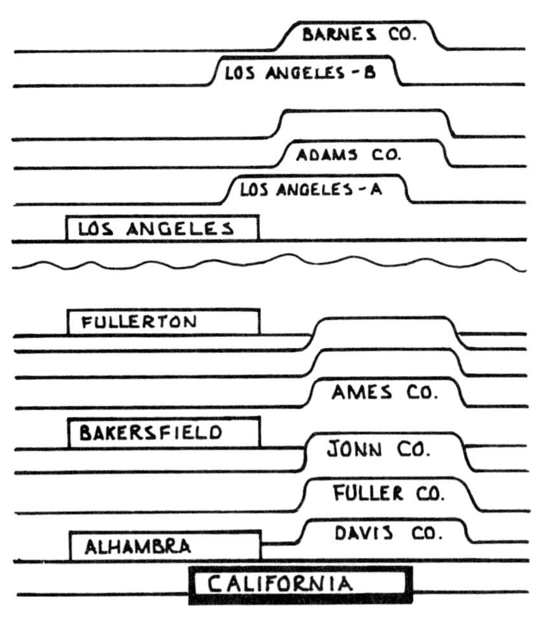

Source Joyce Kupsh and Carol Lundgren, *Records Management*, National Instructional Systems, Inc., 1985. Used by permission.

Figure 6.3 Geographic Arrangements by Name and Street

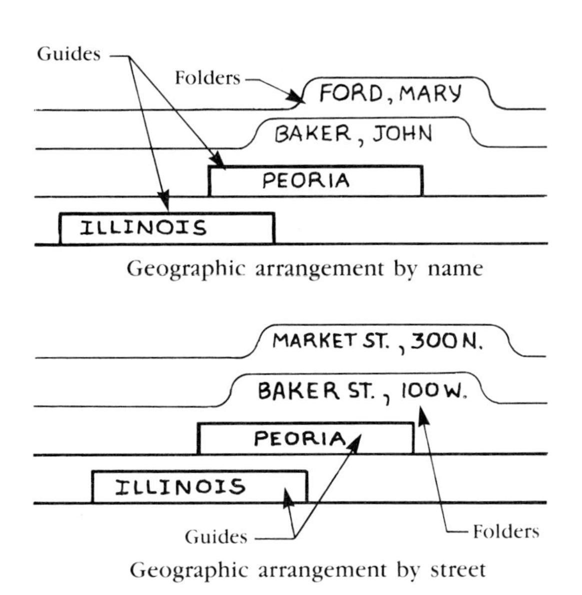

listing or card file is called a cross-reference or *relative index.* A relative index is needed because even though records are filed by number, they are often called for by name. This type of system is also used for material inventories, for example, in the storage of small machine parts.

Two common types of numeric classification are straight numeric and terminal-digit.

Straight Numeric Arrangement A *straight numeric system* is one in which records are arranged sequentially from the lowest number to the highest. Figure 6.4 shows straight numeric arrangement of folders. Records that are printed with sequential numbers, such as invoices, may be stored in this way. If the records do not have printed numbers, then a straight numeric system requires some method for knowing what numbers have been used. A *numeric logbook,* which lists numbers in numerical order and shows the record name or topic assigned to each number, satisfies this requirement. A relative index is also needed so that the record can be retrieved if only the record name is known. For example, if John Brown's social security number is 451-66-3020 and his records are filed in folder 3020, his relative index card would appear as follows:

> BROWN, John David   File #3020
> 451-66-3020

Terminal-Digit Arrangement A *terminal-digit filing system* is one in which files are given a number and then physically stored based on the parts of the number, beginning with the last two digits. For example, a file labeled 14-66-82 would be stored in division (drawer or shelf) 82, in section 66 (of division 82) in the 14th location. File 14-66-83 would be stored in division (drawer or shelf) 83, in section 66 (of division 83) in the 14th location, and so forth. The advantage of using this system is that the files are evenly distributed throughout the system, eliminating

Figure 6.4 Straight Numeric and Terminal-Digit File Arrangements

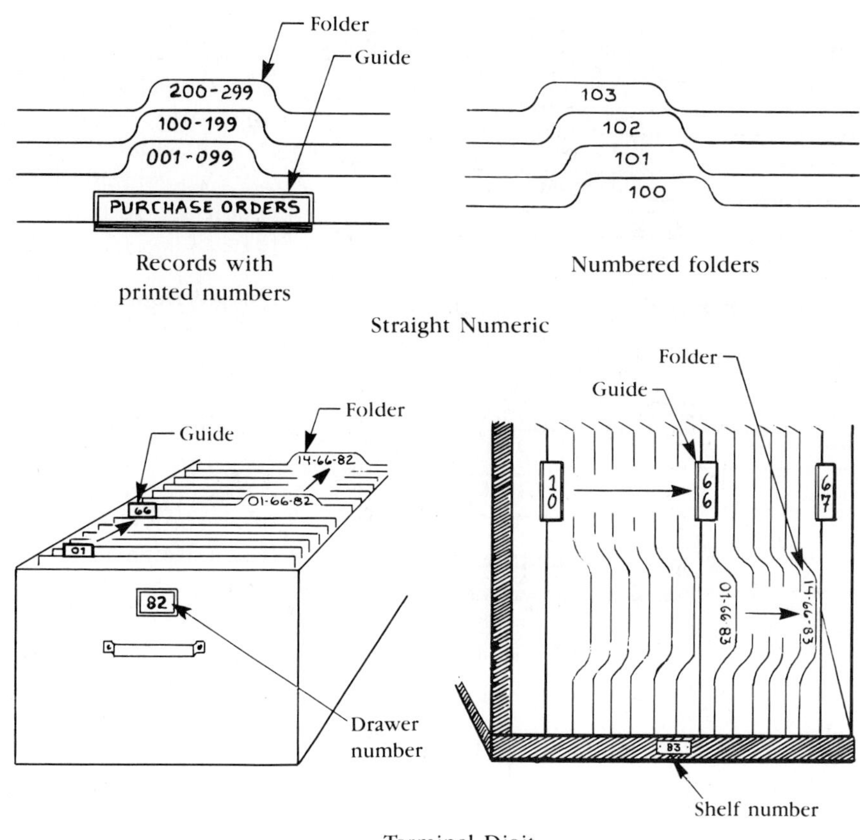

the crowding of new files (and of the people using those files) and the gaps caused by the removal of inactive files. Figure 6.4 also illustrates the terminal-digit arrangement of guides and folders in drawers and on shelves.

Two other types of numeric systems in common use are chronological files and tickler files. A *chronological file* organizes records according to the date they are created. For example, copies of correspondence may be kept in a chronological file by day, week, or month. In a *tickler file*, records are arranged according to the date on which some action must be taken. A tickler file might contain a guide for each month and one set of guides numbered from 1 to 31. In setting up a tickler file for the month of March, you would do the following: Place the March guide in the front of the file followed by the thirty-one day (date) dividers (or folders); the remaining month dividers/guides would be in the back of the file. File records behind the appropriate month and date; only the current month (in our example, March) has date categories. One practical use for a tickler file is to pay bills.

Only copies of documents should be stored in chronological or tickler files because these files are essentially memory aids and a cross-reference usually is not used for these files. Therefore, retrieving an item based only on the date it was created or the date it should be acted on would be difficult.

Subject Classification

A subject classification system may be either alphabetic or numeric or alphanumeric (which is a combination of both). An *alphabetic subject system* lists topics in alphabetical order and subtopics within each category in alphabetical order also. This approach is used in the yellow pages of telephone directories.

A *numeric subject system* is one in which a number is assigned to each topic. For example, numbers could be assigned to each department of a company and the categories pertaining to that department would be assigned an ascending number as shown in the following illustration:

100 Finance Department

- 101 Annual Reports
- 102 Purchase Orders

200 Marketing Department

- 201 Sales Reports
- 202 Advertising Brochures
- 203 Satellite Offices

300 Data Processing Department

When a numeric subject system is used, an index for both the numbers and the topics is needed because the only order to the files is numerical order. The person using the files would need to know what numbers had been assigned and would also need an alphabetical listing of topics. The advantage of this approach is that numbers are easy to keep in order, whereas alphabetical filing rules must be followed if topics are in alphabetical order alone. However, because additional indexes are needed, this approach might be impractical for a large filing system.

Alphanumeric subject systems are often called "dash–slash" systems because the classification levels are separated by dashes and slashes. For example, suppose there are ten initial categories indicated by the numerals 0 through 9. These categories might represent the major divisions of a national corporation with regional offices in various states.

Number	*For category*
0	Sales and advertising
1	Production and manufacturing
2	Data processing
...	....
9	Administrative services

Within each category, the records might be classified geographically by state, and then within each state by a three-digit purchase order number. The resulting labels would look like the following:

0-ILLINOIS/222

3-ALASKA/713

7-IOWA/001

Naming and Classifying Computer Records

The automated office typically has a computer component. Thus, in many offices, records will include both paper records and electronic records that are computer stored, maintained, and retrieved.

Electronic records present some unusual problems because the names of the computer records and their contents are distinct and separate from the files containing the hard (printed) copies of the files. For example, a file folder contains its information and name as a single physical unit. To the extent that the information in the file folder is separated from its file, the same situation exists with computer files. The computer takes care of the physical storage and retrieval of files; all one need do is present the computer with the name of the file and it will store and retrieve it. However, storing the paper record of that file is a separate and different operation.

To make the best use of a computer's capabilities, one should coordinate the paper filing system with the computer system. An understanding of how computer files are named is necessary to accomplish this.

Naming Computer Records

Names of computer records often are restricted to eight characters. Some systems allow two or more of these eight-character names to be combined into a giant name. The most common microcomputer convention allows the eight-character name followed by a dot or period and then a three-character extension, like XXXXXXXX.YYY. This is called the "eight-dot-three" format.

A recent development for microcomputers has been the introduction of a structure for the names. In this structure, a name can, as usual, represent a file; however, a name may also represent a directory, that is, a "primary" name for names that represent files. Therefore, a group of files all can have the same primary name and are accessed with that name in addition to their secondary, or file, name. One convention separates the names with back slashes; for example, SALES\JAN84 is a valid name. SALES is the name of the directory in which the file, JAN84, is stored. Therefore, SALES is the primary name and JAN84 is the filename. To access the file JAN84, one must use the two names together; hence, SALES\JAN84. A complete structure of files and names is referred to as a "tree"; actually an upside-down tree with the main or "root" name (the name of the entire directory) at the top.

A second restriction of naming computer files is associated with the use the computer can make of the names. All computer operating systems are capable of displaying all the names on a physical storage device. The listing of names is called the *directory*. The directory listing also can include other information about the files, such as their sizes and times and dates of last access.

The filenames also are used in file operations, such as erasing and copying, which allow wild card characters in name specifications. A *wild card character* is one that can be substituted for another character. For example, "*" is often equivalent to any sequence of characters and "?" represents any single character. A command like "ERASE TDL*.*" means to erase all files that have TDL as the first three characters. This wild card capability can be a powerful tool for the manipulation of files if the filenames have been structured to take advantage of the capability. However, this structure requires that a *naming convention* refer uniformly to the columns of character placement.

Computer Naming Conventions

One example of uniform character placement with an eight-character name would be to use the first four characters for the main characteristic and the last four characters as a unique identifier; for example, NAMELAST, NAMEFIRST, and NAMEMIDL. The principle is always to use exactly the same number of characters for each element of the name; for example, four and four as in XXXXYYYY. Since the convention must yield names that will be meaningful during retrieval, a "dictionary" that specifies the meaning of the elements of names is also necessary.

Suppose that monthly budgets for various departments are stored on a disk entitled "Monthly Budgets—1985." The files (budgets) could be given the following filenames: JANBUDGT.MKT, JANBUDGT.PER, MARBUDGT.ADM. The month (first three character locations), document identifier (next five character locations), and the department (three character extension) form the filename. Any arrangement of the elements can be used as long as it conforms to the established naming convention. The following are possible candidates for naming parts:

person's initials	XXX
date	MMDD
sequential order	I, I=0, 1, . . .
type of document	YYY

Using initials for part of the filename, for example, the three-character extension, would seem to be a reasonable approach to identifying a computer record, since names are common identifiers. However, this approach may lead to identity problems or the accidental replacement of a file. Because many computer systems do not recognize duplicate names, if you give a new file the same name as an existing file, the computer will store the new file and erase the old one! As it turns out, after 100 people, the probability of two people having exactly the same three initials is at least 50 percent (Parzen, 1960). A practical limit with three-character initials is about seventy-five persons.

An example of two types of naming conventions are shown in Figure 6.5. The production report files use the first seven characters for an abbreviated name (the additional character position could also be used); the first two digits of the extension are the month; and the last digit of the extension is the year. Because only the last digit of the year (7 in 1987) is used, this method assumes that only records for the 1980s are included on this particular disk. In the second example in Figure 6.5, the first six character locations are used for an abbreviated name; the next two locations are used for the year; and the extension is used for the month. If a location for the year is used, then documents pertaining to the 1980s and 1990s could be stored on the same disk. (The use of naming conventions is discussed in further detail in Chapter 14.)

Matching the File Name with the Paper Record

With magnetic media, there are three possible elements to every file: the magnetic or electronic file; the name of the file on the media (in the directory); and the physical file, such as a printed copy of the magnetic file. The name of the file allows direct and

Figure 6.5 Conversion of Standard Record Name to Naming Convention for a Computer Record

ITEM NAME	COMPUTER FILENAME
PRODUCTION REPORT, OCTOBER 1987	PRODREP.1Ø7
PRODUCTION REPORT, MAY 1988	PRODREP.Ø58

NAMING CONVENTION __ __ __ __ __ __ __ • __ __ __
(abbreviated name) (month) (year)

ITEM NAME	COMPUTER FILENAME
BOARD MINUTES, JANUARY 1989	BDMINS89.JAN

NAMING CONVENTION __ __ __ __ __ __ __ __ • __ __ __
(abbreviated name) (year) (month)

easy access to the magnetic file, which can be used to produce the paper record. However, because the media name of the file is usually not on the paper record, it can be difficult to match a physical file to the magnetic file. The most straightforward solution is to put the computer record name on the document also. The printed document can then be filed by name, but it will have its associated computer name on it. Sometimes the person who created the document does not want that "funny" computer name on the document and an explanation of the reason for it will be necessary. Another suitable approach is to ask the user to suggest a name within the naming convention restrictions and to use that name on both the computer file and the paper file copies.

Indexing Records

The use of indexes in records management has not been widespread and their potential has not been fully realized. With increasing understanding of indexing, as compared to classifying, and the significant benefits of indexing for electronic records, we expect to see indexing used more frequently in developing efficient and effective retrieval systems (Acton, 1986).

Indexing Concepts

An index always assumes the existence of ordered items. The ordered items are intended to be retrieved by use of the inherent order. Thus an index is a list that uses some other characteristic of the items for ordering while containing the original ordering. The most general definition of an *index* is that it is a pointer to the desired information. In this sense, an index is an indirect method of retrieval.

A good example of an index would be a name and address file that is ordered by arrival. As each new name and address is created, it is given the next available number in a series starting with 0001. After one hundred entries, the names and addresses are ordered from 001 to 100. This is an easy system to create and it is meaningful for retrieval by entry order; but suppose that we wish to retrieve an entry alphabetically by name. The solution is to have an index that contains the name and the series number alphabetically ordered by the name. We look up the name in the index, which then gives us the series number that is used to retrieve the file. This same principle is followed in creating a relative (cross-reference) index.

Indexing Applications

Manual applications of indexing with paper records are not common for a variety of reasons. First, people are accustomed to being able to retrieve paper files based on only the classification system and are unaware of the potential uses of indexing. Consider the example of a legal firm that has grown rapidly in the last decade and now has thousands of paper (client) records. The firm eventually notices a conflict-of-interest problem because different partners in the firm are inadvertently handling both sides of a case! If the client records were indexed by type of case, major participants, and who handled the case, then the firm could easily determine potential conflicts of interest.

Second, indexing and maintaining the index may not be economically feasible for paper records. The time and resource costs to index paper records manually often is not worth the increase in information. However, many computer systems can do indexing easily and efficiently. (An in-depth discussion of computer indexing methods is provided in Chapter 15, "Computer-Based Records Management Systems.")

Indexing Problems

The biggest problem in indexing is keeping the index updated as changes are made to the records. As records are altered, added, or deleted, the index must be updated. An index that is out of date is useless. Keeping even one index updated in a manual system is time-consuming, but a computer system easily can keep multiple indexes up to date. Also, the relative index for a file folder system can be kept on computer, making updating simpler and less time-consuming.

Another problem is deciding on what the index will be based. Of course, some characteristics are obvious. In a word processing application, the originator's name, the date, the time, or the subject are candidates for an index. Many libraries use a keyword indexing system for books or articles in which the keyword is chosen from the words in the title or suggested by the author. For typical business records, the choices for indexing may not be so clear. When choosing an index, keep in mind that an index exists to help retrieve information.

Color Coding Records

Color coding refers to using color to mean something, usually a letter or number. For example, the letter A, the category Marketing Department, or the number 21 may be coded yellow; that color then has a meaning that will be understood even if no verbal identifier is used. *Color accenting*, on the other hand, means using different colors in different parts of a filing system for a decorative effect or to make various parts of the filing system stand out. For example, folders may be yellow, labels brown, and dividers green. The effect is pleasing visually and the colors aid the user in distinguishing guides from folders, but the colors have no particular meaning.

Color coding can be used to designate file status or type. *File status* refers to the level of activity of a file. *File type* refers to a category or physical type of record, such as a folder, disk, or notebook. An example of color coding by file status would be to use brown labels on all inactive files. An example of color coding by file type would be to use orange folders for divorce files, in a law office, perhaps.

One of the most common applications of color is for coding names and numbers. Several commercial systems are available for this purpose. A less common use of color is for indexing files. The clearest example of color indexing is the use of shades of a color for files. In an alphabetic system, for example, the darker the shade, the further the file is toward the end of the alphabet. As people become used to a color system, the color itself becomes a natural pointer to the file.

Using color in a filing system can create some problems. If the person using the system is color-blind, it becomes a hindrance rather than a help; some employees could have an aversion to certain colors. A color filing system should be coordinated with existing office colors to avoid potential color clashes.

In general, though, color can be a helpful retrieval aid in both numeric and alphabetic systems.

Color Coding in Numeric Systems

In a straight numeric system, any part of the number can be color coded. A simple, straight numeric system can be color coded on the first digit. In this case, ten colors are needed for the digits 0 through 9. Following this system, the second digit in the system could be similarly coded, with the first digit color followed by the second digit color. This progression of color coding can be continued as long as there is physical room on the file. Color in a terminal-digit system is used to code each part of the number, but as in any numeric-based system, only ten colors are needed. The coding occurs in the arrangement of colors and numbers. For example, a color block may be used for the first four numbers of file 14-66-82. The color used for that block would be based on the last digit of the four-number group. Each of the last two numbers would have different colors. Therefore, if 6 is purple, 8 is red, 2 is blue, and 3 is green, then files 14-66-82 and 14-66-83 would be coded as follows:

1466	8	2
purple	red	blue

1466	8	3
purple	red	green

If file 14-66-82 were filed in division 83, the misfile would be apparent.

Color Coding in an Alphabetic System

In an alphabetic system in which names are used on folders, colors are associated with letters of the alphabet. Several commercial file folder systems that use a different color or combination of colors for each letter of the alphabet are available from office suppliers. In the simplest systems, each letter of the alphabet is assigned a color, so that all names starting with A may be green, all names starting with B, red, and so forth. In other systems, when each letter category may have hundreds of files, a color or combination of colors is used for the first letter of a person's last name and a different color is used for the second letter of that person's last name. In still another approach, a single color is assigned to a block of letters.

Consider how the system would be handled if the first two letters of the surname were color coded and a single color was assigned to a block of letters. Five colors could be used to represent the following parts of the alphabet: ABCDE = red, FGHIJ = green, KLMNO = blue, PQRST = yellow, and UVWXYZ = violet. Then the name Baker, coded by the first and second letters, would have a two-part red label; the name Blair would have a red/blue label. Further, a tab position would be assigned to each of the letters in each group: Those names beginning with A would occupy first position; those names beginning with B would occupy second position, and so forth. Therefore, although the names Baker and Carter were both coded two-part red, the tabs would be in different positions across the file drawer or shelf.

Self-adhesive labels are available in a variety of types and colors, and many commercial color coding systems are on the market. Often, simply purchasing preprinted colored labels is the most cost-effective approach; however, colored tape, which can be cut to any size and simply attached to existing folders, can be used instead. Self-adhesive, plasticized paper tape can be purchased in rolls (like scotch tape) in widths of ½ to 3 inches in a variety of colors. The following diagram illustrates a colored-tape approach:

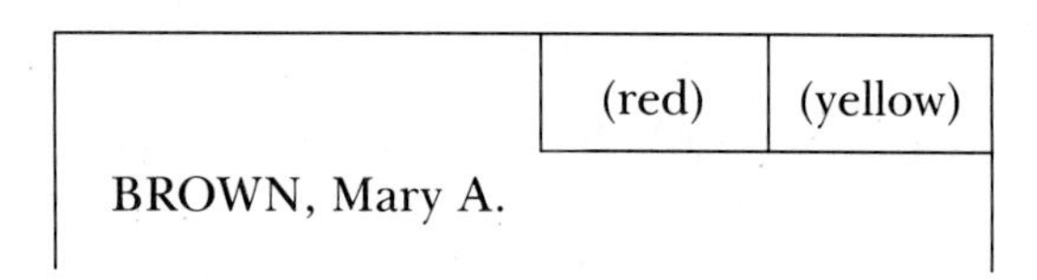

Color Coding for Microcomputer Disk Systems

The following three methods are practical approaches for using color to organize magnetic media.

The most common method of color coding floppy disks is to use color on the labels. Packages of disks sometimes include labels with different colors, but office supply stores also sell disk labels. The labels are colored on the edges and the colors can be used for identification purposes. The colors usually include red, blue, yellow, green, and purple. A typical label, about actual size, is shown in the following diagram. The lined area is for writing the disk name and other descriptive information.

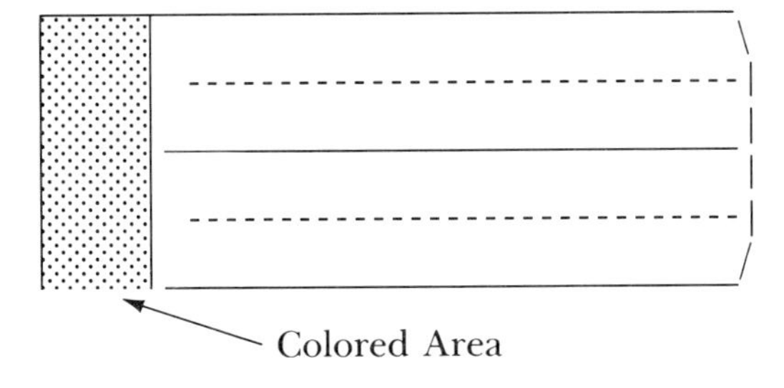

While many microcomputer users ignore the colors on the labels, they can be a practical and useful organization tool. Colors can be used to distinguish major categories of disk use. For example, red could be used for system and utility disks, blue for application programs, green for text files, and yellow for backup disks only.

A second approach in which the color labels are combined with colored envelopes and colored jackets can be used for more sophisticated systems. The envelopes are the holders for the disks and usually contain the manufacturer's identification information. The disk jacket contains the disk itself sealed inside and is usually plain black. (Both the jackets and envelopes are available in a variety of colors.) Color coding in microcomputer systems will probably follow the naming convention used for the files and disks. Because most naming conventions are subject oriented, the color coding, too, should be organized by subject.

Color coding the storage containers for the media and associated material is a third possibility for using color in microcomputer systems. Magnetic media containers include disk boxes, which may hold from ten to one hundred disks, file-folder page systems, which usually hold from two to four disks per page, and larger file systems. In combination with color labels, envelopes, and jackets, colored disk boxes or cases can provide excellent disk organization. If disks are filed in file pages, then color systems can be used in the same manner as traditional paper files and the system has an additional advantage. It is easy to store paper documents (for example, documentation or directory listings) with the disk. The next step is to proceed from having only disks filed in file pages to the notebook method of organization. The notebook would contain both the disk and its associated information in a convenient format for storage and retrieval of disparate groups of materials. By using color codes for the notebooks, a quick and convenient system can be developed for the storage of microcomputer software and materials.

Summary

Business records require systematic naming and arrangement. The simplest methods for both naming and arranging records is by alphabetical or numerical order. The naming, arranging, and indexing of records is called the classification process. The first step in the classification process is naming the record; the second step is arranging them. Different approaches to naming records are required, depending on whether the record is a paper file or a computer file. A common identifier and systematic arrangement of parts of the record label are required for a paper file. A naming convention is required for a computer file.

Paper records can be classified in alphabetic, numeric, or subject systems. An alphabetic system uses letters of the English alphabet for general identifiers—correspondence is often filed alphabetically. Geographic systems are a subset of alphabetic classification in which records are filed by location. In a numeric system, records are filed by number. Two common numeric systems are straight numeric and terminal-digit.

Numeric systems require the use of logbooks and relative indexes. Subject classification systems may be either alphabetic or numeric, or a combination of the two. Subject systems also require relative indexes.

An index is a pointer to desired information and may be based on name, date, keyword, or some other item that aids retrieval. Two problems of indexing are choosing a suitable item or items on which to index, and keeping the index up to date.

Color coding records can enhance both numeric and alphabetic classification systems. Many commercial color coding packages that associate color with letters and/or numbers are available, but individuals can use colored labels or tape to create their own systems. Color is also very useful in setting up microcomputer disk and notebook systems.

List of Terms

indexing unit
index
identifier
classification system
alphabetic classification system
correspondence arrangement
primary guides
secondary guides
geographic arrangement
numeric classification system
relative index
straight numeric system
numeric logbook
terminal digit system
chronological file
tickler file
alphabetic subject system
numeric subject system
directory
wild card character
naming convention
alphabetic color block
color coding
color accenting
file status
file type

Discussion Questions

1. What are the most common methods for classifying records?
2. What are the advantages and disadvantages of the numeric classification system?
3. What are the three ways in which you could set up a geographic classification system in which states, counties, and cities are the divisions under which company folders are filed?
4. What are some examples of a computer naming convention?
5. What is the difference between color accenting and color coding?
6. What are two approaches used for color coding alphabetic files?
7. What are two common problems in naming computer files?
8. Why are naming conventions useful and necessary for computer files?

Activities

1. All working records systems must, by definition, already have a classification system. An interesting way to delve into the beginnings of a classification system is to examine the storage/retrieval system in a

small office or the business records at an individual's desk. Do so and report on the classification system in use.

2. Research suggests that terminal-digit, numeric classification systems are best suited for large volumes of active records. But is the reverse always true—do large, active systems always work best with a terminal-digit system? Can you describe a vast, active records system that would work well *not* using a terminal-digit system?
3. Color accenting tends to follow "fashion" trends, although putty and walnut seem to be permanently popular. Visit an office supplies store and write a report on the latest "fashion" in color accenting.
4. Personal records usually are kept with an implied subject classification system. What are the major subject categories in which you keep your personal records?
5. The sophisticated use of color coding for computer media has not developed very far. Visit a mainframe computer center or a business that has several microcomputers in use. Write a report suggesting how color coding might be used effectively in these environments.
6. Would it be reasonable to file and retrieve student files according to a straight social security numeric system? (Hint: What would be the range of numeric values?)

References

Acton, Patricia. "Indexing Is Not Classifying—And Vice Versa." *ARMA Quarterly* (July 1986): 10–15.

Lundgren, Terry and Norman Garrett. "An Unusual Topic in Data Processing Courses: Naming Conventions." *Journal of Business Education* (December 1984): 106–8.

Parzen, Emanuel. *Modern Probability and its Applications* (New York: John Wiley & Sons, 1960), pp. 46–47.

Chapter 6 Highlight

Decimal Classification

Nearly all libraries use a numeric subject system developed by Melvil Dewey in 1873. Commonly known as the Dewey decimal system, it is based on the use of decimal numbers for classification. In the same way that an alphabetic system has twenty-six (A–Z) major categories, a decimal system has ten (0–9) major categories. Each category can have ten further subdivisions; each subdivision can have ten more divisions, etc.

The Dewey decimal system is based on an XXX.YYYY naming convention. The Ys are the numbers after the decimal and they represent increasing subdivisions. There is no limit to the number of Ys possible, but few libraries use more than four of them. Consider that an XXX.YYYY naming convention can have one million categories and subcategories and you can see why more decimals usually are not necessary.

The X00 part represents the first ten general divisions as follows:

000 General Works
100 Philosophy
200 Religion
300 Social Science
400 Language
500 Pure Science
600 Applied Science
700 Arts
800 Literature
900 History

Subcategories must fit into the ten major categories. For example, a chemistry category is assigned number 540 and subcategories under it are assigned using a 54X.YYYY naming convention.

The advantage of such a system is that new divisions are easily added, and grouping by subject makes browsing useful. The books are arranged on the shelves in numerical order, so if the Dewey decimal number is known, retrieval is straightforward.

Obviously, a relative index is absolutely necessary for this type of system. Since books are often searched for by author, title, or subject, an index by each of these areas is required. This index is the traditional library card catalog with three cards for each book.

The major disadvantages of a decimal system are:

1. The system is inflexible; categories that seemed meaningful in the past may not be relevant today.
2. With a number of relative indexes and a large number of subcategories, keeping the indexes up-to-date becomes difficult.
3. If the records are misfiled, it will be extremely difficult to locate them, if they can be located at all.

What was a reasonable categorization in 1873 is less applicable today. A typical university library of a million items overwhelms any manual index system, and strict rules must allow only authorized personnel to reshelf materials to reduce misfiling.

Libraries are now computerizing their holdings. Computerized searches are fast and efficient, and computer technology offers many possibilities for reorganizing the physical arrangement of library materials. Perhaps by the year 3000, libraries will have only digitally stored data—and books (and the Dewey decimal system) will be found only in museums!

Chapter 7

Filing Equipment and Supplies for Paper and Computer Records

Learning Goals

1. To become familiar with a broad range of equipment for storing paper and computer records.
2. To become acquainted with the supplies available for use with paper records and computer records.
3. To understand how to make the best use of filing equipment and supplies for paper records and computer records.
4. To know the factors to be considered in making equipment purchase decisions.

Introduction

Business records must be stored and cared for not only to avoid damage to the physical record, but also to make them readily and conveniently available when needed. Because paper records are produced in different sizes (for example, letter size and legal size) and because the records themselves may be letters, maps, blueprints, or cards, one type of equipment is not suitable for all paper records. People also have preferences for durability, portability, style, and color; or the type and use of the record may dictate the need for a particular type of equipment. Therefore, a wide variety of office equipment has been designed for storing paper and computer records.

Computer records present some special storage problems because they are often generated in both paper and magnetic form. Computer records are stored first on magnetic disks and tapes. Then the hard copies of those records are printed on single-sheet or continuous (tractor-fed) paper of various sizes. Equipment and supplies are needed for those records in paper and magnetic media form.

Obviously, the variety of records stored by a business requires a wide variety of equipment, but just about any configuration of equipment one wishes to use for filing paper and computer records is available today, along with an extensive array of supplies.

In this chapter, we will describe many of the types of equipment and supplies used for storing and maintaining paper and computer records. (The information on equipment and supplies for micrographic records is provided in Chapter 8.) We also focus on the best or most common uses for records management equipment, including those with unique features. After becoming familiar with features and uses, you will find the section on purchasing records management equipment helpful in making wise and economical equipment choices. The chapters in Part 2, which deal with specialized records management situations, explain specific, practical applications for the equipment described here.

Filing Equipment for Paper and Computer Records

The basic types of manual filing equipment for paper and computer records are vertical, suspension, lateral, shelf, tray, box, and rotary. Many different styles of these types of equipment are sold to accommodate the variety of paper and computer records used in businesses today, including mechanized versions of shelf and rotary file cabinets. Also, equipment may be designed for a specific record. Certain types of equipment are recommended for certain sizes and types of records. Storing records in equipment that was not designed for that record is not only inefficient, but may also result in damaged records and damaged equipment.

Vertical Files

Vertical files are drawer files designed to store paper records that are letter size (8½ × 11 inches) or legal size (8½ × 14 inches), as well as card records. Cards are made in a variety of sizes also: 3 × 5 inches, 4 × 6 inches, and 5 × 8 inches are common. Any equipment in which records are stored upright (individually or in file folders) in a drawer is considered vertical filing equipment. However, in popular usage, a vertical file is one in which records are filed from the front to the back of the drawers. Vertical filing equipment is sold in letter and legal sizes with one to six drawers. The equipment is suitable for filing correspondence, reports, magazines, catalogs, or most any paper records that fit the equipment dimensions. Vertical files also are constructed with many small drawers to hold index cards, microfiche, or cassette tapes. Figure 7.1 shows two types of vertical files—for cards and for folders.

Important features of vertical files are (1) full-suspension drawers, which provide adequate support and smooth operation; and (2) locks, which provide security for records. A full-suspension drawer allows access to the entire drawer because it can be pulled out to its full length without collapsing or warping. The suspension feature consists of additional arms and rollers built into the body of the cabinet that connect the drawer to the cabinet and support its weight. A non-suspension drawer can be pulled out only about two-thirds of its length. If pulled all the way out, non-suspension drawers literally will fall out of the cabinet, although they may have built-in stops to prevent them being pulled out further than two-thirds of the way. Clothing dressers and desks often have non-suspension drawers.

Full-suspension files are more expen-

Figure 7.1 Vertical Files

sive than those with non-suspension drawers. However, if the cost is measured in terms of accessibility per inch, then the full-suspension unit is the better value even though its initial cost is higher.

(Suspension drawers should not be confused with suspension or hanging files, which are explained in the following section.)

Suspension (Hanging) Files

Suspension files are those that allow items to hang suspended from a frame (drawer-type) or rod. *Drawer-type suspension files* are made to be used in a filing cabinet; some suspension frame files are constructed to stand alone. Figure 7.2 shows two types of suspension frame files: a drawer-type and a free-standing-type for computer binders.

The drawer type of hanging file equipment is a metal frame that fits inside of a file drawer. File folders that are especially designed to hang from the metal frame are needed for use with the drawer-type suspension file. Drawer-type suspension files have several advantages. Because the files slide on the metal frame, they can be moved back and forth easily without falling into the drawer. Also, each hanging file can be used as a separate folder or can hold several paper file folders. The latter arrangement is especially useful for keeping a master and several copies of a document. The master is kept in the paper file folder with the copies stored behind it. Both the file folder and the copies are in the hanging file folder. Free-standing suspension files also are used for storing computer printout binders. The

Figure 7.2 Suspension (Hanging) Files

Drawer-Type Suspension (Hanging) File

Source Courtesy of Fidelity Products Co.

Computer Binder Files

Source Courtesy of Moore Business Products.

computer printouts are first bound and then suspended from the frame by their spines. The advantage of this suspension file is that it stores large, nonrigid items easily and conveniently.

Another less frequently used type of suspension equipment employs a rod (wooden or metal) from which the record or document (for example, a newspaper or map) hangs. Libraries sometimes have this rod-type suspension file for storing current copies of newspapers, atlases, and other large paper items. Retail stores use a variation of this equipment for displaying posters.

Lateral and Shelf Files

Lateral and shelf files share several of the same features. Therefore, the distinction between them is somewhat arbitrary. *Lateral files* have drawers or slide-out shelves. Folders may be arranged across the width of the drawer or shelf (from right to left or vice versa). Figure 7.3 shows a lateral file. Lateral files become a type of vertical file when the records are stored upright in the drawers in the front-to-back arrangement on suspension frames. Figure 7.4 shows the lateral and vertical methods of arranging records in a lateral file cabinet.

Lateral filing equipment is sold with two to five drawers and in a range of widths (36 inches and 42 inches are common) and heights. This equipment may be purchased in 18-inch depth to accommodate both letter- and legal-size folders. Lateral files are suitable for filing reports, correspondence, magazines, and catalogs. The unique aspect of a lateral file is that it takes up less aisle space than a vertical file because the drawers are only 18 inches deep. When users are accessing records from a lateral file drawer, they usually stand to the side of the drawer rather than in the aisle. Also, accessing records from a lateral file causes less fatigue because the drawer fronts may flip up or drop down for easier access to folders. Full-suspension drawers are an essential feature of lateral files to ensure efficient access to the records. Locks are an additional important security feature.

Shelf files are sometimes referred to as lateral files because records are stored across the width of the shelf. However, the distinction is that shelf files have only shelves

Figure 7.3 Lateral Files

Source Courtesy of Dept. of Business Information Systems and Education, Utah State University, Logan, Utah.

Figure 7.4 Filing Arrangements in Lateral Files

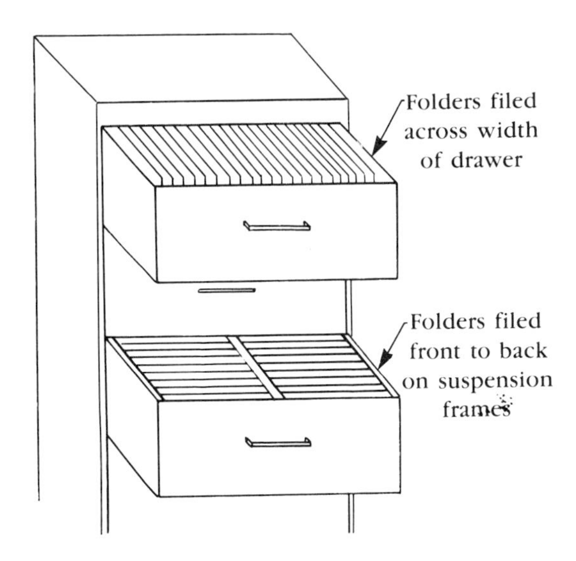

and lateral files may have drawers, shelves, or a combination of the two. One type of shelf file is simply an open bookcase in which books and other similar documents are stored. Another type is a lateral file similar to the lateral drawer file described previously. (The difference between a lateral drawer file and a lateral shelf file is that the former type has drawers that pull out; the latter has shelves, some of which pull out.) The type of shelf file with sliding shelves also may have a lid for each shelf that can be pulled over the shelf front and locked—called a "drop-lid file." This shelf file is recommended for storing file folders or other labeled records. It is especially suitable for important records if shelves have the front lid that can be locked, and one or more of the shelves slide out for easy access to records.

Still another type of shelf file has a series of small compartments about 9 inches wide for storing literature, forms, or other loose

Figure 7.5 Shelf Files

Compartment File

Source Courtesy of Fidelity Products Co.

Drop Lid File

sheets. Figure 7.5 illustrates drop-lid and compartment shelf files.

Mobile Shelf Units

Mobile shelf units are shelf files that move along tracks in the floor. The units are mounted so that they can slide along the tracks either by a mechanical-assist device or electronically. The unique aspect of this equipment is that it occupies much less floor space than conventional file cabinets, since only a certain number of aisles are open at a time (see Figure 7.6). The units, which may be single- or double-sided, are moved apart to access records. One type of mobile shelf system has a mechanical assist system that allows one pound of force to move 3,000 to 10,000 pounds of load. A control, located on the end of the cabinet, moves the units to open the desired access aisle. This equipment also has safety features to prevent closing aisle space in which someone is working.

Mobile shelf units are suitable for high-density storage of both active and inactive records, but the weight and size of the equipment can create special problems. The floors in most commercial buildings are designed to support the weight of office desks, copiers, and filing cabinets, but in relatively low-density situations. Installation of high-density equipment can easily place a weight load on the floor that exceeds the maximum weight per square foot limits of a building. Commercial building floors typically are designed for loads ranging from 50 to 100

Figure 7.6 Mobile Shelf Units

Source Carol Lundgren and Joyce Kupsh, *Records Management*, National Instructional Systems, Inc., 1985.

Figure 7.7 Flat, or Tray, File and Layered Tray File

Flat File

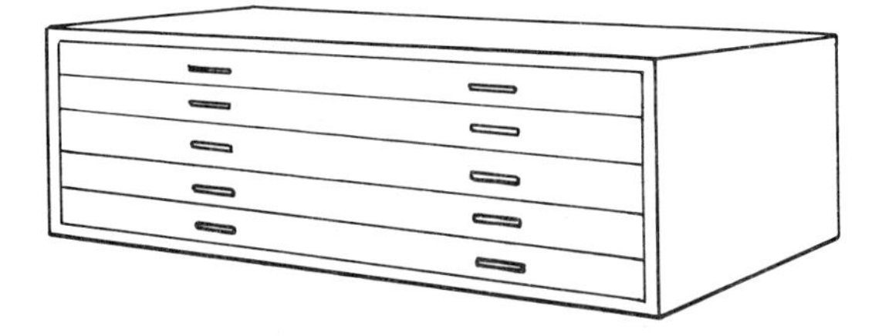

Layered Tray File

Source Courtesy of Kardex Systems, Inc.

pounds per square foot. Mobile file shelves can impose weights of almost double those limits. If mobile files are being considered and there is any doubt as to the weight-bearing capacity of the proposed space, then a construction engineer should be consulted. Vendors of this type of equipment are well aware of this situation and can provide aid and advice. Also, most office ceilings are 9 feet high, but in some buildings, ceilings may be lower and mobile file units need to be low enough to allow room for ceiling sprinkler systems (*Modern Office Technology*, 1984).

Flat Files

Files that consist of a single paper record are sometimes easier to access and work with if they are stored flat. Figure 7.7 illustrates two types of flat files: a *flat drawer*, or *tray*, *file* with several large, shallow drawers, and a layered tray file.

Some records, such as personnel or accounts receivable cards, are inserted in plastic, transparent jackets and stored in a *layered tray file*. The jackets are attached to a flat rack so that the records are layered and an inch or so of the bottom of each record is visible. An individual name, company name, or some other identifier is printed at the bottom of the card so the identifier shows when the cards are layered. Although the jackets are removable for rearrangement if necessary, these files are best suited for records that do not change frequently.

Maps and blueprints may be laid flat and stacked in a flat drawer (or tray) file, with only a few items to each drawer. Because the user must go through the stack to find an item, these files are recommended for records that are used only once or infrequently. For example, geological maps that will be sold to interested users are stored in flat drawer files.

Box Files

Box files are cardboard, metal, or plastic boxes. Some box files have hinged or detachable lids; others are simply upright boxes. Figure 7.8 shows two types of box files: an archival box file with an attached lid and a cardboard (upright) box for storing magazines.

Box files often are used for storing inactive records because the boxes are portable and may be stackable. These features also make box files suitable for storing frequently used records that need to be moved from place to place.

Box files that are used for storing inactive records generally are made of heavy cardboard construction, chemically treated to retard deterioration of the records they hold and prevent attack by vermin. The cardboard boxes may be reinforced with metal bracing to allow convenient stacking to almost any height. The boxes are a uniform size so that 8½-×-11-inch files (or individual records) may be stored in the box from front to back, or legal-size (8½-×-14-inch) files may be stored across the width of the box. Box lids keep dust and other debris out of the contents, and the boxes have areas for labeling on one or more sides.

The upright cardboard box file used for storing magazines or catalogs is shown in Figure 7.8. The advantage of this type of box file is that it supports the sides of nonrigid items such as magazines.

Metal box files are available with hinged lids, the type most commonly in use. The small versions are used to store cards, and the large versions are mounted on wheels so they can be rolled from one location to another. Because of their low cost and durability, metal box files are recommended for storing active records.

Plastic or wooden box files are used for storing small microcomputer disks (known as floppy disks). Because the disks encode data magnetically, metal containers are inappropriate. Figure 7.9 on page 108 shows both plastic and wooden disk box files.

Some disk box files are constructed to hold forty to fifty disks and have hinged or roll-top lids. They may be single– or double-width, and generally are a uniform width (approximately ½ inch wider than the disks).

Another type of disk box file is only a few inches deep and completely encloses the disks. These boxes can be attached to each other and stored on shelves. All of the types of disk box files described are recommended for storing floppy disks. They are inexpensive, durable, and portable.

Rotary Files

Rotary files store items so that the contents can be accessed by turning the equipment. Large rotary files, several feet high, have shelves for storing file folders, cassette tapes, or films. This equipment turns like a carousel on a centered post; hence, the name "carousel file." Desk-top rotary files may be small card wheels used for keeping phone numbers or business cards, or a larger carousel-type file on which cards or individual pages are attached. The pages may hold microfiche, cards, floppy disks, or simply strips of information. Figure 7.10 on page 109 shows three types of rotary files: a strip file, a carousel-type rotary file, and a desktop rotary file.

Figure 7.8 Cardboard Box Files

Archival Box File

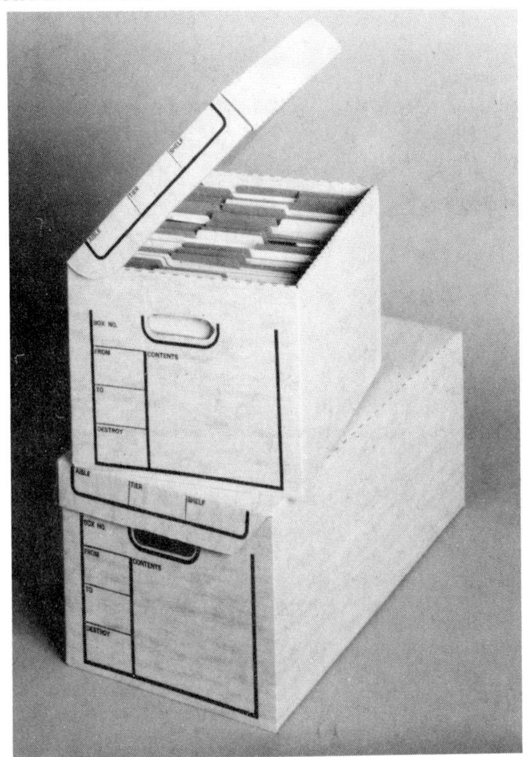

Source Courtesy of Fidelity Products Co.

Cardboard Box File for Magazines

Source Courtesy of Fidelity Products Co.

Figure 7.9 Disk Box Files

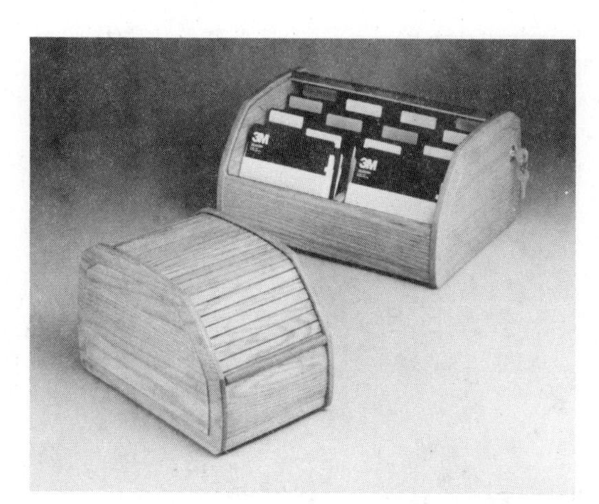

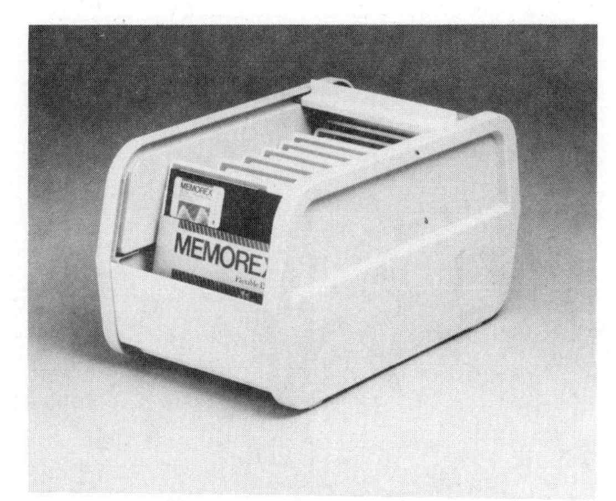

Source Courtesy of Moore Business Products.

Special Purpose Files

Some filing equipment is designed for a particular type of record and is seldom used for anything except that record. Pigeonhole and notebook files fall into this equipment category.

Pigeonhole (or roll) *files* are files with several small compartments (holes). Rolled maps or blueprints fit into the holes with only a single or one type of record occupying each compartment, and the compartments are labeled. These files are suitable for maps and blueprints that do not need to be rearranged, since changing one label usually necessitates changing all the others. Figure 7.11 (page 110) shows a pigeonhole file.

Notebook files serve both paper and computer filing needs. Plastic page inserts for floppy disks can be incorporated into common 3-ring binders. Notebooks that are mounted at an angle on metal racks are used for reference materials. This equipment is recommended for frequently updated reference records such as automobile parts books, telephone books, or computer documentation.

Supplies for Paper and Computer Filing Equipment

Some supplies (for example, labels) are used for both paper and computer records. Other supplies are designed uniquely for either paper records or computer records. In this section, we will describe the unique supplies: file folders and guides for paper records, and floppy disks for computer records.

File Folders and Guides

Paper records are stored in file folders of various sizes and shapes. Folders for vertical, lateral, or shelf files are for standard 8½-×-11-inch or 8½-×-14-inch records with a tab at the top or side for labeling. The folder may have internal fasteners and usually is scored at the bottom to allow for expansion. File folders are designed to hold a maximum of about ½ inch of material.

The tab position on a file folder is important for incorporating folders into an existing filing system or in creating a new system. As you will recall in Chapter 6, tab

Figure 7.10 Rotary Files

Strip File

Source Courtesy of Kardex Systems, Inc.

Desktop File

Carousel-Type Rotary File

placement was used in a filing system to organize and identify records. The tab width is called the *cut*, and folders are manufactured in full cut (tab all the way across) or partial cut (half, third, or fifth) to accommodate almost any filing arrangement. For example, third-cut folders will have three possible tab positions across the top, with each tab about 3½ inches wide on a folder designed for 8½-×-11-inch paper. In a box of 100 folders, approximately one-third of the folders will have a tab in the left position, one-third will have a tab in the middle position, and one-third will have a tab in the right position. Figure 7.12 on page 111 illustrates file folders of various cuts.

The tab is positioned on the side of the folder for shelf filing, with the same choice of cuts. Hanging file folders have slots along the top edge of both the front and back parts of the file in which plastic tabs are inserted, so the user can change both the tab width by using a wider tab, or cut, as well as the tab position by simply moving the tab to a different position (see Figure 7.12).

Guides are used in conjunction with file folders as dividers and identifiers for sections within a drawer or shelf. Guides are

Figure 7.11 Pigeonhole (Roll) File

Source Courtesy of Fidelity Products Co.

constructed of plastic or heavy weight cardboard for durability and have two major uses. *Division guides* are usually rigid, heavyweight cardboard and are used to divide and label sections in a drawer or shelf. *Out guides* may be plastic or heavy paperweight. Out guides are used to indicate that a file folder has been removed and to provide information about the absent folder. An out guide is inserted when the folder is removed, and the name of the individual who has the folder and the date it was taken are written on the guide (see Figure 7.12). Some out guides have plastic inserts for holding items that must be filed before the folder is returned.

Microcomputer Disks

Flexible, or floppy, disks are one of the most common computer supplies. The *flexible disk* is a circular piece of pliant mylar plastic, coated with a magnetic layer and encased in a jacket. The jacket is lined with a soft, low-friction material that continually cleans the disk and allows it to rotate freely in the disk drive.

Flexible disks are available in 8-inch and 5¼-inch sizes, single- or double-sided, and of various densities. The *disk density* refers to the quality of the coating on the disk. Single density is "thinner" than double density so less data per unit is usually stored on single-density disks. More dense coatings, for example, quad density, are also available. However, the actual amount stored on a disk is determined by a computer's hardware and software, not the disk itself. A 3½-inch *non-flexible disk* is sold for use on some microcomputer equipment. This disk is enclosed in a plastic, very durable, and rigid case about ⅛ inch thick. The most common 3½-inch disk has about twice the capacity of the most common 5¼-inch disk. The general trend has been toward smaller disks of higher density. Color labels are usually packaged with floppy disks and the disk jackets themselves also may be different colors. Vinyl notebook pages for storing up to four disks per page are sold, too.

Making Equipment Purchase Decisions

Equipment represents a significant cost for any organization. Often the investment in records management equipment is so great that new equipment will not be purchased even though the present equipment is obsolete. For this reason, a business must carefully consider what equipment will do the best job for the greatest number of records over the longest period of time. More effi-

Figure 7.12 Folders and Guides

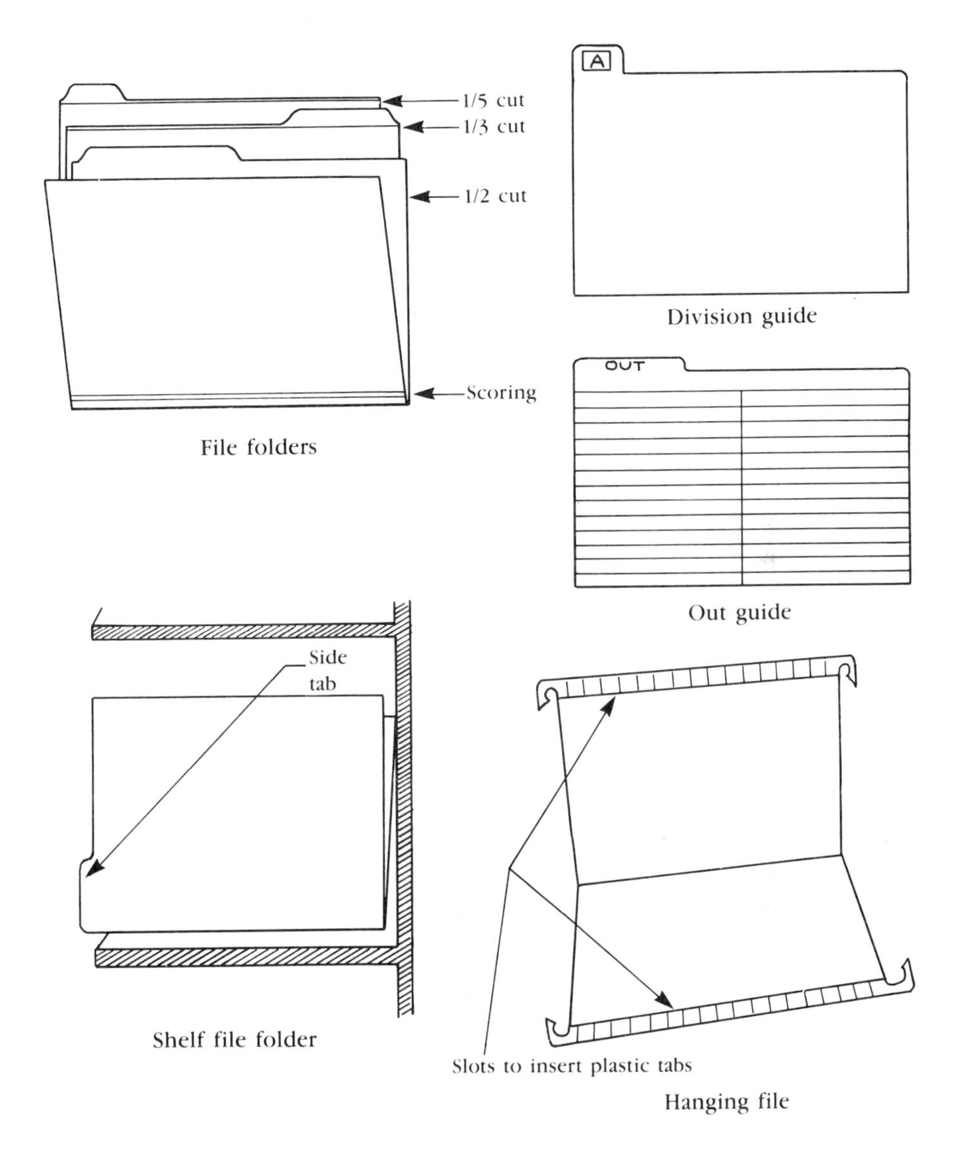

cient and attractive equipment is being designed constantly. Technology is creating the need for different types of equipment. Sometimes the best decisions are thwarted by new technology, relocation of offices, or some other factor over which the purchaser has little control.

Clerical staff sometimes will be asked to participate in selecting equipment, but the responsibility for making equipment purchases will rest with management. The major factors to be considered in any equipment purchase decision are cost and use. These two factors must be weighed carefully, especially if even the least costly equipment being considered is very expensive. For example, vertical filing cabinets range in price from approximately $80 to over $300. One reason for the difference in price is construction. The less expensive filing cabinets will have suspension units of lesser quality and would not be suitable for the heavy use to which filing cabinets are subjected in a business, but may be practical for a home office. Non-suspension units, as mentioned, are rarely a good filing value unless they are not used to store records. Purchasing the least expensive filing cabinet would save money in the short run, but the poor operation of the equipment in day-to-day use would hinder productivity and cost more in operation costs in the long run.

Since equipment and floor space for records storage equipment represent a large portion of the cost in a records system, cost justification is required. A cost-justification study should be made to determine how much the planned-for equipment will cost and in what ways that cost is justified. Then the equipment selection should be based on cost effectiveness and suitability, including the following factors:

- □ degree of protection and security offered
- □ initial cost and cost of maintenance
- □ design and floor space occupied
- □ frequency of use
- □ efficiency of equipment operation.

The purchase of expensive mechanized equipment may be justified by the increase in efficiency of staff or prohibited by the additional expense of making structural changes in the building to support the additional weight.

Other factors to consider in making equipment selections include style, color, and compatibility with other equipment. Compatibility is a particularly important—and increasingly difficult—factor to consider when computer equipment and supplies are being purchased. Vendors can provide information on the features of computer equipment, but they seldom are the best sources for determining if new equipment will be compatible with old. Trade magazines such as *Modern Office Technology* and *PC Week* regularly print equipment evaluation articles that list and objectively ssess equipment features. (Appendix B on pages 273 to 274 contains a list of publications in which office equipment and supplies frequently are reviewed and evaluated.)

Finally, it is sometimes possible to use equipment on a trial basis, or lease it and delay the purchase decision until the suitability of the equipment can be determined.

Summary

Records management equipment should be designed for the records it will store. A wide variety of equipment for storing paper and computer records is available. The basic types of filing equipment are vertical, suspension, lateral, shelf, tray, box, and rotary.

Vertical files are drawer files for letter and legal-sized paper records. Suspension files are drawer-type, for use in vertical and lateral files, free-standing frames, or rod-type. Lateral files have drawers or slide-out shelves on which folders are arranged across the width. Shelf files are bookcase, drop-lid, or compartment-style. Mobile shelf units offer high-density storage and reduce floor space requirements, but may create installation problems due to their excessive weight when full. Flat drawer (tray) files are suitable for large paper records, such as maps, which can be stored flat; and layered tray files are ideal for some individual records.

Cardboard box files are used for storing inactive records and magazines. Small metal box files are suitable for active records. Plastic and wooden box files are used for floppy disks. Rotary files may be carousel floor files, small desk-top wheels, or carousel strip files. Some filing equipment, such as a pigeonhole (or roll) file, is designed for items that can be rolled into a cylinder for storage.

Because equipment represents a significant investment for most businesses, careful consideration must be given to increased productivity and the balance between cost and use in equipment purchase decisions. The purchaser should determine the cost and justify the purchase of the equipment in terms of its durability, usefulness, style, and purpose.

List of Terms

vertical file
suspension file
drawer-type suspension file
rod-type suspension file
lateral file
shelf file
mobile shelf unit
flat drawer file
layered tray file
box file
rotary file
pigeonhole (roll) file
notebook file
cut
guide
division guide
out guide
flexible disk
disk density
nonflexible disk

Discussion Questions

1. Why are suspension drawers an important feature in vertical and lateral files?
2. What is the difference between a shelf file and a lateral file? How are they alike?
3. What are some of the common uses for suspension (hanging) files?
4. What are the ways (types of equipment) in which you could file newspapers? What would be the best way?
5. What is the basic operation of a mobile shelf unit?
6. What are the advantages and disadvantages of using mobile shelf units?
7. What are the advantages of lateral and shelf filing equipment?
8. What are three types of rotary files? Which type would be best suited for filing cassette tapes? business cards? phonograph records?
9. What are the major factors to consider in selecting equipment?

Activities

1. Suppose that you have been hired by an insurance agent to handle all of the office duties in the agent's small office. One of your duties is to select the equipment for the office records, which are now stacked in various places. The records include insurance forms (many different

types), client file folders (current and inactive), insurance announcements (paper), floppy disks (both blank and used), and reference manuals. You have room for just two or three pieces of equipment, and whatever you decide to buy will have to last for quite some time. Decide what equipment you will purchase, how it will be used, and explain the reasons for your choice.

2. Review the popular and trade magazines that carry microcomputer supplies. List the different types of magnetic media (disks) available by nominal size, storage capacity, price, and special or unique features.
3. Visit an office and describe the equipment used for paper records. Try to determine when it was purchased and when it is expected to be replaced. Make an estimate of the total value of the equipment.
4. Visit a large "everything except food" store (e.g., K-Mart) and list the types of office equipment for records storage that are available. Is any of it suitable for daily office use? What do you think the typical purchaser has in mind for the equipment?
5. Visit an office that is using lateral files as opposed to vertical drawer files. Are they taking advantage of the reduced space needed to access the records? Draw a diagram to illustrate their effective use of floor space, or show how a different arrangement would be a more efficient use of floor space.

References

"No Visible Means of Support." *Modern Office Technology* (November 1984): 72–78.

"Paper Free, Not Paperless." *Modern Office Technology* (May 1986): 56–60.

Chapter 7 Highlight

Microcomputer Disk Magnetic Media

Magnetic media in the form of disks for microcomputers has been available since about 1980. The general trend has been toward smaller disks of higher capacity. Unfortunately, not all disks and disk drives are compatible. For example, a 5¼-inch disk will not fit in a 3½-inch disk drive, but there are other limitations, as well. For disk magnetic media to be used, it must be formatted using software provided with the microcomputer operating system. This software, in conjunction with the disk drive, determines the actual usable capacity of the disk. (See the Highlight in Chapter 16 for information on media capacity.)

The general rule for disk usage is that the latest disk drive and software can read/write any previous disk that is physically compatible. But an early disk drive may not be able to read a disk written by the latest model even if it is physically compatible.

Physical compatibility means that a disk is the same size and sidedness. Microcomputer disks presently have three sizes, 8 inches, 5¼ inches, and 3½ inches in diameter. "Sidedness" refers to capability of the disk to be used on one side only or both sides. Single-sided disks are referred to as SS and double-sided disks as DS.

The following table shows the magnetic media used in IBM and compatible microcomputers today.

Size	*Media*	*Capacity*
5¼″	Single-sided disk	160/180KB
5¼″	Double-sided disk	320/360KB
5¼″	High-capacity disk	1.2MB
3½″	Double-sided disk	720KB
3½″	High-capacity disk	1.44MB

In terms of capacity, a KB, or kilobyte, is about 1,000 bytes. A byte is equal to a single character. An MB, or megabyte, is about 1,000 KB.

The higher-capacity disks can be used at a lower capacity, but the reverse usually does not work well. For example, a 5¼-inch SS disk can be put into a high-capacity drive and the software will try to format it properly. The result typically will be unsatisfactory, as the formatting program will mark much of the disk as unusable. This is the capacity factor. Higher-capacity disks have a higher density or superior-quality media that is capable of more accurate reading/writing.

Disks prepared for use by formatting on one type of microcomputer may not be usable on other types of hardware. In general, there are IBM and compatible, Apple/Macintosh, and CP/M microcomputers. Even physically compatible disks cannot be used between these types of microcomputers. Because of this problem, a number of hardware and software manufacturers sell devices and programs that will allow one type of machine to read the disks formatted by another type of microcomputer. Even though a disk can be used on two different types of microcomputers with special hard/software, only data can be shared. An applications program (for example, a spreadsheet) that runs on one type of microcomputer will not run on another type of machine.

Chapter 8

Micrographics

Learning Goals

1. To become familiar with the field of micrographics.
2. To become aware of the variety of supplies and equipment available in micrographics.
3. To explain how micrographic retrieval systems operate.
4. To be able to differentiate between manual and computer-assisted retrieval (CAR) in micrographic systems.
5. To become knowledgeable about micrographics system selection.

Introduction

The area of micrographics refers to the making of graphic images. The original materials are often paper but can include optical and magnetic media. Micrographics means reproduction, on a smaller or reduced scale, of an original on film. If we were to reproduce the original to the same scale, we would then call the process "reprographics." (Reprographics will be discussed in Chapter 9.)

The goal of micrographics is to make one or very few smaller copies of the original for backup purposes. The development of modern micrographics is generally attributed to the banking industry, which needed an inexpensive, efficient method to record the checks passing through a bank to replace the laboriously handwritten (and error-prone) descriptions of checks. Hardly a bank today exists that does not use check microfilming.

The Field of Micrographics

Surveys and sales in micrographics consistently show that this is a steadily growing area of records management. On a regular basis, claims are made that computer technology will soon render micrographics obsolete for records management, but the advantages of *microforms* (the various types of micrographic materials) for records storage are not likely to be eliminated for many years. Research studies have shown that more firms plan to begin or increase use of micrographics than to begin to expand use of computers for records management. Generally, micrographics is popular because traditionally it has been, and continues to be, an effective method for storing records. Records managers are more familiar with micrographics equipment and processes than they are with data processing. As computers continue to proliferate and suitable computer hardware and software for records management are developed, computers undoubtedly will invade the micrographics arena. Nevertheless, the unique properties of micrographics assures its future for a long, long time.

Definition and Scope

Micrographics is a technology that records information as miniaturized images on film. It has been available since film technology became cost effective, around 1900. Probably the earliest reported use of micrographics occurred during the Franco-Prussian War of 1870 when carrier pigeons were used to carry reports that had been microfilmed. Microfilm has also gained a certain ignominy because of its use by spies in the classic "hollow heel" and the "spy dot," an entire document hidden as a dot or period at the end of a sentence in an ordinary document.

Micrographic systems are used mainly in accounting, records storage, engineering, information distribution, and computer reporting. Each of these areas takes advantage of the unique aspects of micrographics. A relatively new area of use is *micropublishing*. Specially designed micrographic equipment is used to store and retrieve efficiently and quickly published and unpublished books and manuscripts on microfilm.

Advantages and Disadvantages

The four major advantages of micrographics over paper are space reduction, improved accessibility, cost, and security of data.

When paper is replaced with microforms, the space saved runs between 90 and 98 percent. (A popular analogy is that a football field of paper can be stored in a small room on microfilm.) Although the precise space savings are dependent on the nature of the media involved, it will always be significant.

With microforms, it is possible to access images in seconds and the possibility of misfile or damage is greatly reduced. Most micrographics systems can be integrated with a computer to allow sophisticated, fast storage and retrieval, which would be almost impossible in a paper records system.

In terms of costs, a 100-foot roll of microfilm with 2,000 to 4,000 images can be duplicated for $5 to $10; microfilm costs less than 1¢ an image to duplicate. Although film is inexpensive, the associated equipment is rather costly. Initial costs for a complete micrographic system are high, but normally cost return can be realized in three to seven years.

An unanticipated advantage of micrographics is the enhanced security of the information. Because microforms are difficult or impossible to read without special equipment, they are not as susceptible to casual observation as, for example, a letter left on a desk might be. On the other hand, the portability of microforms can make them easy prey for theft.

Two general disadvantages of micrographics are (1) the time required for a system conversion (for example, from paper to microfilm, which depends on the equipment used) and (2) the cost of equipment and training, particularly if a computer system is used. For converting a large paper system to micrographics, the cost is estimated in multiples of $50,000 and time is estimated in years.

Micrographic Equipment and Supplies

Virtually all micrographic equipment and supplies are designed for black-and-white operations, although full-color operation is possible with suitable media and equipment changes. Most records are or can be filmed in black and white with no loss of information. (Color options are discussed in the Service Bureaus section of this chapter.) The following description of equipment and supplies assumes operations using black-and-white film.

Micrographic Media

Media for micrographic operations comes in a variety of forms. Two of the most common are roll microfilm and sheet microfiche. Other types include cartridge and jacketed microfilm, ultrafiche, ultrastrip, and aperture cards.

Roll microfilm is the most common type of microform. The roll of film comes on a reel or open spool, as shown in Figure 8.1. It is used for sequentially organized documents. Normally, data is added sequentially and requires little updating and infrequent retrieval. The common widths are 16, 35, and 105 mm. Common thickness is 5.5 mil (5.5 thousandths of an inch). The common lengths are 100 or 215 feet. The actual amount that fits on a standard reel depends on the thickness of the film. One 100-foot roll can contain about 4,000 images.

Cartridge microfilm is a roll permanently encased in a cartridge that protects the film and is self-threading (see Figure 8.1). The automatic threading feature speeds up han-

Figure 8.1 Roll and Cartridge Microfilm

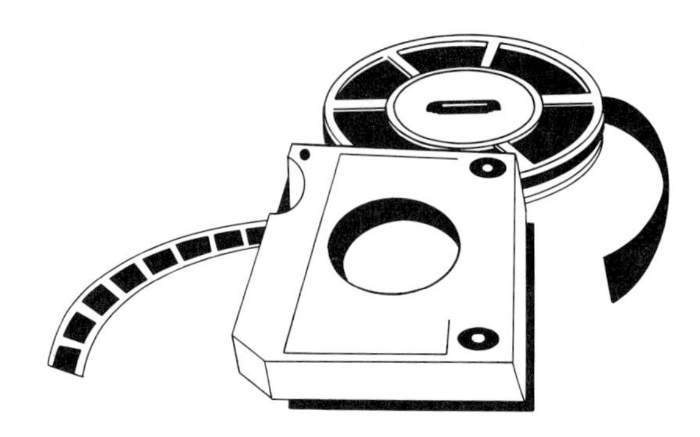

Figure 8.2 Jacketed Microfilm

dling, and multiple cartridges can be used in a "jukebox" type of retrieval system. After a roll of film or a cartridge has been selected, location of a specific image within the 4,000 images on the film takes only seconds. Given the price in the $5 to $10 range (Kodak $5.40, 1987) for a 16-mm-×-100-foot roll, the media is a relatively inexpensive format for records storage.

Jacketed microfilm is a plastic sheet with channels or slots for microfilm, as shown in Figure 8.2. Jackets come in a variety of sizes from 3 × 5 inches up to 5 × 8 inches. They are used for "unitizing" microforms where several types of records are combined in one jacket. A standard 4-×-6-inch jacket can hold up to seventy-five images depending on the size of the film. Images can be read or copied directly without removing the film from the jacket. Jackets can be written on, color-coded, or notched, and they are easily

Figure 8.3 Microfiche

filed. One hundred jackets are only about one inch thick. Jacketed microfilm allows strips of film to be added or changed, making it a particularly flexible microform for records storage.

Figure 8.3 shows *microfiche*, which is a sheet of film of grid images. The most common size is a sheet of 105-mm film measuring 4 × 6 inches. It is easily duplicated, relatively inexpensive, and easily handled. A microfiche can contain from 30 to 500 images, but the most common number of images is from 75 to 98. One of the images can be large enough to be read without magnification and thus is used as a title strip or index page. Also, microfiche can be color-coded, notched, or labeled for manual storage and retrieval.

Because microfiche can be produced economically and is easily mailed, inventories and directories are excellent candidates for this media. A central office can produce the microfiche and mail it to regional offices where a microfiche reader will retrieve the image. Updates can be produced inexpensively and mailed on a regular basis.

Ultrafiche is used for greatly reduced grid images. It is possible to put up to seventy-five microfiches on a single 4-×-6-inch ultrafiche. It is possible to put 5,000 images of standard 8½-×-11-inch paper records on ultrafiche. The entire 1,200 pages of the Bible can be reduced to two square inches of film with no loss of information! This enormous storage capacity makes ultrafiche suitable for large-volume records. The equipment for producing and reading ultrafiche differs from that used for microfiche. It must be highly calibrated and the environment kept extremely clean. The requirements for the production and use of ultrafiche has discouraged its use.

Similar to ultrafiche is *ultrastrip*. An 8-inch segment of 16-mm film can contain up to 10,000 images with no loss of information. In general, the problems and advantages of ultrastrip are the same as those for ultrafiche. Ultrastrip can be stored in jackets with fifteen strips in an 8½-×-11-inch jacket. Such a jacket could contain 150,000 pages of information with the added advantage that any given strip could be changed to update the entire jacket.

An *aperture card* is shown in Figure 8.4. It is a data processing card with a microfilm insertion. The card is a standard computer keypunch card measuring 3¼ × 7⅜ inches and made of heavy stock paper. The aperture card facilitates computer sorting and retrieval. The window typically holds a 35-mm film chip with from one to eight letter-size (reduced) images. The window can hold other microforms; for example, a miniature jacket with three slots for 16 mm film strips.

Aperture cards have been used widely for engineering applications in which the window holds a 35-mm film chip of an engineering drawing and the card contains a description of the drawing. This application may decrease in the future as the develop-

Figure 8.4 Aperture Card

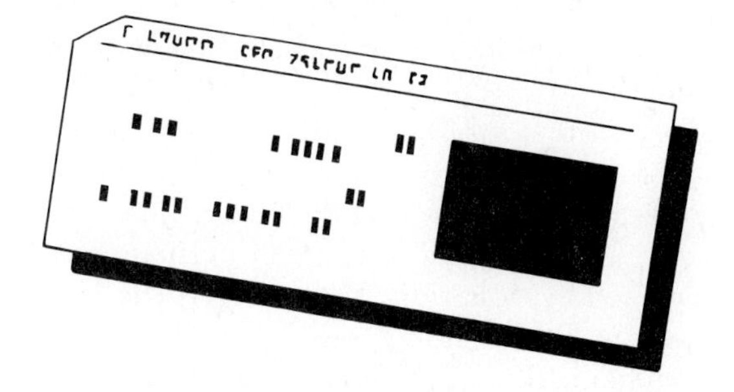

ment of sophisticated and affordable hardware and software allows all of the information, description, and image to be stored on a computer.

Another factor in the use of aperture cards is that computer keypunch cards are not used in present computer systems. The storage of computer programs and data has evolved from cards to video and magnetic media. Expensive equipment such as card sorters, which were used to sort computer cards, are no longer used in contemporary computer systems. Thus, aperture cards should be carefully evaluated if computer sorting and handling are envisioned.

Does this mean that aperture cards should be abandoned? Not necessarily. Because they are cards, they can be used in the same way as a card file with appropriate manual storage and retrieval. They can be color-coded, labeled, notched, and used as any manual card system with the additional advantage of significantly increased storage capacity. A single card easily can hold twenty standard pages of information.

Micrographic Equipment

Because micrographics always involves the creation and use of smaller film images, the equipment needed will be (1) cameras and duplicators to capture the images on film, (2) film processors to develop the film, (3) readers to view the images, and (4) miscellaneous devices to efficiently handle the film. Before describing the equipment, we will define some general terms used in micrographics, including reduction ratio, indexing capability, resolution, and density.

Reduction ratio refers to the image size produced in relation to the original document. For example, 48:1 or 48X means the image is forty-eight times smaller than the original. With standard film, reduction ratios are usually in the less than 50:1 range, though ultrafiche may have a reduction ratio of 1000:1 or greater. For cost effectiveness, reduction ratios of less than 50:1 are preferred because of the cost of the associated equipment and procedures. Higher reduction ratios require proportionally costlier equipment.

Indexing capability refers to the capability of the equipment to number or code the film automatically as the image is created. This process can be as simple as putting a sequential number with the image, or as complex as recording a binary code pattern with key words and a description with the image.

Resolution and *density* refer to the amount of detail and contrast in the images. These are standard film processing terms used to describe the quality of the image. Resolution can be measured by the number of lines per original inch that can be preserved on the microform image. For example, if the original has 1,000 lines per inch and those 1,000 lines are distinguishable on the microfilm, then the resolution is said to be "at least 1,000 lines per inch." Density is measured by the degree of light transmission. Under standard conditions, the best density occurs when 100 percent (all) of the light passes through the microfilm in a "clear" place, and 0 percent (none) of the light passes through a "dark" place. Of course, when there is no difference in transmission anywhere on the image, then the density is uniform and nothing can be distinguished. The important point is that resolution and density must be sufficient to preserve the image information. With contemporary film and equipment, resolution and density are not a problem.

The creation of a micrographic film image starts with a camera. Although a popular 35 mm camera can be used, since the media and procedures are virtually the same, a micrographics camera is designed specially for speed and efficiency in producing images of standard-size documents. There are three major types of micrographics cameras: rotary, planetary, and step-and-repeat.

In a *rotary camera* system, documents are fed automatically into the machine that films them at high speed. The camera is usually designed with a fixed reduction ratio and feeding mechanism for specific-size originals such as checks, 4-×-6-inch cards, or 8½-×-11-inch paper files. Modern rotary cameras can film documents up to 10 per second, or 600 per minute. Feeding mechanisms are available to flip the original so that both the front (obverse) and back (reverse) of a document, such as a bank check, can be filmed in sequence.

A *planetary camera* is designed for large and uniquely sized documents. It photographs them on a flat surface, somewhat the reverse of photographic enlarging. The camera can be used to film different size documents and can have a variable or fixed reduction ratio; it also can be used to produce aperture cards. Large planetary cameras are capable of photographing engineering drawings, maps, and other large documents. Desktop models are designed for letters, cards, and other smaller documents.

A *step-and-repeat camera* films documents in a grid pattern to produce microfiche. Essentially, it exposes a small portion of the film and then moves a step for another exposure on the same film sheet. The operator can control placement of the images on the fiche.

Duplicators begin with the microfilm and produce a film copy. Although most duplication occurs when the film is processed, duplication may be required for an infrequent copy to mail or for backup. For low demand levels, table-top duplicators are available. These create a complete copy ready for use in minutes.

After the image has been captured on film with a camera, it must be processed. Of all the equipment associated with micrographics, the film processor is usually the most expensive and complicated. Chemicals are required and a slipup here probably would require that the documents be retrieved and sent through the camera again. Because of the potential problems, film processing is sometimes sent to a service bureau for development and duplication. However, the latest technology has decreased many of the problems associated with film processing and it is now possible to purchase relatively clean, fast desktop units for film processing.

In order to view a retrieved image, a special device called a *reader* is required. Basically, readers are devices that provide sufficient illumination and enlargement through a lens system for normal reading. They can be used with all microforms, including roll film, cartridges, and jacketed microfilm (without removing the jacket).

A *plain-paper reader-printer* allows printing hard (paper) copy of the displayed image on low-cost bond paper. Options available allow enlargements, printing on paper, vellum (parchment), or polyester film, automatic adjustment for contrast, and image rotation. Those reader-printers that can accommodate different microfilm formats are called "multiformat." More sophisticated reader-printers are linked to microcomputers that can allow editing of an image before printing. Special microcomputer software converts the image to a digital format that can be edited. More sophisticated software allows the image to be automatically enhanced, for example, to increase density. A *reader-filler* allows reading of the microfilm, selection of images, and automatic insertion of film sections into microfilm jackets or aperture cards. This type of equipment can significantly reduce handling of the microforms in preparation for filing.

Miscellaneous devices include microfilm cleaners which remove static, dust, oil, and other debris usually prior to review or duplication to prevent scratching or damaging masters. Film cutters, both automatic and manual, cut film into standard sizes. Aperture card handling equipment encompasses card-to-card duplicators, keypunches, and sorter/collators.

A chronic problem in micrographics is the I/O or input/output obstacle. The input side involves getting valid images into the system and the output aspect involves getting the micrographic image into a format acceptable by other systems. We will briefly examine the equipment solution to the I/O problem: scanners.

A *scanner* is a device that converts an image into a digital format. For example, a microcomputer can display an image on its display screen, but that image actually is represented in a digital format in the microcomputer's display memory area. The microcomputer expects and requires the digital format. A scanner does the converse; it starts with the image and converts it to the digital format. Scanners occasionally are called "digitizers" because of their function, and they come in different degrees of discernment. A *dumb*, or *graphics*, *scanner* is just like a camera in that the image is simply transferred to a digital format with no knowledge of the contents of the document. The digital format cannot be processed as text or picture; but it can be transferred to another device, for example, by facsimile (electronic copy transmission).

Optical character readers (OCRs) are scanners that can capture the information content of an image. For example, an OCR can recognize a page of text printed with a Courier pica font and convert the document to a format that can be edited with a word processor. In the last few years, OCRs have evolved from expensive, slow, error-prone devices to cost-effective, reliable, and effective tools for input operations. More specialized OCRs can ignore graphics and read only text, or they can be programmed to read only text at specific locations on a page; this type of OCR is particularly suitable for reading filled-in forms.

Computer Output and Computer Input Microfilm

Computer output microfilm (COM) produces microfilm media from computer digital data. An on-line system transmits the data from the computer directly to microfilm in the same way that it would be transmitted to a display screen, a printer, or any other output device. An off-line system transmits the data to another device, for example, computer tape or disk. In this format, the pre-COM can be retrieved and converted to an image on a microcomputer for editing before converting the image to film. More complex systems use a microcomputer to control the COM operation with job accounting, storing and using job setups, allowing operator interaction with the system, and displaying error messages and conditions in the system operation.

In a COM system, the film typically is processed in an automated developer with output speeds ten to twenty times faster than a line printer. The obvious advantages of COM are the speed of creation, the reduced storage costs and problems, and reduced distribution costs. COM can be incorporated into a sophisticated computer storage and retrieval system. Such systems are described later in this chapter.

Computer input microfilm (CIM) is a fairly new development. CIM refers to the transfer of microfilm images to electronic data for input to a computer. The standard arrangement combines COM and CIM to allow the exchange of information (both input and output) between computer and microfilm. A significant advantage of this arrangement is that the technology is very easily adapted to merge facsimile transmission into the system. (Facsimile) is a method of electronic transmission, which is explained in detail in Chapter 9.) Another possibility, rather than using magnetic media or paper, is a COM/CIM arrangement that uses microfilm as a backup for the computer system's electronic data.

Micrographic Retrieval Systems

For most people it is not immediately obvious how a micrographics system can improve retrieval speed and accuracy. The essence of a micrographic system is that the documents, images, and so forth are captured on contiguous (adjacent) pieces of film that require special equipment to view. The contiguity significantly reduces the chances of losing or misfiling an image; for example, it would be difficult indeed to lose the fiftieth image on a roll of microfilm without losing the entire roll! The requirements for viewing present an opportunity to increase the retrieval efficiency, especially since the images have an explicit order; for example, the images on roll film are in sequential order.

To take advantage of these inherent characteristics of roll microfilm, it is necessary to use indexing. You will recall that indexing was referred to in Chapter 6 as a pointer. Indexing has a similar meaning in this context and is referred to often in later chapters. For now, note that in micrographic operations, indexing simply associates a specific element (such as a number) with an image. The image file is in order by the index element. An index file is a listing of the images in any order one prefers; for example, the images may be in alphabetic order by description with each image numbered. To find images, the operator first locates the desired image in the index file and then uses the obtained index element (number) to get the image from the image file.

Micrographic Retrieval

The concept of *micrographic indexing* is that each image is associated with an identifiable marker that is easy to locate. A simple example is to associate each film image on a roll of 100 images with a sequential number from 00 to 99. The index file would contain the numbers from 00 to 99 with a brief description of each image associated with each number. The descriptions are kept in alphabetic order in the index file. The process of retrieval would involve first looking at the index file for the description of the image and then noting the associated sequence number from 00 to 99. With the sequence number, the operator can go directly to the correct image on the roll of film.

There are many ways of creating an indexing system. A manual system would associate colors, notches, numbers, characters, or some other marker with each image. The images would then be filed and retrieved by the marker, similar to a paper file system. Automated systems use mechanical or electronic means to index. For example, a mechanical reader for 100-image cartridge film can move easily to the desired sequence number from 00 to 99.

There are two basic approaches to indexing microfilm, which also apply to microfiche. One approach uses manual methods and the other integrates the indexing operation with a microfilm reader. Manual methods are comparable to the indexing and retrieval of regular paper records. These manual methods include notching, color coding, and labeling for storage and retrieval. (An example of a jacketed microfilm system using these methods is given in Chapter 13.) Microfiche and jacketed microfilm are good candidates for manual methods if the volume is small and retrieval is infrequent. When the microform is located manually, then a reader is used to examine the images.

Roll film, by its physical qualities, is a poor candidate for manual indexing. Most often, roll film is indexed in a way that requires a special reader to locate the image, which is then immediately available for inspection. Figure 8.5 illustrates the common methods for indexing roll microfilm.

Using *flash cards* for indexing microfilm is similar to using guides in a file drawer. Records are grouped before filming and a flash card identifying the group is prepared. Then the records are filmed with the flash card preceding the group. To retrieve a particular item in a group, the operator first locates the flash card that precedes that group. The index consists of a list of the flash cards and their associated groups of records.

Figure 8.5 Microfilm Indexing Methods

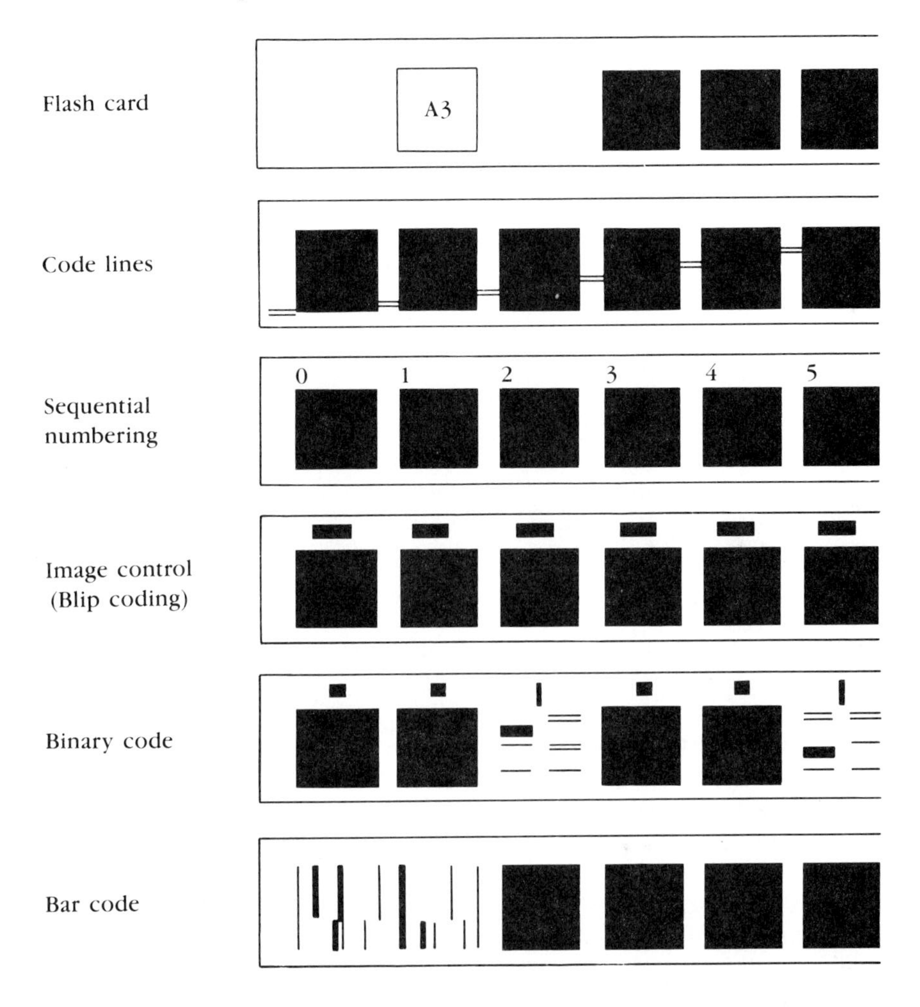

Code lines are lines filmed along with images that indicate the relative location of the image. As shown in Figure 8.5, the first image has the code line near the bottom; each succeeding line is a bit higher. During retrieval, the operator looks for the code line by position, matching numbers or letters on a scale next to the screen.

Sequential numbering involves manually stamping numbers on documents before filming or, as shown in Figure 8.5, having the camera automatically number the document. To locate image 56 for example, the operator simply looks for that number on the microfilm.

Image control, or *blip coding*, counts markers or blips on the microfilm. A small square or blip is exposed on the film next to each image. The index file is a sequential number for each blip from 0001 to the maximum number of images on the film. For retrieval, the operator enters the number of the image and the retrieval equipment counts blips at high speed.

The *odometer* method of indexing is not shown in Figure 8.5 because it requires a mechanical counter. Image positions are associated with linear distances on the film. The retrieval equipment must be able to measure distance on the film. To retrieve the fifty-sixth image, for example, the operator would note in the index file that the fifty-sixth image is 18.7 inches from the beginning of the film and then advance the film to the desired position of 18.7 inches. This method is similar to using the counter indicator on tape recording equipment to find a particular place on the tape.

In a *binary code* method of indexing, as each document is filmed, the binary code corresponding to the subject matter of the document also is recorded on film. The binary code occupies an image location on the film. The images are grouped and marked with one kind of blip and the binary code with another type of blip so the retrieval system knows the difference. The binary code is read as pieces of data that are either present (on) or absent (off). Part, or all, of the binary code will be a unique code number. To retrieve a certain image, the code number is entered and the retrieval equipment electronically scans the film and stops at the image with that code.

In the last decade, *bar codes* have been used to index microfilm (Reid, 1987). This is the same type of bar code that is becoming widely used on products in supermarkets. Similar to binary coding, the bar code contains from thirteen to twenty-one bits or bars. Each bar can be on (present) or off (absent); hence the binary designation. The bar code is associated with the image on the film. The retrieval process is similar to that used with binary code. Bar codes can also be easily extended to microfiche.

Computer-Assisted Retrieval (CAR) Systems

Locating a microform to display it on a reader or make a hard copy of it on a printer is not always a fast and simple process. When a large volume of microforms are involved, simple manual retrieval systems involving color coding or notching may not allow cost-effective retrieval. A solution to this problem can be *computer-assisted retrieval* (CAR) technology (Minicucci, 1986).

Essentially, a CAR system integrates a computer with a micrographics system. This is not a new development as CAR systems have been available for the last fifteen years. The important changes have been occurring in the CAR's computer component. In the past, the computer was the corporate mainframe, which restricted the use of CARs to large organizations. Today, CAR systems are available on minicomputers and microcomputers, which has extended their range to businesses of almost any size.

The working principle of a CAR is an index of the microforms. For example, we can locate any frame in a roll microfilm system by the roll number (NNNN) and the frame number (nnn). With each number set (NNNN: nnn), we can associate key words that identify the frame, such as ACCOUNTING, INVOICE, MM/DD/YY, XYZ CONSTRUCTION, etc. The index consists of the set number and key words. The computer component contains the index and the appropriate software to allow an operator to search the key words. For example, an operator may request the system to search for all frames that are associated with the company XYZ CONSTRUCTION. The software will then provide a list of all frames that contain that information along with their number sets. The operator can then decide which, if any, microforms to access in the micrographic component.

A CAR system can have the micrographic and computer components separate or completely integrated. In the separated systems, the index information is entered separately into the computer component after the microform has been created and stored in the micrographic component. During retrieval, the computer is used to access the *on-line index* for the desired set number(s), which are then used to access the microforms in the separate micrographic system. Older systems may use on *off-line index*, which requires the computer to print the index on paper. These separate systems are characteristic of existing micrographic systems that have been converted to a CAR by adding the computer component.

A fully integrated CAR ties the index creation and retrieval processes together in an *on-line index and retrieval system*. As the source documents are filmed, the key words are entered. The integrated CAR creates the film and index simultaneously. When the system is used for retrieval, the frames displayed from a key word search can be retrieved automatically and displayed on the computer screen and, if desired, printed.

Because roll microfilm and microfiche are physically different, most CARs are designed for microfilm. However, microfiche and jacketed-microfilm systems are becoming available. CARs with microfiche cartridges exist in which up to thirty microfiche are contained in a cartridge so that each fiche is individually accessible in the system. Similarly, a complete CAR jacketed microfilm record control system is available, which consists of an automatic camera and film processor, the jackets, a valet jacket inserter that automatically places the film in the jackets, and microcomputer hardware and software for data search and retrieval. Of course, the filled jackets are stored and retrieved manually.

Micrographic Procedures

In a simple, micrographic, inactive records system, the microform replaces the paper source documents. The original documents may be stored briefly and then destroyed. Duplicate backup copies of a microforms are stored in a secure off-site location as protection against disaster. When the microforms are inactive records, the retrieval system need not be particularly sophisticated and reader integrated indexing may not be necessary. Color coding and notching may suffice.

System Selection

Keeping up to date on the available equipment will enhance the system selection process. Records personnel can do this through contact with micrographic vendors and professional organizations in the field, such as the Association of Records Managers and Administrators (ARMA) and the Association for Information and Image Management (AIIM). Each of these organizations publishes a magazine that is sent to members and keeps them up to date on the latest systems.

A complete micrographic system will contain the appropriate hardware, software, and supplies. Accessory equipment and supplies should also be considered; for example, fiche rotary stands, desk stands, and color-coded panel holders. Modular storage file systems, cabinet storage and retrieval systems, carousels, trays, tables, workstations, and furniture for all types of microforms can be useful and productive tools. Most vendors will be pleased to provide the potential purchaser with a complete catalog of required and optional accessories.

Service Bureaus

Service bureaus can provide specialized micrographic operations, such as film processing, or they can provide virtually the entire micrographic system. As a general rule of thumb, the filming of source documents can rarely be done more economically by a service bureau because of the expense (and possible loss) of transferring the documents. A careful cost–benefit analysis of the entire proposed micrographic operation will help the business decide on the appropriate operations that could be handled by a service bureau.

For some records, *color microimaging*—that is, filming in color (like color slides)—may be considered. Color has been found to increase information productivity for maps, training materials, sales brochures, and similar materials. Service companies sell conversion kits to allow black-and-white microfilm cameras to use color when required. Of course, processing of color film requires special equipment and the service bureau will provide this service, too, for an additional fee.

Summary

The reproduction of images through micrographics is essential to business operations. In micrographic operations, original documents are reproduced on film at a much smaller scale. Micrographics is often considered for records storage because of the savings in space and costs along with improved accessibility and security. Micrographic supplies and equipment include various microforms—roll microfilm, cartridge microfilm, jacketed microfilm, microfiche, aperture cards—and a variety of cameras and readers. Computer output microfilm (COM) and computer input microfilm (CIM) are two electronic applications of micrographics.

Micrographic systems store and retrieve records very efficiently through the use of indexing methods such as blip code and bar code. Some indexing methods are manual, others incorporate a reader. Computer-assisted retrieval (CAR) systems combine micrographic and computer technology. Selection of a micrographic system requires knowledge of available equipment and assessment of the needs of the business.

List of Terms

microform
micrographics
micropublishing
roll microfilm
cartridge microfilm
jacketed microfilm
microfiche
ultrafiche
ultrastrip
aperture card
reduction ratio
indexing capability
resolution
density
rotary camera
planetary camera
step-and-repeat camera
duplicator
reader
plain-paper reader-printer
reader-filler
scanner
dumb, or graphics, scanner
optical character reader (OCR)
computer output microfilm (COM)
computer input microfilm (CIM)
micrographic indexing
flash card
code line
sequential numbering
image control, or blip coding
odometer
binary code
bar code
computer-assisted retrieval (CAR)
on/off-line index
on-line index and retrieval system
color microimaging

Discussion Questions

1. What are the advantages and disadvantages for using micrographics for a records information system?
2. What are the different types of microfilm? Describe each of them.
3. What is the difference between microfiche and ultrafiche? Can you think of some specific situations in which each would be used?
4. What is an aperture card and why might it soon disappear from use?
5. What importance do reduction ratio, resolution, and density have when filming letter-size and legal-size legal documents? (Hint: Would legibility and accessibility be important?)
6. What are the types of cameras used in micrographic operations? Describe how they work.
7. How are readers and reader-printers used in micrographics operations?
8. What are two types of scanners? How do scanners solve the I/O problem?
9. What are the uses and relationships of COM and CIM (computer output/input microfilm)?
10. What is the difference between manual and computer-assisted retrieval (CAR) systems in micrographic operations? Is a CAR always preferable?
11. What are two types of microfilm indexing that use some sort of coding?
12. What is the difference between an on-line index and an off-line index?
13. What services can a service bureau provide for a micrographics operation?

Activities

1. Contact a micrographics manufacturer and obtain information on its products and how it markets the products. Try to obtain several brochures with pictures of various types of equipment to circulate in your class.
2. Consult trade magazines and journals and prepare a report on the range of micrographic equipment available. What is the price and what are the capabilities of a minimum equipment configuration? What is the largest micrographics system and what features does it have?
3. Interview an office or small business and assess its micrographic needs. If micrographics are not used, try to determine whether the use of micrographics would be cost beneficial.
4. Interview personnel in an office that uses micrographics (a law offfice or city government office would be a good choice). Describe the sup-

plies, equipment, and procedures. Find out if the office uses a service bureau for any aspect of its micrographics operations. Ask what changes in micrographics operations are desired or planned.

5. Examine a phone book's yellow pages or business advertisement section. Report on the number of businesses that fall into the categories of micrographics vendor, service bureau, and other businesses related to this chapter. Estimate the importance of the various categories and determine which services a small business in your city could use.
6. Take activity 5 a step further and prepare a manual describing in detail the service bureaus for micrographics available in your area. Include in the manual such information as name of the business (service), address, services offered, costs, pictures and descriptions of equipment used, security features (if any), and any other relevant information.

References

Association for Information and Image Management. "Trends in the Micrographics Market." *Special Interest Package #3* (Silver Spring, Md: AIIM, October 1986).

Minicucci, Rick. "Driving Microfilm with CAR." *Today's Office* 20, no. 11 (April 1986): 26–30.

Reid, Marvin A. "Bar Code on Microfiche." *INFORM* 1, no. 5 (May 1987): 20–23.

Chapter 9

Reprographics

Learning Goals

1. To become familiar with the field of reprographics.
2. To become aware of the variety of supply and equipment options available in reprographics.
3. To explain the different printing processes available.
4. To become knowledgeable about facsimile (fax).
5. To understand the elements of reprographics management.

Introduction

Reprographics and micrographics both involve the making of graphic images or copies of original materials. However, *reprographics* refers to the reproduction of an original image to the same scale. Lately, the term has come to encompass printing processes and facsimile transmission as well as copying and duplicating. Although the concept of duplication remains the basis of reprographics, technological advances are redefining what used to be just a simple paper copy through enlargement, reduction, color, and image editing. Similarly, technology has made electronic copy transmission and in-house printing possible. Few fields have changed as much as reprographics in the last generation and the future is charged with innovations.

The Field of Reprographics

Today, reprographics includes all operations that result in the reproduction of a graphic image, primarily on paper. Such reproduction can have legal ramifications, so anyone working in the field of reprographics must be knowledgeable about legal constraints as well as equipment and procedures.

Definition and Scope

A complete definition of *reprographics* is the management of personnel, equipment, and procedures used for reproduction processes such as duplicating, printing, and copying. A brief historical view of reprographic processes will demonstrate the scope of present-day operations.

Prior to 1950 the major business reprography processes were carbon paper (used on a typewriter), printing processes, and stencil/fluid duplication. The volume of copies was relatively small due to the costs and general inconveniences in obtaining copies of materials. During the 1950s, copiers were small, slow, and not of particularly high quality. The technology was developing rapidly, however, and by the 1960s dry (electrostatic) process copiers became available. These were considered very fast at ten copies per minute. Today, copiers are even faster with sixty copies a minute common on many machines. Copiers have an amazing range of options and cost-effectiveness, which have enabled them to virtually supplant the typewriter and carbon paper, as well as many jobs that previously went to the print shop.

Legal Considerations

The availability and range of reprographic processes in business today is astounding. Almost anything can be reproduced at a reasonable cost, but this capacity also has legal implications. Following are those problems specific to reprographics.

"Fair use," as defined by the Copyright Act of 1976, provides for the fair copying of materials. This is usually interpreted to mean that the copying does not avoid fair payment for the materials. For example, with today's equipment, a hardcover book often can be copied for less than the cost of the book. Is this fair? No, because it deprives the book's author, manufacturer, and others of their fair payment. Although at times it may be difficult to correctly determine *fair use copying*, it is even more difficult to control the reprographic equipment so that it is used only within legal and ethical constraints. The machine does not know if the material being copied is legal or not! Both educational and technological approaches are in use to deal with illegal or unethical copying.

The educational solution is to explain clearly to appropriate personnel what constitutes fair use, what the penalties are for violation, and what the company policy approves. It is assumed that when people understand the legal and ethical environment, they will act accordingly. Most people respond to the educational approach; but when it does not seem to be working or may not be feasible due to a large and changing number of reprographics users, the technological approach may be suitable. One technological approach is to imprint materials that should not be copied so that copying them results in a damaged image. Another possibility is to print materials so that they will not copy reliably. For example, many copiers today will not reliably reproduce materials printed in light blue ink with a low density.

In a reprographic sense, microcomputers allow the copying of magnetic media. It is possible to copy a $1,000 program with a microcomputer and a $1 disk. Manufacturers' methods of copy protection have not been particularly successful and the illegal copying or pirating of microcomputer programs is a significant problem. Under the copyright law, a microcomputer user has the right to make a copy only to guard against the circumstance whereby the original disk may no longer function. (See Chapter 2 for a complete discussion of the problems associated with copying software.)

Reprographic Equipment and Supplies

The technological changes that have occurred in the field of reprographics have changed the nature of the field. Although the definition of operations has stayed the same, the major equipment and procedures now encompass copiers, printing operations, and electronic copy transmission.

Copiers and Duplicators

When reprographics deals with multiple paper copies of an original paper image containing text and perhaps graphic images, the objective is to generate copies of appropriate quality for distribution to end users. In this application, reprographics includes making many copies of a single original (e.g., mail promotions, newspaper inserts, or meeting handouts), as well as making single copies of several original documents (e.g., copy of a scholarly article, portions of a book, or patent pages in a search).

Copiers and duplicators have become increasingly sophisticated—from "dumb" copiers that produced a readable image on relatively poor quality paper to "intelligent" copiers that produce high-quality reproductions through electronic transmission. Copiers and duplicators perform a wide range of functions and now offer a range of options that are almost overwhelming. The traditional distinction between a copier and duplicator, which is still valid, is that a copier reproduces from an original, whereas a duplicating machine requires a specially prepared master. In the past, copiers could not produce copies with the same speed and economy as duplicators, but this is no longer true. Because the distinction between the two types of machines is becoming increasingly blurred, we will concentrate the following discussion on the major options available on copiers (Rowh, 1988).

Color A single-color option allows the output to be in the selected color such as black, blue, brown, red, and so forth. Single-color is the standard for copying text with maximum clarity through the elimination of tonal gradations (see discussion of photo mode on page 134). Full-color processing is designed to accurately reproduce color images with tonal gradations. The cost of full-color copying is presently about fifty times greater than single-color reprographics.

Dual Page When copying from bound materials, the dual-page option will copy two pages at once, making the appropriate size adjustment as necessary. An associated feature is edge erase, which cleans up the fuzziness that can occur on the edges and center (guttering) of bound volume copies.

Duplexing *Duplexing* is the process of making copies on both sides of a sheet from one- or two-sided originals. An automatic duplexer can copy both sides of an original and produce the selected number of duplexed copies without operator intervention.

Electronic Editing *Electronic editing* involves a grid overlay with an electronic pen that allows the user to delete or relocate parts of the original image.

Image Overlay With an *image overlay*, two or more originals can be imaged to the same sheet. Each original is "copied" to the same sheet. The effect is as if the originals were on transparencies, so that the images are merged on the copy. This option can be used creatively with different color toners (the "ink" used in copy machines).

Image Shift Also known as margin shifting, the *image shift* feature allows the operator to shift the image of the copies without touching the original. Sophisticated image shifting even allows some rotation of the image to "square up" the copy.

Photo Mode When copying continuous-tone materials, for example photographs, the *photo mode* option adjusts the process to capture the tonal gradations (also called "halftones"). Tonal gradations are the grays between white and black. An image with no tonal gradations would be all white with all black lines, characters, or symbols. This is maximum density or contrast as you would see on a page of black-and-white text. Normally, a copier is set for maximum contrast, which eliminates or severely reduces tonal gradations. For text, the elimination of tonal gradations will generally increase the clarity of the image. The more the tonal gradations, the more levels of gray. For example, a typical black-and-white photograph has a wide range of grays or tonal gradations. If a copier can be set to preserve the tonal gradations, then photo images can be copied rather well.

Miscellaneous features include reduction and enlargement capabilities at various scales, a computer forms feeder to easily copy odd-size and connected documents, automatic feeders so that a stack of separate pages can be fed to the copier unattended, a sorter and collator for the finished copies, and various finishing options such as cover sheet insertion, stapling, and hole drilling.

Intelligent copier-duplicators combine data processing, photocopying, duplicating, and phototypesetting technologies. They can take input from other sources in other media formats such as a computer, word processor, microfiche, or other systems. The image can be edited on the copier and reproduced to other media and locations.

Printing Processes

Printing processes are reprographic processes, but printing at some point involves typesetting. Printing can produce high-quality, volume reproduction that is unmatched by any other method. Printing uses complex, expensive equipment and requires experienced personnel. Therefore, printing operations are usually in a department separate from records management or even reprographics. Often, documents that require printing are sent to service agencies. Desktop publishing is a fairly recent development that has, in a sense, combined the areas of word processing and reprographics. *Desktop publishing* is word processing software that allows the use of fonts, various type sizes, graphics, and sophisticated formatting to produce copy that looks very much like it was printed.

The typical role of records management is to decide when the unique capabilities of printing processes are required. In order to make reasonable decisions, records personnel must be aware of the various printing processes. The major types of printing operations are offset, engraving, gravure, screen, and letterpress.

Offset is a popular printing process that can produce high-volume, excellent quality reproductions with color and halftones. It is also called "lithography," "multilith," and "multigraph." The term "offset" describes the printing operation that prints from one drum which is offset to another. Offset printing should be considered when photographic-quality images, color, and a large volume production are involved.

Engraving and *gravure* processes both involve the creation of an image through materials removal through etching, carving, or cutting on a metal plate. The resulting metal image is used for the reproduction process. Neither process is suitable for most office operations, but is very applicable for color, graphic reprography such as currency (money), fancy invitations, business cards, mail order catalogs, and newspaper supplements.

Screen, or *silk screen*, is a process that can reproduce color, graphic images on a wide variety of surfaces such as metal, glass, cloth and paper. It is suitable for putting images on shirts or creating custom brochures.

Letterpress is used for newspaper and similar printing jobs. It is distinguished by its direct printing operations in which the paper (letter) is pressed against an inked plate. Although letterpress can be of good quality, it cannot compete with offset. Small-scale letterpress equipment is suitable for handbills, circulars, labels, and other similar jobs.

Electronic Copy Transmission

Up to this point, we have discussed processes that reproduce images solely by a mechanical process. Computer technology allows images to be reproduced electronically. Two processes which reproduce this way are facsimile and intelligent copiers.

Facsimile, or *fax*, has been available since 1924, but interest and expansion of this process didn't begin until the 1970s. Fax combines a scanner, printer, and synchronous modem to send and receive special format bit-mapped images (graphics or text) over standard telephone lines. In simpler terms, with a fax machine in one office in New York and another in Los Angeles, a user can send an image across the United States by simply inserting the image document into the facsimile machine and pressing a few buttons; you don't actually send the document, but a reasonable "facsimile."

Fax can be thought of as *telereprographics*. Instead of making a copy of an original at the same location, the original and copy are separated by a telephone line. The original is converted to an image, sent across the telephone lines, and converted back to paper at the receiving end. The major benefit of facsimile is that it gives an exact reproduction of the information and yet costs a fraction of what overnight delivery services charge ("Facsimile . . . ," 1988).

Fax add-on boards are available for microcomputers. These boards enable the microcomputer to send and receive image documents. There are different standards or levels of fax, from group 1 to group 4, with higher levels generally allowing faster, higher-quality image transmission. Most fax hardware is at group 3 today. Of course, the fax hardware must have the same standards (group level) to send and receive images. Facsimile features rival and surpass those available on copiers. Reduction, automatic document feeding, contrast control, and telephone number storage are just a few of the possible features.

Intelligent copiers can combine compatibility with microcomputers and fax with their reprographics capability to allow transmission of images to different mediums and locations. Images can be created, sent, received, managed, and displayed with possibilities barely envisioned a few years ago. How the potential of this equipment ultimately will be utilized remains to be seen.

Reprographics Management

Because records managers are responsible for much of the paper created through reprographic processes, they are often involved in the management decisions involving reprographic operations. Careful attention to reprographics management can make a significant difference in the productivity of the operations. Reprographics management involves conscientious matching of the equipment to the organization's reprographic needs. Also, monitoring of the ongoing operations is essential to ensure that the equipment is being used properly.

The management of copier equipment is especially important because the copier needs in a business can change quickly, and the technology continues to produce many innovations in the equipment. The vast range of equipment available should be studied carefully to meet the specific needs of the business. This task should not be left to the vendors. The management of reprographics equipment consists of selecting appropriate equipment, determining the equipment location, conducting a cost analysis, and establishing control procedures.

Equipment Selection

Equipment selection should match the needs of the business. Following a systems approach, one should first inventory the present situation; then the question of what additional equipment is needed can be addressed. Other considerations should include whether it is best to (1) upgrade to better equipment, (2) replace present equipment, or (3) add different equipment. In general, a checklist of criteria for equipment selection should consider machine downtime, environment, speed, special features, and training.

Machine Downtime An estimate of the average *machine downtime*—the time that a machine is not operating due to malfunction—if available, can provide good comparative information for choosing equipment. In addition, information on the anticipated service call time, how often to expect paper jams, and how often supplies must be loaded is useful. The point is to assess the expected "good" operating capacity of the machine. Vendors are sensitive to this issue and may provide more information than expected. (A popular industry joke is that the salesperson boasts that each machine comes with a special accessory—an OUT OF ORDER sign that is easily attached to the equipment.) In many cases, however, downtime is related to overestimating the production capacity of the machine. If a machine designed to produce 1,000 copies a week is pressed to produce 10,000 copies in that time period, downtime will almost certainly occur. A copy machine should be purchased that is best suited to the actual volume of work anticipated.

Environment The environment question is whether the equipment will be a walk-up unit or a central reproduction unit. The walk-up unit is situated in various locations in the business for making a few copies. It should be less sophisticated and suitable for low-volume, fast reproduction. Walk-up units are also known as convenience copiers.

The central reproduction unit would be located in a central reprographics department, where much of the organization's copying is done. Therefore, it should be highly sophisticated, suitable for high volume, and able to accommodate all of the desired options.

Speed The speed of the machine and its related factor, volume, must be prudently evaluated. Manufacturers generally rate their machines by a maximum monthly capacity, the lowest being 1,000 copies, through ranges up to 500,000 copies per month. As mentioned, probably the single most important factor in machine downtime is that the machine is expected to perform beyond its rated capacity.

Decisive special features are those that the machine must include to do the jobs for which it was purchased. Decisive features often involve the size and type of originals that the machine must handle, reduction or enlargement capabilities, and duplexing. If duplexing is needed and the equipment will not do that one special operation, then it is not suitable. For example, if an engineering department must copy 17-×-22-inch originals and reduce them to 8½ × 11 inches, then a machine that will not perform this one special operation is worthless to that department. Changing machines to obtain an additional feature will almost certainly cost much more than choosing the correct equipment in the first place.

Training A complex copier cannot be used to its capacity without training the personnel who are expected to operate it. Letting users "figure it out" is wasteful of resources and can pose a real threat to the maintenance of the equipment. Formal training by the vendor should always be considered in an equipment purchase and the training should include more than simply providing an owner's operating manual.

Equipment Location

The decision for equipment location should be made prior to obtaining the machines. Criteria for the decision should include the location of the most frequent users and the physical sites available. Obvious, but too often neglected, criteria include space availability for supplies and clearance for getting the machine to the desired location! The equipment supplier should also be consulted in this decision. For example, some equipment may have certain ventilation requirements or require a dedicated power line with specific voltage and amperage levels. The vendor can and should inform buyers of these types of special requirements.

Cost Analysis

A cost–benefit analysis may be performed at various levels—from a simple cost comparison to spreadsheet present-value calculations. Most companies have standards for appropriate cost–benefit analyses. Regardless of the format of the analyses, the major decision factors are (1) what equipment will provide the best value, and (2) how to acquire the equipment; for example, purchase, lease, rent, or some combination of purchase and lease.

A cost–benefit analysis should consider the costs of maintenance. It may be tempting to base a purchase decision on the cost per copy, but other factors such as maintenance may be decisive. The reprographics manufacturers generally offer maintenance contracts that provide for regular service under specific conditions. Because copier use is often perceived by users as a need that cannot be "put off until later," a maintenance contract that guarantees immediate service can be valuable even at exorbitant rates. Many companies offer same-day service as a part of a maintenance contract or under a warranty provision.

Reprographics Control

A chronic problem associated with copiers is that actual copy use often exceeds the perceived required number of copies. This situation often surfaces when a business acquires a new copier. Probably the expected use of the new copier was based on the volume estimates of previous copier use and, in the first few months, the actual use significantly exceeds the original estimates. The cry then is to "control the copier."

Given the cost investment in copiers today, management is anxious to use the equipment properly and avoid excessive use. This is a particularly sensitive issue and one that deserves consideration. First, what are the possible reasons for excessive use of a copier?

- ☐ illegal and improper use such as copying for nonbusiness (personal, social, church groups) purposes
- ☐ frivolous use, such as copying a person's hand or a dollar bill
- ☐ wasted copies due to improper use caused by unfamiliarity with machine, poor documentation, or insufficient training
- ☐ legitimate use due to the superiority of the new machine (for example, it may now be cost effective to copy rather than use carbon copies, or the new duplexing feature makes using the copier more attractive).

Since it may not be easy or productive to precisely determine which of the above reasons are responsible for excessive copying, a comprehensive plan that deals with all possibilities is suggested (Epstein, 1984).

First, consider centralizing the equipment and personnel in an obvious, visible location so that it is clear who is using the copier and for how long. This approach implicitly provides control of users and items being duplicated. Another solution is to make it difficult to use the machines in off hours. For example, removing the paper trays at the end of the day helps limit abuse.

The point is to structure the situation to discourage abuse of the equipment rather than using a more obvious approach that may encourage sabotage. For example, it is common practice to post a sign reminding workers that the copier is for company use only. What is the purpose of the sign? The abusers already know the copier is not for their personal use, and legitimate users may feel harassed. In fact, research shows that a sign does not deter abuse.

Another approach is to investigate cost-saving alternatives to copying. Preprinted forms with a sufficient number of copies to be distributed may solve the need for making copies of certain items. For occasional single copies of items stored on floppy disks, simply allowing the file to be viewed by interested parties may be the answer.

It is crucial to pinpoint responsibility for copying costs. This means keeping track of the number of copies being made and deciding how the cost for those copies will be assigned. Although it is tempting to post a sign asking users to write down the number of copies they make, a more effective solution is a *key accessory*. Key accessories are devices that must be used in order to operate the machine. The key may be a credit-card device, a small plug-in box, or simply an account number that is entered into a keypad on the copier (Lefcourt, 1988). The keys can be distributed so that a machine can be used only by a particular group or department. The machine has a counter that records the copies made. The group or department making copies can be charged for the total number of copies made during a certain time period—or advised if copies made during a certain time period are exceeding the expected number. The copier may be capable of producing regular reports that detail copier use by department and allow a complete accounting of all copies made in a given time period.

Although the key approach sounds virtually foolproof, copier keys are not a foolproof solution. They incur additional costs and, in practice, the keys may be traded or abused. Also, the keys may interfere with legitimate use and lead to low morale and machine sabotage.

An effective structural solution, if feasible, is to centralize the equipment and operations. By physically restricting access to authorized operators, much control can be gained. When equipment is centralized, users fill out copy request forms that list the number of copies, type of paper, and options desired, such as stapling, duplexing, or enlargement. An operator then does the copying; other employees do not access the equipment directly.

No one solution fits all situations. To reduce copy costs, the business should look closely at the cost of paper, toner, and other supplies. Supplies purchased in large volume may be eligible for discounts. Also, different departments with different equipment and requirements may be able to use compatible paper so that the combined orders result in a significant discount. Finally, it is wise to work with the vendors. They can provide a wealth of information and suggestions.

Summary

The reproduction of images through reprographics is essential to business operations. In reprographics, the reproduction is at a scale similar to the original and usually on paper.

Reprographics includes copying and duplicating processes, printing processes, and electronic image transmission. Reprographics primarily involves paper copying operations, although electronic image transmission (facsimile and intelligent copiers) is growing rapidly. Today copiers provide a vast array of options, including color, duplexing, image shift, and photo mode. Printing processes include offset, engraving, silk screen, and letterpress.

Managing reprographics equipment includes selecting appropriate equipment, determining the equipment location, conducting a cost analysis, and establishing control procedures. Several approaches can be used to control copy use unobtrusively, the best being to centralize the copying equipment and operations.

List of Terms

reprographics
fair use copying
duplexing
electronic editing
image overlay
image shift
photo mode
intelligent copier-duplicator
desktop publishing
offset printing
engraving and gravure
silk screen printing
letterpress printing
facsimile (fax)
telereprographics
machine downtime
key accessory

Discussion Questions

1. What is the difference between reprographics and micrographics? Consider the procedures involved and the functions served by both processes.
2. Could a service bureau feasibly provide reprographics services to an organization? to a small business? to an individual?
3. Do you think the definition of reprographics could be expanded? Redefine that term.
4. Within the concept of fair use, are there legitimate nonrecord uses of reprographics? Why or why not?
5. What are four features of copiers that would be particularly useful for copying photographs? Explain why they are.
6. In what situation might you make practical use of the image overlay and image shift features of a copier?
7. When might it be cost-effective for a business to purchase a complete offset printing outfit?
8. Under what circumstances could copier usage be effectively controlled with a user copier log?
9. What are the four criteria that should be considered when selecting reprographics equipment? Which one do you think is most important and why?

10. What is facsimile (fax) and how do you see it being used in the future—in addition to the use described in Chapter 8?

Activities

1. Contact a reprographics manufacturer or a business that sells reprographics equipment and obtain information on its products and how it markets the products. Try to obtain several brochures with pictures of various types of equipment to circulate in your class.
2. Consult trade magazines and journals and prepare a report on the range of reprographic equipment available. What is the price and what are the capabilities of the smallest and least sophisticated copier? What is the most advanced copier available and what features does it have?
3. Interview an office or small business and assess its reprographic needs. If the office has a copier, find out what problems the office has experienced with misuse and/or abuse of the copier and how the office deals with those problems.
4. Interview personnel in an office that has a high level of reprographics use (a school/college office or city government office would be a good choice). Describe the supplies, equipment, and procedures. Find out if the office uses a service bureau for any aspect of its reprographics operations. Ask what changes in reprographics operations are desired or planned.
5. Visit a printing business and determine the typical kinds of materials it prints and the clients it serves. Describe the type and approximate costs of the equipment.
6. Review the microcomputer popular magazines (for example, *PC World*, *Byte*, *Personal Computing*) and from the articles and advertisements, try to determine the present state of software piracy. Look for articles, manufacturer's statements of copy protection, and how both copy-protected and noncopy-protected products are advertised.
7. Examine a phone book's yellow pages or business advertisement section. Report on the number of businesses that fall into the categories of reprographics or copier vendor, printing services, service bureau, and other businesses related to reprographics. Estimate the importance of the various categories and determine which services a small business in your city could use.
8. Take activity 7 a step further and prepare a manual describing in detail the service bureaus for reprographics (copy centers) available in your area. Include in the manual such information as name of the business (service), address, service offered, costs, pictures and descriptions of equipment used, security features (if any), and any other relevant information.

References

Epstein, David. "Copier Buyer Commandments." *Modern Office Technology* (November 1984): 112–113.

"Facsimile Offers More and Experts Tell Us Why." *Office Systems '88* 5, no. 5 (May 1988): 44, 46, 48, 50.

Lefcourt, David. "Curtailing Frivolous Use—and Costs of a Copier." *The Office* 107, no. 3 (March 1988): 76, 77.

Rowh, Mark C. "Today's Copiers: They Cost Less and Do More." *The Office* 107, no. 3 (March 1988): 71–72.

Chapter 10

Records Centers and Archives

Learning Goals

1. To become familiar with the purposes for records centers and archives.
2. To recognize the advantages of and requirements for using company facilities for a records center.
3. To identify the features of commercial records centers.
4. To become familiar with the methods for protecting records in long-term storage.
5. To understand the procedures for planning or selection of a records center.
6. To appreciate the importance of historical records and the need for their preservation.

Introduction

Two of the major components of the records information system are storage of inactive records and final disposition of archival records. These functions are important in any organization and, as the records in an organization increase, the need to maintain inactive records and preserve historical records becomes even more critical.

Chapter 10 explains these functions. First, we discuss the criteria for a records center. Next, the circumstances surrounding the choice to use a company-owned center versus a commercial center are examined, and the general features of records centers are explained. The discussion of commercial centers focuses on the services they provide. Finally, archival storage is discussed.

The terms "records center" and "archives" can easily be confused because both facilities are used for long-term storage of records. Whereas records centers and archives have several features in common, the purpose for each facility is different, and the types of records stored in them are usually different, too.

Criteria for a Records Center

In the simplest terms, a records center is a centralized facility for the bulk long-term storage and retrieval of records that have been designated as inactive. Although the term *records center* may be used to refer to active records storage and retrieval, this discussion of the records center is oriented toward records that are in the storage phase of the records information system. An *archives*, on the other hand, can be considered a specific type of records center in that its purpose is the permanent storage of records with potential historical value. The records in a records center retain their primary purpose, and their value is defined in terms of their original introduction into the records information system. The records in an archives are basically inactive, have lost their primary value, have acquired a historical value, and may also have monetary value because of their historical significance. Because archives are a specialized subset of records centers and share many of the same physical features and procedural requirements, the focus will be on records centers throughout most of this chapter.

Although a location in a business may be used to store active records and may be called a "records center," the term is meant to describe the facility for long-term storage of inactive records. The general purpose of a records center, therefore, is to provide a centralized location for inactive records with well-defined procedures for storing records and provisions for retrieval when that function is needed. In some companies, inactive records are stored in basements, warehouses, and back rooms with little or no concern for their retrieval. This type of records center fulfills only the storage function and bears no resemblance to a professionally operated records center. Simply putting all records in one location does not fulfill the requirements for a records center. The criteria for a records center include:

1. identifying the types of records to be stored, particularly vital records, and the purposes for their storage
2. having a suitable storage site, which requires analyzing what type of facility to use.

In addition, planning a records center includes:

- □ space and architectural requirements
- □ security and protection standards
- □ proper equipment
- □ an efficient layout
- □ procedures for transfer and retrieval
- □ adequate staffing.

Identifying Vital Records

Records serve various functions in an organization: administrative, fiscal, legal, historical, and research. Some records in each of these areas may be classified as vital; that is, they are essential for the continuous operation of the business. One purpose of a records center is to preserve and protect vital records, which usually comprise 2 percent to 4 percent of a company's total records.

A *vital records program* helps to ensure that vital records are identified and adequately protected. The program should include an overall plan for equipment, personnel, and procedures that is supported and approved by management. The essential components of the program include:

- □ one person in each department responsible for identifying vital records
- □ one or more specific locations for storage, such as a safe or vault
- □ a suitable medium for storage, which may be paper, magnetic media, optical media, or film
- □ facilities and equipment for protection against deterioration
- □ a disaster recovery plan.

The vital records program should be incorporated in records center planning.

Although a records center may be quite small, perhaps only a large room with several thousand records, it still represents a significant investment of personnel and equipment. A state-of-the-art records center that houses hundreds of thousands of corporate records is a considerable expense. A small business may not feel it has sufficient records to justify the expense involved. A large business may not wish to make the considerable initial investment to begin a records center. In these situations, or for other reasons, a business may decide to have its inactive records stored by a commercial records storage firm rather than incur the expense for its own facility.

Choosing the Type of Facility

At some point, a business may have accumulated so many inactive records that the pile-of-records-in-a-storeroom approach is, not only inefficient and costly, but presents a safety hazard, as well. Ideally, a plan for long-term storage of inactive records should be created when the business begins operation. However, this is rarely the case because when a business begins operation it has no inactive records! Even when the need for records storage becomes apparent, the solution to the problem of too many inactive records and inadequate storage for them is not simple. Many options for records storage are possible, and the decision about what records to store and where to store them requires careful consideration. When a business plans inactive records storage, the first step is to purge unnecessary records, and the purging will be most efficient if the eventual storage location for inactive records that will be kept is known. Therefore, the business should decide whether it wants to store records in a company-owned records center (on-site or off-site), in a commercial center, or in some combination of the two before the purging process begins.

Several factors influence the decision to use a company or commercial center to store inactive records:

- ☐ How many boxes of records need to be stored?
- ☐ Does the business own land and a building that could be used for a records center?
- ☐ Does the business own land on which a facility could be built?
- ☐ Could the business lease the space it needs?
- ☐ Is inexpensive space available in the company's existing facilities?
- ☐ What is the cost of storage in a commercial records center versus the cost of storage in the company's own facilities?
- ☐ How frequently will the records need to be accessed?

The answers to these questions will help management decide whether to establish a company records center, either on its present site or in another location, or use the services of a commercial records center (Constantini, 1986).

The advantages of using in-house storage are convenience, easy access, and control. The major disadvantage is cost, and other disadvantages may include inadequate protection and insufficiently trained personnel.

Commercial records centers are in the business of renting records storage space to companies. They buy or lease land and buildings, and then rent storage space to businesses. They also provide professional management of inactive records such as records control, retrieval, transfer, and microfilming. The advantages of using a commercial center are security, trained personnel, and minimal cost. The disadvantages are that these centers are less convenient and accessible than an on-site center, and the company has less control over personnel, procedures, and facilities. Also, agreements to rent space from a commercial center are often on a contract basis of three to five years, which represents a considerable investment. The following considerations are of major importance in a company's decision to use company or commercial storage for inactive records (Culton, 1987).

Cost of Space The first consideration is the cost of space. If a business leases a building for records storage, the choice must be a building with adequate space and facilities for the company's records. On the other hand, a large commercial center will have the space and appropriate facilities for ten, fifty, or more companies. The commercial records center can take advantage of overlapping resources; for example, they need only one security system and each fork-lift truck can service the records for multiple companies. Also, it is usually a simple matter for a commercial center to increase the storage space for a particular company. These advantages, in addition to other economies of scale, allow the commercial center to rent space competitively. The costs of a commercial center should be obtained to determine if they represent a more economical alternative to a company-owned facility. The typical expenses for a company-owned records center providing approximately 10,000 square feet of storage space are shown in Figure 10.1.

If the business owns the building, it does not pay rent but does pay taxes, building maintenance, and repair costs. Also, the building becomes a capital investment and that money can be earning interest or income. The cost of storage in a typical commercial records center in the Chicago area in 1987 was about $3 per box, per year, and that included steel shelving, taxes, utilities, profit, insurance, and certain overhead expenses. Additional expenses for a client business include file retrieval, refiles, destructions, and other special services that may be required. Based on 1987 costs, if a business stores 12,000 boxes in a commercial center at $.24 a month per box, the cost is $35,000 annually for space; an additional $5,000 per year would cover retrieval and delivery charges for a cost of $40,000 annually. Most records management consultants agree that unless a business has more than 20,000 boxes, it cannot justify the cost of having its own records center (Culton, 1987).

Figure 10.1 Typical Expenses for a Company-Owned Records Center (per year)

Salaries	
Supervisor	$25,000
Records center specialist	20,000
Telephone/light/heat	5,200
Security system	1,500
Office supplies	500
Rent	12,000
Steel shelving	3,000
Records center boxes	1,000
Misc. overhead expenses	2,000
Insurance	1,000
Overtime	500
Total	$71,700

Source John D. Culton, "Commercial Records Center vs. Private Center: When Should You Build?" *ARMA Chicago Chapter Newsletter,* February 1987.

Cost of Personnel The second consideration in choosing between a company-owned center and a commercial center is the cost of personnel for the center. Even with a small records center, a minimum equivalent of two full-time people will be needed to staff it so that someone will always be available to provide services and guarantee continuity of services if personnel changes occur. Also, for a large, full-service center, at least one person must be trained adequately for records center management. If a business decides to construct its own center or use its own facilities to establish one, several decisions will need to be made to ensure a successful center.

Corporate Records Centers

When a company decides to set up its own center, the following steps must be accomplished:

1. Obtain management's approval for a records center program.
2. Determine the needs of the corporate records program and the records capacity required.
3. Determine the functions to be performed in the facility and who will pay for them.
4. Determine whether the facility should be on-site or off-site.

Management support for a records center program is critical for the success of the center. To get that support, the records manager can cite the advantages of consolidation of the records function: increased control and security of records; cost savings on office space, furniture, and filing equipment; and cost savings over using a commercial storage facility. Also, top management's support of systematic procedures for operating the center will ensure that the center does not become a dumping ground. This point should be strongly emphasized, for if long-term resources are not committed, the records center will degenerate into a junkyard of records. Once this situation occurs, it is very difficult and costly to turn it around.

The records program should include a definition of inactive records, criteria for storing records in the center, and a clearly defined procedure for storing records. Then an estimate of the capacity needed in the center can be made. (One method for estimating the amount of space occupied by records is described below in our discussion of space and architectural requirements.)

The functions that could be performed in the facility include storage and destruction of only inactive records or the maintenance of all records (active and inactive), microfilming and vault storage, forms management, and any other services required by the business. In any case, the costs of services should be charged back to the various departments that use the center. A *chargeback system* discourages records hoarding and encourages departments to destroy unnecessary records on a regular basis and to use the center efficiently.

Site selection considerations for a corporate center would include proximity to corporate users, turnaround time for user requests, security and fire or flood hazard potential, and costs of owned or leased space. For an on-site facility, the strength of the structure of a proposed location would be an important consideration. Stored records are very heavy, especially when stacked. Other considerations would be access to the facility after business hours and whether employees are unionized. A chronic problem of on-site storage is encroachment by other departments. If the company's records center is too close to the corporate offices, management may be constantly moving the center to use the space for what they perceive to be a higher priority requirement.

After the initial decisions are made, the actual planning of the center begins with attention to the following details:

- ☐ space/architectural requirements
- ☐ security/protection
- ☐ equipment and layout
- ☐ transfer and retrieval procedures
- ☐ staffing.

Space and Architectural Requirements

A physical measurement of all records must be made to identify space needs. This is achieved by counting all the equipment in which records are housed and/or estimating the volume of records filed in this equipment. This measurement includes paper, film, and magnetic media records. The volume of records normally is figured in cubic feet of space. A four-drawer vertical file cabinet holds about 6.5 cubic feet of records. This measurement is based on the contents of each drawer being 8½ inches high × 11 inches wide × 30 inches deep or 2,805 cubic inches. This figure is divided by 1,728 and the result is 1.6 cubic feet per drawer (times 4 drawers = 6.5 cubic feet).

If departments know definitely what they will store, the capacity needed in the center can be figured precisely. However, for a ballpark figure, about one-third of all the records in an organization normally will be eligible for long-term storage. Additional square footage for aisles, doors, work space (desks or viewing areas), and processing areas also must be included in the planning. The amount of space for potential growth of records can be determined to some extent by the estimated growth of the company, but initially a 100 percent growth potential should be planned.

The center should be constructed to meet certain minimal physical requirements: steel and masonry one-story construction with a brick exterior and a metal roof, an automatic sprinkler system, a waterproof interior of unpainted cinderblock, hard-surfaced concrete floors, and temperature and humidity controls. Ceiling height in the records storage area should be a minimum of 16 feet to accommodate metal shelving and still leave about 18 inches of clearance below ducts, pipes, and sprinkler heads (Smart, 1978). If the center is not on a ground floor, then floor load capacity becomes a consideration. *Floor load* refers to the amount of weight per square foot a floor can support without collapsing. Boxed records stacked on steel shelving are extremely heavy; therefore, the floors in the center must be structurally capable of supporting the weight. An architect can be consulted to determine if a particular above-ground-level location will be suitable for the intended records center, if structural supports are required, or if the proposed location is not structurally feasible.

Security and Protection

Record storage areas should be protected with intrusion and fire detection/control systems. All records should be protected against theft, mutilation, fire, or water damage. Publications from the National Fire Protection Association provide information on reducing fire hazards in records centers. A written disaster prevention and preparedness plan should be part of the organization's vital records program, and duplicates of records considered essential to the organization should be housed off-site. Therefore, protection for records includes both security measures to prevent vandalism, theft, and mutilation and measures to prevent deterioration or destruction of paper, film, magnetic, optical, and other media.

Paper deterioration is a problem of massive proportion for information specialists. It is estimated that more than 90 percent of the books published in the United States between 1900 and 1939 will not be available for general use by the year 2000 because of deteriorating bindings and paper (Lowell, 1979). The factors that cause paper deterioration are biological, physiochemical, and mechanical; they include acid contamination, heat and moisture, light, damage by fungi and vermin, natural disasters, and vandalism or accidental damage by people. Most paper used to register information during the past century has a high acid content, which will destroy the paper. Worse, acid has the ability to migrate from one piece of paper to another so that a document prepared on acid-free paper will be contaminated by storing it in an acidic file folder. Records managers can protect against acid contamination by using both acid-free storage materials and permanent/durable paper for creating and maintaining paper records that are destined for long-term storage.

Temperature and humidity in the center should be maintained at between 55 and 70 degrees Fahrenheit and 30 to 50 percent relative humidity. Generally, the lower the storage area temperature, the longer paper will last. Too high humidity in a records storage area promotes mold and bacteria growth and accelerates acid deterioration. If the humidity is too low, paper becomes brittle. Therefore, temperature and relative humidity should remain constant, and a records center should have a means for controlling temperature and humidity constantly.

Another factor in paper deterioration is ultraviolet radiation. The effects of ultraviolet radiation can be minimized by insuring that paper records are not left in direct sunlight for any period of time. A classic example is a newspaper left in the direct sunlight in Phoenix, Arizona; it is unusable after one day. Ideally, records storage and use areas should have incandescent lighting because it emits no harmful light radiation.

Rodents and insects thrive in records storage areas where they feed on cellulose, gelatins, and starches. High temperature and humidity favor propagation of these pests. Infestation can be reduced by fumigating any records suspected to house mold or vermin before they are stored. Regular inspection will avoid these biological problems.

The general storage requirements for photographic film and magnetic tapes or disks are low temperature (60 degrees Fahrenheit) and relative humidity no lower than 20 percent. Film should be stored in a storage room or vault separate from any other type of medium, especially paper, since some types of film give off acidic fumes. Oil-based paints in a freshly painted room emit peroxides that are particularly harmful to film, so film should not be stored in such an environment for at least four weeks. The shelf life of magnetic tape varies greatly from one product to the next. The National Bureau of Standards provides test criteria for determining the archival quality and life expectancy of magnetic tapes. The optimal temperature and humidity for magnetic tape and magnetic disks is 65 degrees Fahrenheit and 40 percent relative humidity. Relative humidity lower than 35 percent can produce static electricity, which attracts dust and may degrade data on magnetic disks. Magnetic tape should be enclosed in a container and stored in a filtered air environment. Magnetic disks also require a filtered air environment, as well as periodic checking for data errors.

Both mediums should be backed up on duplicate tapes that are stored at another site. Cosmic rays and other stray radiation can adversely affect the validity of magnetic media. Most experts agree that magnetic media should be rewritten at least every three years to preserve the validity of the information.

Equipment and Layout

For the low-cost storage center, steel shelving is an inexpensive and safe choice. Self-stacking, steel reinforced boxes, which eliminate the need for any type of shelving, also are available. Mobile files are a suitable choice for semi-active records, but they are an expensive alternative for records that are accessed only a few times a year ("Filing . . . ," 1985). Shelving that provides the most filing space per square foot of floor space, while permitting convenient access, is the most desirable. Therefore, shelving that is 42 inches wide and 30 inches deep, erected back to back (double-wide) is usually a good choice. The most common type of storage container is the 15-inch-×-12-inch-×-10-inch heavy corrugated cardboard carton with a shoe-box-type lid. These boxes can accommodate both legal- and letter-size records, are inexpensive and durable, and their filled weight is about 15 pounds.

The layout of the center will include the records storage area, work space within the storage area, a receiving and destruction area, and some provision for expansion. In addition, the center may need to have designated areas for microfilming, user viewing of records, equipment storage, general office space, one or more vaults, and rest rooms. In planning specific equipment, supplies, and locations, the manager needs to plan for single- and/or double-depth reinforced shelving, storage boxes, microfilming equipment (if designated), copiers, telephones, and telecopiers. Connection capability planning includes ensuring adequate power supplies (regular and emergency), lighting needs, sufficient outlets for the proposed equipment, and satisfactory terminal cable hookups. Security considerations encompass the number and type of entrances to the facility, and security, fire, and water detection systems. Finally, planning should consider the capabilities of the physical plant to carry out the proposed operations efficiently; for example, ease of access to a loading dock (if off-site facility), automobile parking space, water drains, and floor load capacity (see Figure 10.2).

The layout of a records center needs to incorporate a *shelving address system* for the stored boxes; in other words, each space on the shelving must have an address. The shelving address system enables records personnel to know what spaces are available (empty) and provides a method for locating stored boxes. Numbering systems for double-wide shelving use some combination of row number, unit number, space number (and sometimes shelf number), for the address. In a *row, unit, and space numbering system* (RUS), each row of shelving is assigned a sequential number, which is posted on the aisle end of the row. Each row is then subdivided into units, which also are numbered sequentially. The units consist of a particular number of spaces, depending on the height of the shelving. As illustrated in Figure 10.3, boxes are stacked two deep and three wide on three tiers of shelving. Each

Figure 10.2 Interior of Company Records Center

Source Courtesy of Hughes Aircraft Company.

Figure 10.3 Row, Unit, and Space Numbering System

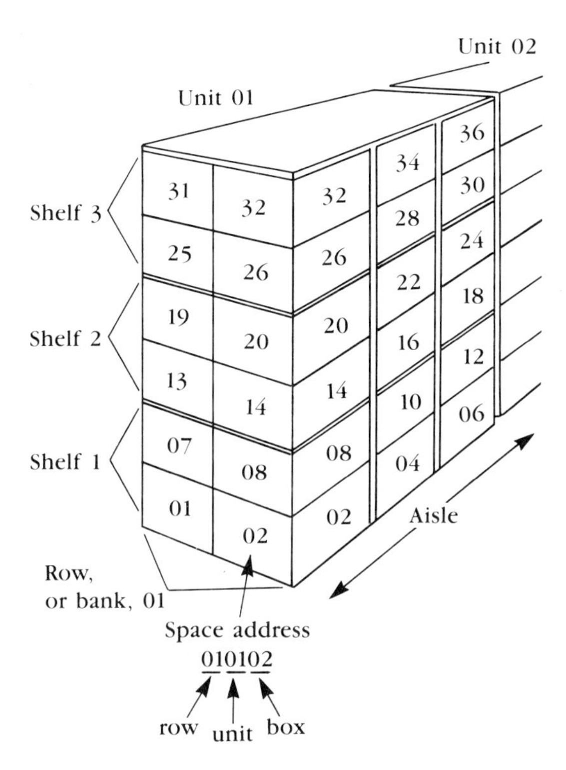

unit consists of thirty-six spaces, numbered from back to front and bottom to top. In addition, space 01 is behind space 02, so that all even-numbered spaces are in the front and odd-numbered spaces are behind.

When the center is set up, the spaces available are entered in a card system (manual) or a computer database. As each box is shelved, the contents of the box and its address are recorded. Sections of space, or units, can be assigned to particular departments. However, a more efficient approach is to fill spaces sequentially. In any case, a listing of stored records by department name (or some other identifier) is needed. For example, let's assume that the marketing department stores two boxes of sales records for March 1987. The boxes are stored in row 8, unit 2, spaces 01 and 02. With a card system, the cards numbered 080201 and 080202 would be used to record the department name and box contents as follows:

Space No. 080201
Marketing Sales Records, 3/87 only

In addition, in the alphabetical card file or computer database, the following entry would appear:

Dept: Marketing	Space No.
Sales Records, 3/87	080201
	080202

A fairly simple alphabetical card system could be maintained by department and record type within each department. However, a computerized system is more efficient, especially in a center that stores several thousand cartons, since the computer can easily search a database of departments or record types to find the location addresses. The numbering system also can incorporate the shelf number, or be simplified to use only a row and space number. The principle is to provide a unique address for each storage space.

Transfer and Retrieval Procedures

Whether the records center facility is on-site or off-site, a well-defined procedure for transferring records to the center is necessary. The *transfer procedure* requires a transfer list, which is prepared by the office or department that is transferring records. The list should provide all pertinent information regarding the records being transferred: name of office or department, official name of the records series, brief description of the records series, time span covered by the records, intended destruction date, date of transfer, authorization for the transfer, and temporary box number. When the list is received in the center, it is checked against the cartons received and location numbers are assigned to the cartons. The office or department may receive a copy of the transfer list with the assigned location numbers, but security can be a problem if this information is provided.

Another part of the transfer procedure is the actual transportation of the records. If the center is off-site, delivery trucks can make scheduled runs to pick up records. If the center is on-site, the records manager must establish a suitable procedure for pick-up and delivery. In either case, the records are in transit, and this fact must be recorded.

The retrieval procedure requires a request or *charge-out form* that should include the name, phone number, and location of the requestor; the date, record description, and the space address if it is known. The request form is usually filled out in triplicate with one copy replacing the record, the second copy attached to the record (or box) as a routing slip, and the third copy kept in a suspense (or tickler) file for follow-up or billing information. When the record is returned, it should be refiled immediately. The copy of the request form that is attached to the record is marked "refiled" and may be kept for future reference on file activity; the copy of the request form that was used as a marker is destroyed.

Staffing

The number and type of personnel needed for the records center will vary depending on the size and activity of the center. Even in a small center, however, at least two people are needed so that one person always will be available to provide service. Also, security guards may be employed, as well as personnel to staff the center after regular business hours if twenty-four-hour access is provided.

Commercial Records Centers

The commercial records center is a low-cost alternative for storing inactive records, especially if those records must be stored for many years. Commercial centers compare favorably to certain forms of in-house storage, such as microfilm. While microfilm may ease storage space requirements, it is an expensive option for records that may never be retrieved until it is time for them to be destroyed. Commercial center storage can also be less expensive than in-house, off-site storage since space can be rented on an as-needed basis.

In a commercial center, each document is indexed and its description and location are stored on computer. Such indexing is necessary to handle requests for stored documents that come in each day. With the computer indexing and records storage, a document can be located in five minutes or less. Since fast return of filed documents to clients is an important selling point, commercial centers often have twenty-four-hour "hot lines" to fulfill emergency requests. Commercial centers also provide monthly and yearly summaries so their clients know exactly what documents are stored, as well as storage costs. The monthly billing statement may include a listing of all documents, as well as a breakdown of document requests by department so that the client company can charge storage costs back to departments if it wishes to do so. The yearly report for each client may list retrievals, refiles, deliveries, number of cubic feet used, cost, and other items of interest to the client company.

Underground Vaults and Storage, Inc., in Hutchinson, Kansas, is a commercial storage facility that offers more than 102 million cubic feet of storage space for client companies (see Figure 10.4). The facilities and services provided by this company include semi-private vaults for microform storage with temperature maintained at 68 degrees Fahrenheit and 38 percent humidity, private rooms for viewing records, and storage for paper, film, and magnetic tape. Security is provided with closed-circuit TV, security personnel, and controlled access to the underground storage area. Records sent to or from the client location may be transported

Figure 10.4 Commercial Records Center

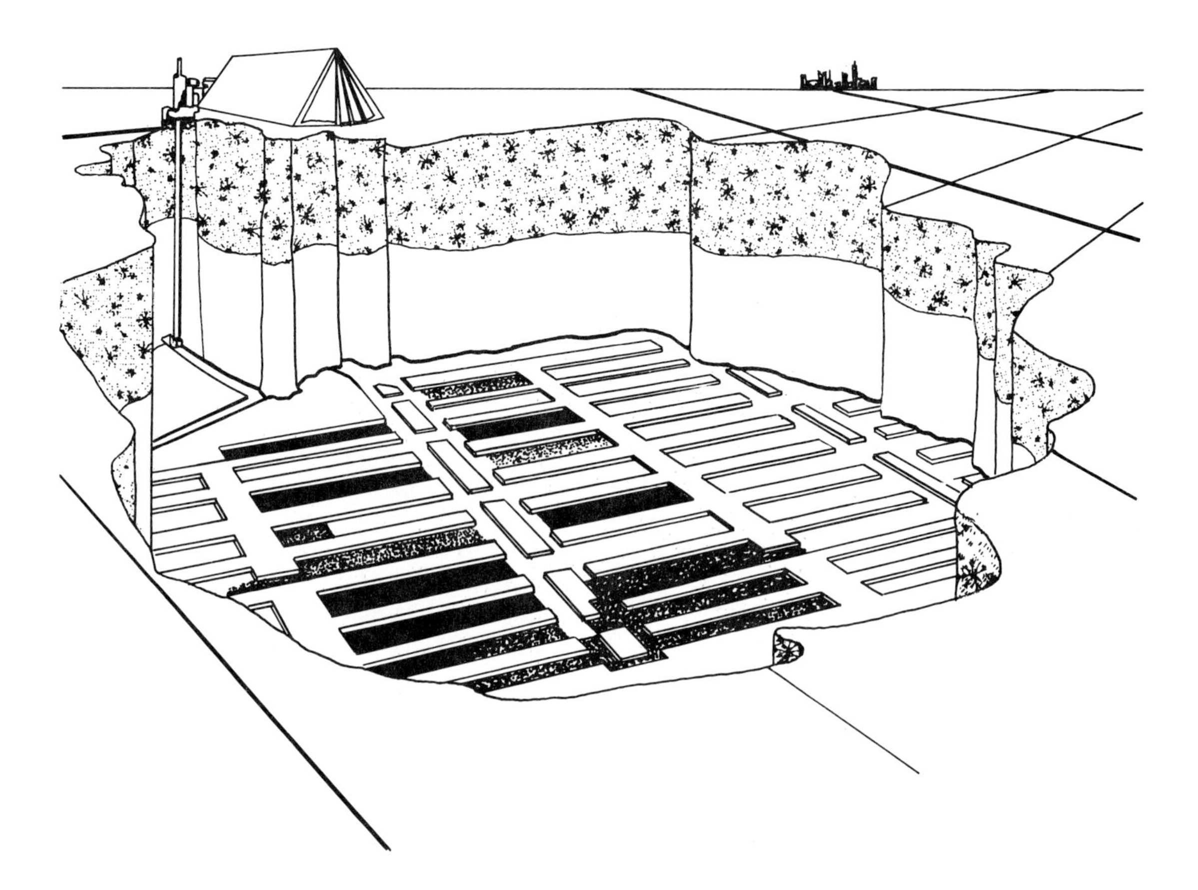

electronically (for example, by telecopier) or by a variety of mail or freight transport systems, such as air freight, bus or private carrier.

The features described for a commercial center also are contained in many corporate (in-house) records centers. (A thorough description of the records center for Hughes Aircraft Company, which has many of these features, is given in Chapter 13.)

Archives

Archival storage traditionally has referred to the preservation of historical documents. Although the role of the archivist has expanded to include other types of records management, the distinction between archives and records centers is still based to a large extent on the type of records stored. In fact, in records management circles, archivists are sometimes unkindly referred to as pack rats, since their primary concern is the permanent preservation of all records that have or may have historical value.

The importance of archival storage should not be minimized, however, since without it we would not be able to view such awe-inspiring documents as the original Articles of Confederation or the original text of the preamble to the Constitution. Archival management requires highly specialized skills and knowledge of sophisticated preservation techniques. Methods of preservation and the other concerns of the archivist are illustrated in the following example, which describes the preservation of the *Domesday Book* (pronounced "doomsday"), a 900-year-old book that is a historical record of landholdings in eleventh century England (Ker, 1986).

The *Domesday Book,* in its two volumes, gives a minute and accurate account of the state of England in 1086 A.D. The book is the oldest public record in the United Kingdom, and it is the most remarkable statistical record produced in any medieval kingdom. In 1085, William the Conqueror ordered a survey to determine

> *"how much land and livestock the king himself owned in the country and what annual dues were lawfully his from each shire. . . . The survey recorded how much land was held by each and every landholder, how much livestock, how many ploughs, how many villeins, cottiers and slaves he had, how much land was in use, and how much more could be put to use . . . not even one ox, nor one cow, nor one pig escaped notice in his survey. (Ker, 1986)*

The custodian of this priceless treasure is the Public Record Office in the United Kingdom. The Public Record Office is the national repository of records deriving from the actions of central government and the courts of law. It holds millions of documents from the eleventh century to the present day. In 1986, on the 900th anniversary of the *Domesday Book,* the Public Record Office was concerned with transferring the book to microfilm; the original sheepskin parchments had been rebound several times, and photographing information from it was very difficult because of the curvature caused by the deep spine. The description of that process provides a typical example of the preservation procedures that archivists employ:

> *It was decided . . . to unbind both books, carry out any necessary conservation repair work, and microfilm the original manuscripts. At the same time color separation negatives would be made so that facsimile reproduction could be carried out using a continuous tone printing process. [The process also included translation of the text which is in Norman Latin.] (Ker, 1986)*

In a security cage in the Public Record Office building, the books were unbound and restored by specialist binders, then photographed to provide the four separate negatives and microfilmed. One film was sealed in a time capsule and "the container was filled with an inert gas and elaborate precautions were taken to ensure that the film was not damaged in sealing the capsule." (Ker, 1986) The second roll of film serves as a master to make duplicate copies whenever necessary. The preceding description is typical of the types of documents found in archives and the procedures used to preserve them.

A challenging problem for any archive facility to solve is the selection of an appropriate classification system for the archival materials. Most materials accepted into an archives were active records at some time and have a classification system. For example, archives often accept old billings and receipts, personal files of retired executives, out-of-date materials, catalogs, photographs, and other materials that have their own, unique classification systems (numeric, alphabetic, alphanumeric, and so forth) or perhaps no system at all.

In order to make archival materials accessible, a general classification system is required and for the wide collection of materials, only a subject classification system will suffice. For this type of classification, a general overview of the materials should be done to determine about twenty-five major subject classifications. Within the major subjects, each coherent group of materials is given its own subject classification and then the original classification system, as feasible, is used. This is a form of the dash–slash system of classification, with the dash and slash respectively separating the overall primary and secondary subject classifications.

Sometimes archives simply are dumping grounds for records. The records are not stored according to an organized classification system and so are virtually unretrievable. Even if this type of archives has a records management system in place, the budget is rarely adequate to effectively maintain the system. Ideally, an archives is the museum of the business, where valuable and irreplaceable historical records are preserved and protected with impeccable care.

Summary

Records centers and archives are used for long-term storage of inactive records. Archives usually are designated for permanent storage of historical records. A records center, on the other hand, may be used for both active and inactive records, but its primary purpose is for centralized storage of inactive records. A vital records program is an essential part of records center planning. In the planning process, the business must decide whether to use a commercial center or its own facilities for storing inactive records. Two factors that influence this decision are cost of space and cost of trained personnel.

The planning for a corporate records center includes determining the space and architectural requirements for the room or building, providing security systems, protecting records against deterioration, choosing appropriate equipment, designing the layout of the center, setting up a space numbering system, developing transfer and retrieval procedures, and staffing the center.

Commercial records centers can provide a low-cost alternative to company-owned records centers, and offer a wide range of services to client companies.

Archives serve a unique purpose and require expert personnel and facilities. The preservation and protection of valuable historical documents is one important purpose of an archives.

List of Terms

records center
archives
vital records program
charge-back system
floor load
shelving address system
row, unit, and space (RUS) numbering system
transfer procedure
charge-out form

Discussion Questions

1. What are the differences in purpose between a records center and an archives?
2. What are the criteria for a records center?
3. What are the essential elements of a vital records program?
4. What are some of the factors that determine whether a business should have a company-owned records center?
5. What are the advantages and disadvantages of an in-house records center?
6. How does the cost of space influence the decision to use a company records center versus a commercial center?
7. What are the typical costs incurred in a records center?

8. What space and architectural factors should a business consider in planning a records center?
9. What factors affect the deterioration of paper?
10. What equipment is suitable for a records center?
11. What should be included in records center transfer procedures?
12. What are some of the advantages and disadvantages of using a commercial records center?
13. What steps are necessary in creating a numbering system for a records center?
14. What are the reasons for a business having a records center and/or archives?

Activities

1. Design a records center for a small business that plans to store approximately 200 cartons of records per year and has at this time 400 cartons. Include the layout of furniture and shelving in your design and a justification for your choices.
2. Devise a numbering system for carton storage that could be kept on computer. Explain how space would be assigned and how retrieval and refiling of records would be accomplished in your system.
3. If available, visit a commercial records center and describe the physical facilities and operations. Could any of the records stored in the facility be correctly classified as active records? vital records?
4. Visit an archive facility and describe its classification system. Interview the personnel and determine what types of material they accept for the archives. Based on your observations and interview(s), state the criteria that is used to determine the archival value of materials.
5. Write a report that describes how a computer could be used in an archive. Consider that the main use for a computer most likely would be to increase the efficiency of storage and retrieval of materials.
6. Because of the nature of archives, some experts believe that they should be open, public facilities like museums. What are the advantages and disadvantages to turning an archive into a public facility?

References

Constantini, JoAnn M. "Considerations for Constructing a Records Storage Facility." National ARMA Conference, Kansas City, Mo., October 8, 1986.

Culton, John D. "Commercial Records Center vs. Private Center: When Should You Build?" ARMA Chicago Chapter Newsletter (February 1987).

"Filing—Cheaper by the Billion." *Modern Office Technology* (February 1985).

Ker, Niel. "900 Years from Doomsday." *IMC Journal* (November/December 1986).

Lowell, Howard P. "Preserving Recorded Information—The Physical Deterioration of Paper." *Records Management Quarterly* (April 1979).

Smart, Lora L. "Getting It All Together." *Records Management Quarterly* (October 1978).

Chapter 10 Highlight

Do-It-Yourself "Micrographics"

Many of the advantages of micrographics can be realized for personal and home records systems. The minimum equipment you will need is a camera and film. In the same way that most micrographics systems are used for vital or inactive records, you can use camera and film. The following list suggests some of the records you might wish to film.

- ☐ household furniture
- ☐ valuable goods (jewelry, coins, silver, etc.)
- ☐ garage/utility room items
- ☐ important papers (investments, deeds, etc.)

In the case of a disaster, film that verifies the existence of items can be extremely useful. Of course, the film should be stored off-site in a secure location. A safety deposit box would be an appropriate storage place.

The equipment for filming is easy to find. We suggest using a 35 mm camera and film because of the variety available. If only images are necessary, such as pictures of furniture, then virtually any commercial camera and film will be adequate. If some detail is required, then the camera and film should be of a higher quality.

For most purposes, the detail needed will be the ability to read standard printed text such as a book page, a legal document, a computer display screen, or the serial number on a piece of equipment. To do this efficiently, the following equipment is recommended.

35-mm camera with 45 to 60-mm lens

adjustable lens with minimum f/4.0

ISO/ASA 400-speed film

The film can be color print film, which is the most widely available; but prints are not really necessary for this type of filming, nor is color often required. Either color slide film or black-and-white (b & w) print film will work fine. Prints can be made from slides or negatives should they be required. There are a number of excellent films available that meet these specifications.

The camera can be manual or automatic with the capability of focusing to 12 inches or less. Plan on about one 8½-×-11-inch standard page per image. In order to maximize the depth of field (i.e., the range that will be in focus), try to use the smallest possible lens opening (largest f/stop) with a minimum speed of 1/30 of a second. Use a support to hold the camera steady or go to a slightly higher speed, perhaps 1/60 or 1/125 of a second. With a very stable tripod and remote shutter release, you can go to 1/15 or even 1/8 of a second with satisfactory results. As necessary, add lighting to meet the minimum conditions.

As you film, keep an index describing each image. You might want to film the index as the last image on each roll of film. Keep the slides or negatives in a secure location with the index, and update your filmed records regularly.

Part

2

Records Management Applications in Business and Government

Chapter 11

Careers and Professional Growth in Records Management

Learning Goals

1. To become acquainted with the requirements for various records management positions.
2. To recognize the desirable skills, knowledge, and personal qualities of records personnel.
3. To learn the advantages of professional organizations.
4. To become familiar with the requirements to become a Certified Records Manager (CRM).
5. To understand how professional organizations and professional certification increase career opportunities.

Introduction

The records management field offers a wide variety of career opportunities for people with the interest and aptitude for managing information resources. People in the records management field may work in records and information retention, integrated technologies applications, records center operations, vital records security, forms and reports management, correspondence management, and historical document preservation, to name just a few. Many job positions are available, and the education and experience required for those positions range from a high school diploma to a doctoral degree, and from no experience to many years of experience.

The records management field has evolved from primarily filing tasks to include the management of information resources in a variety of formats and in an increasingly complex business environment. Roles of records personnel have changed accordingly and continue to evolve. Anyone who seeks employment in records management should be aware of contemporary job requirements and the career opportunities that exist in the field. In addition, joining a professional organization and knowing the benefits of professional certification will help aspiring records personnel advance in their careers.

In this chapter, we will describe various positions in the records management field and the specific requirements needed to acquire them. Also, the discussion of job positions will include the typical duties performed, along with examples of position announcements and job search information.

Since records management professional organizations significantly influence the field, we provide a brief history of those organizations and their objectives, plus the benefits those professional organizations offer to their members. Finally, we give the requirements for professional certification and provide an outline of the Certified Records Manager examination.

The Changing Roles of Records Personnel

What image does the title "records clerk" form in your mind? Many people still envision someone working with paper file folders in a job with little future. That image belongs to a previous age. Today even entry-level positions at the lowest skill level are likely to require computer literacy and other technical skills. Furthermore, almost any ambitious employee at any level on the records management career ladder has an excellent chance of advancement to a wide variety of positions. The field of records management is bursting with opportunities for men and women, and that situation will continue to improve for many years to come.

Businesses are vitally concerned with productivity. The increased efficiency found in an effective records management program using today's computer technology contributes to increased productivity. As businesses discover this fact, they turn to records personnel, especially the records manager, to solve productivity problems associated with information management. The result is that records personnel are found in every type of business and at all levels of management. When records operations such as word processing and mail management are linked to the records management department, records personnel must understand word processing technology and telecommunications. When micrographics and/or reprographics are linked with data processing operations, records personnel must have knowledge of that area. Increasingly, records managers coordinate more and more aspects of the information resources of the business.

As information specialists or *chief information officers* (CIO), the role of the records manager requires knowledge of all operations within the company, the ability to work with all types of people at all levels, and technical ability in the traditional areas of records management as well as in electronic data processing. Records and information management has evolved considerably from the days of conventional hard (paper) copy filing systems. Today, a professional records manager must be knowledgeable, not only in the traditional approach to information management, but also in the newer technologies such as automated systems, integrated networks, and micrographics.

Not long ago, the definition of records management was the efficient storage and retrieval of paper records and film media. With the realization that information is a resource that can be profitably administered with the principles of records management, the field has expanded to include many diversified areas that deal with information management, as follows:

- ☐ *Records and Information Retention* is involved with developing schedules indicating the length of time and in what format each record is to be maintained, and assigning value to the record.
- ☐ *Integrated Technology Applications* involve automated state-of-the-art technologies that are used in the creation, storage, and retrieval of information. These technologies include micrographics, word processing, electronic data processing, telecommunications, and emerging applications that use optical and video disk technologies.
- ☐ *Records Center Operations* involve developing specifications and procedures for economical and efficient management of inactive records, including reference and retrieval services for users.
- ☐ *Vital Records Security* involves protecting those records that are crucial to the continuity of an organization in the event of a disaster and using the most economical media to ensure security.
- ☐ *Forms and Reports Management* involves designing the most economical and useful forms and reports, as well as controlling their number and distribution. Today, forms management is rapidly shifting to computer technology for management as well as distribution as videotext forms.
- ☐ *Correspondence Management* involves developing the most efficient techniques for letter writing, copy control, and the use of word processing equipment. A new direction toward the use of expert systems for producing correspondence has developed.
- ☐ *Historical Document Preservation* involves providing permanent preservation for those records that reflect the organization's history. This area includes both assessment of document value and consideration of a wide range of potential media, from paper to optical disk.

In addition to dealing with old and new technologies and a wide range of operations, records personnel need a broader perspective of business operations than in the past. The business world has become a global community, and the challenge of managing records on an international scope has affected every records position. With all of the changes in the way we do business, there is little doubt that anyone wishing to do so can find an interesting and rewarding career in records management.

Career Opportunities in Records Management

Most positions in the field require general mechanical aptitude, the ability to analyze data, and human relations skills such as cooperativeness and the ability to relate well to others. The requirements for a particular job and the salary will depend, of course, on the level of the position. Entry-level positions often require only a high school diploma and place the employee on the bottom rung of the career ladder. Professional mobility and higher salaries, however, require at least a bachelor's degree and progressive experience in the field.

Several job titles are provided by the Association of Records Managers and Administrators (ARMA) and those titles are used in the descriptions in this section. Although every business does not use precisely these titles, the tasks performed will be similar to those described.

The following positions minimally require a high school diploma. However, a person with one or more years of college education or a bachelor's degree may have more opportunity for advancement than others with only the minimum education required to obtain the job.

- *Records and Information Clerk* Analyzes systems and microfilm needs; destroys records according to retention schedules; files and retrieves documents; follows up on charged-out records; indexes and codes records for filing; inserts microfilm into jackets; prepares documents for filing; types reports, labels, schedules, and so forth; assists in training of personnel; answers telephone; processes and distributes mail; orders and checks office supplies; performs clerical tasks related to office.
- *Records Center Clerk* Assigns location numbers; maintains request controls and location logs; locates records for reference purposes; files and retrieves documents and records boxes; checks incoming transmittal lists; delivers documents and records storage boxes to requesting departments; maintains security controls in records center; charges out records; screens requests for access to confidential records; microfilms documents; destroys records.
- *Micrographics Clerk or Technician* Microfilms documents; duplicates microfilm; establishes procedures for filming a project; files and retrieves documents and film; indexes microfilm; maintains record of documents to be filmed; maintains record of film to be processed; mounts aperture cards and/or inserts film in jackets; prepares monthly, quarterly, yearly reports.

The following positions require a junior college or community college (two-year) education. Unless the educational background involved substantial coursework in records management, experience in the field also is required.

- *Records and Information Supervisor* Assists in program evaluations and decisions regarding maintenance, protection, retrieval, and destruction of records; recommends records retention schedules; supervises inventories of active records areas; supervises destruction of records; supervises records storage areas; verifies notices for the destruction of records; assigns/directs work of other employees; assists in training of employees; evaluates employees for promotional and salary increases; prepares job descriptions and interviews prospective employees.
- *Records Center Supervisor* Enforces security controls in records center; oversees charge-out and follow-up systems, and transfers of records; supervises inventories of records, microfilming of documents, and destruction of records; supervises maintenance of equipment; evaluates employees; assists in training of employees and directs their work.

The following positions require the appropriate combination of a college or university education and several years of experience in the field.

- *Records and Information Manager* Designs corporatewide records management programs; prepares goals and objectives for program; prepares and oversees department or division budget; coordinates various aspects of program, including personnel, equipment, and procedures. (In addition, the general responsibilities of records managers are provided in Chapter 4, "Responsibilities of the Records Manager." Figure 11.1 describes the job requirements for a records manager in a large corporation with branch and field offices.)

Figure 11.1 Records Manager Job Description

JOB TITLE: Records Manager

DEPARTMENT: Office Management

Job Responsibilities:

Record Storage and Retention Initiates, institutes, and maintains the computerized record storage/retention/destruction program for inventory, handling and destruction of 19,000 boxes in storage by the corporate office. Coordinates storage of all inactive records with commercial records centers, including daily flow of records between corporate departments and storage (approx. 12,000/year); purchasing, packing and shipment of boxes; contract negotiations; approx. 536,637,800 documents in storage. Initiates, institutes and maintains a comprehensive retention policy for all field offices nationwide, meeting legal requirements for all fifty states, plus operational needs. Collects, tabulates, and applies legal, tax, and operational requirements to all records. Locates off-site storage and negotiates contracts. Publishes and distributes the Field Retention Policy to all office managers and store managers along with instructions in use, purging, and destruction.

Records Library Houses, maintains, microfilms, and performs filing operations for 13,000 files. Real Estate, Construction and Licensing (approx. 3,606,400 documents; 115,000 pieces of filing received per year. Supervises delivery and pickup of files to requesters daily in thirty-two departments; 35,000 files per year checked out. Maintains efficient lending, returning, and security procedures for all records.

Filing Systems for Corporate and Field Offices Responsible for records inventories, analyses, and appraisals. Develops filing systems, correspondence control, equipment, hardware, software, recommendations, and growth projections for both the corporate departments and field offices.

Microfilming Investigates, develops, and implements the corporatewide microfilming system, standardizing as much as possible on format, filming procedures, and equipment. Makes recommendations on microfilming programs to field offices.

Vital Records Protection Insures the protection of vital corporate and operating records in case of loss, fire, or disaster. Identifies vital records, provides security and fire protection, places duplicate copies off-site in either hard copy or microfilm.

Budget Establishes and maintains budget covering the library, record storage, and microfilming functions. Does cost analysis and maintenance analysis in all areas of responsibility.

☐ *Records Analyst* Serves as liaison with other departments in the company regarding records needs; conducts research for requesting departments; reviews, designs, consolidates, and controls company forms; reviews/recommends documents for microfilming; conducts periodic audits of active and inactive records areas; reviews supplies and equipment used and/or needed; may be involved in evaluation, training, and direction of other employees.

Figure 11.2 Position Announcements

Records and Information Management Systems Analyst Leading manufacturer of medical devices seeks Records and Information Management Systems Analyst to design systems, prepare retention schedules, and establish forms management; will also write procedures and provide training. B.A. in library science preferred or equivalent experience in records management. Knowledge of IBM PC and automated office technology a plus. May consider bright beginner.

Records Management Administrator This position is responsible for the administration of the records management program of the Department of Archives and History. Duties include the development of policies and procedures for state and local records management programs and management of the department's staff in carrying out those programs. Qualifications are a bachelor's degree with a major in public administration, general business administration or management, records management, archival administration, systems analysis, information sciences, or a closely related field (prefer master's degree in one of these fields) and four years of experience in records systems analysis program in a state or local agency including one year of supervisory experience. Salary range: $25,168–$38,142.

Records Systems Analyst One of the fastest growing research-oriented pharmaceutical companies in the United States is currently recruiting several Records Systems Analysts. Responsibilities include developing and communicating records management policies and procedures to internal clients; training corporate staff on records management philosophies and services; and providing records systems consultation and implementation processes to ensure policy compliance and retention schedule adherence. Position requires a bachelor's degree and three to five years experience in implementing policies and proposals.

Records Manager Responsibilities include: organize and implement a comprehensive university records management program, design record forms, prepare and submit retention/disposition schedules, develop microfilming activities, supervise assistants, and instruct appropriate university personnel as to proper records-keeping techniques. Qualifications: bachelor's degree with relevant graduate work preferred and at least two years experience working in a records management program, extensive knowledge of records management principles and techniques, skill in document research and preservation, experience with microfilming and automated records-keeping systems and equipment preferred, supervisory experience, ability to effectively communicate orally and in writing. Salary: $20,439 plus excellent state employee benefit package.

Records Manager Multi-billion dollar financial institution located in the Southeast is recruiting an individual to head up a newly created position. This individual will be responsible for the design of a state-of-the-art system for the management of the institution's records. Individual must have experience and education equivalent to that of a CRM.

Manager, Records Systems A pharmaceutical company is seeking applicants for the position of Manager, Records Systems. This individual will be responsible for all aspects of a corporatewide records management program. The manager will have responsibility for a nine-member staff. The successful applicant should have a strong background in records management principles and practices. In addition, she or he should have a familiarity with systems and technologies such as personal computers, CAR, COM, and optical disk.

Figures 11.2 and 11.3 are representative examples of position announcements that have appeared in various professional publications.

Professional Growth

Membership in a professional records management association is worthwhile for managers and for those who aspire to management positions. Professional organizations offer affiliation with people of similar career interests, opportunities for training, professional publications, recognition and awards for achievement, and a commitment to continued improvement of the field.

More subtle advantages of professional associations include the dissemination of trade information about the latest equipment and operations, as well as the exchange of information with colleagues in similar industry positions. With the fast pace of change in the field, no one in records management can afford to ignore the equipment and operation innovations that are constantly occurring. The conventions of professional associations can provide a rich opportunity to efficiently review the latest procedures and equipment.

Professional Organizations

The *Association of Records Managers and Administrators* (ARMA International) was founded in 1955. The association as it exists today was formed on July 1, 1975, as successor to the American Records Management Association. In the fifteen years from 1972 to 1987, the membership grew from 950 to over 9,000 members representing twenty countries. ARMA International has over 115 chapters in the United States, Canada, and Puerto Rico, and members throughout the world.

Figure 11.3 Additional Position Announcements

Records Supervisor Seeking mature, well-organized person to supervise the communications and current records/archives/mailroom operations for a public organization. Qualifications: good English and spelling, typing, telex skills and experience. Salary: $20,000. Good vacation and medical benefits.

Records and Information Clerk Northeastern fiduciary firm is seeking a self-starter who would have responsibilities to retrieve, sort, classify, index, and file records. Additionally, this individual would enter data into an information system and control access and retention activities. High school diploma and a minimum of two years of office procedures work experience is required. A bachelor's degree in business or information related area preferred.

Court Records Analyst Supreme Court library, seeks person with five years records management experience or a combination of education and experience; court records experience preferred. NHPRC grant for twenty-four months $27,920—first year, and $29,143—second year.

Records Consultant Trainee Bachelor's degree in government, history, public administration, business, or related field supplemented by courses/seminars in records management; familiarity with center operations, micrographic systems and applications, records automation training programs. Preferred: CRM, master's degree in appropriate field, experience with local government records, experience with micrographics. Starting salary $18,180 with increase to $23,628 after completion of 6–12 months training.

All professional organizations have a commitment to the professional growth of their members. ARMA has three major objectives:

1. Promote and advance the improvement of records and information management and related fields through study, education, and research.
2. Advance professional knowledge and techniques by sharing and exchanging experiences and information related to the field of records and information management.
3. Develop and advance standards of professional competence in the field of records and information management.

The benefits of ARMA membership include continuing education that develops professionalism through local chapter meetings, regional seminars, and an annual conference. The association publishes a professional journal, the *Records Management Quarterly*, which is provided to all members, that presents technical articles and case studies. The ARMA newsletter provides members with current news on chapters. In addition, ARMA monitors legislation that may have an impact on records and information management and rallies support for pending legislation that will be helpful to the records manager.

During its annual conference, the association gives awards and recognition to those who accomplish outstanding achievements in the field. ARMA is one sponsor of the Institute of Certified Records Managers. The association also sponsors the *Industry Action Committee* program, which enables records managers within the same business or industry to communicate regularly and solve common problems.

ARMA International has a four-part job referral service that offers members the use of a nationwide, custom-designed, job search database. The database is available through Lockheed's Dialog Information Service. It permits employers to customize a candidate search based on the skills and experience they require. ARMA members place their resumes in the database for a fee; data entry forms are provided by local chapters or are available from ARMA.

In recent years, ARMA has become increasingly concerned with the educational needs of records personnel and future educational requirements for positions in records management. Consequently, the association has prepared several curriculum guides to aid junior/community colleges and four-year institutions in setting up records management programs. ARMA also encourages student memberships and offers a special membership fee to any student who meets their eligibility requirements.

The *National Association of Government Archives and Records Administrators* (NAGARA) was founded in 1974. Its purpose is to improve the administration of government records and archives and to raise public awareness and increase understanding of government archives and records management programs. The goals of NAGARA are to:

1. Act as a forum for members and foster exchange among government archives and records management agencies in order to improve their programs and services.
2. Promote research, development, and use of archival management methodology.
3. Encourage research and examination of problems in the administration and preservation of government records.
4. Create and implement professional standards of administration of archival and government records.

The *Society of American Archivists* (SAA) was founded in 1936 and presently has about 4,000 members. It is a professional association of individuals and institutions concerned with the management of current records, archival administration, and the custody of historical manuscripts in government, business, and semipublic institutions. The society awards the Waldo Gifford Leland prize for outstanding published contribution in the fields of archival history, theory, or practice. The SAA has an annual convention, maintains a placement service, and conducts regular seminars and workshops.

The *Association for Information and Image Management* (AIIM) was founded in 1943 and has approximately 8,500 members. AIIM consists of manufacturers, vendors, and professional users of micrographic equipment and software. The AIIM monthly publication, *INFORM*, provides articles and information in the area of traditional micrographics management, as well as the newer technologies involving other image-based media such as optical disk and facsimile. The annual conventions and educational programs are aimed at stabilization and improvement in the technical production and use of all microforms.

The Certified Records Manager Program

The *Institute of Certified Records Managers* (ICRM) is a nonprofit, certifying organization of professional records managers and administrative officers who specialize in the field of records and information management programs. The ICRM membership is composed of individuals experienced in information requirements, records and information systems, and the related office operations and technologies. All members have met certification requirements and have received the *Certified Records Manager* (CRM) designation.

The concept of ICRM and of certification for professional records managers was developed by the American Records Management Association in 1966. That organization and the *Association of Records Executives and Administrators* (AREA) initially financed and staffed the institute. The sponsors of the institute now include the present ARMA organization as well as NAGARA, SAA, and AIIM; but the Institute of Certified Records Managers is a separate and independent organization from its sponsoring associations.

The qualifications for obtaining the credentials of a Certified Records Manager and thereby becoming a member of the institute include:

1. A minimum of three years full time or equivalent professional experience in records management in three or more of the following categories:
   - ☐ Management of Records Management program
   - ☐ records creation and use
   - ☐ active records systems
   - ☐ inactive records systems
   - ☐ records appraisal, retention, and disposition
   - ☐ records protection
   - ☐ records and information management technology.
2. A bachelor's degree from an accredited institution (professional experience may meet some portion of the required education).
3. Successful completion of all six parts of the CRM examination within a consecutive five-year period (ARMA, 1987–1988).

The certified records manager must continue to meet any requirements set by the Board of Regents to remain a member in good standing of the ICRM.

CRM Examination Outline

The CRM examination has six parts, as follows, all of which require rigorous study. (As of 1987, approximately 500 people held the CRM designation.)

Part I: Management Principles and the Records Management Program This part of the examination requires the applicant to know the characteristics of the classical, behavioral, and scientific schools of management and to apply the general management principles of planning, organizing, staffing, directing, and controlling. Further, the applicant must understand each management function and how it would be implemented into a records management program. The ability to identify problems, identify the steps in the decision-making process, and write goals and objectives is also necessary. The applicant should know the history of records management and how records management has developed through the years, as well as the role of professional organizations. Finally, the applicant must have a thorough grasp of the life cycle concept of records management and its relationship to costs and productivity in an organization.

Part II: Records Creation and Use In this part of the examination, the applicant will be required to know the interaction of all phases of information flow, to discuss intelligently cost considerations in records creation, and how correspondence, directives, and reports can be managed effectively and economically. An extensive knowledge of the latter three areas at a practical and experiential level is required.

Part III: Records Systems, Storage, and Retrieval The applicant must understand the system concept and how it applies to records management to successfully pass this part of the examination. Part III requires knowledge of all types of filing systems (alphabetic, numeric, and so forth), information retrieval systems and related technology, active file systems, active and inactive file operations with particular attention to records center operations, and the requirements of storage of nonstandard records. Further, the applicant must know what is involved in converting from one system to another, for example, from paper to film, and how to manage automated paper and film systems.

Part IV: Records Appraisal, Retention, Protection, and Disposition This part of the examination covers such topics as vital records, records inventories, and retention schedules. The applicant must understand thoroughly all aspects of a vital records program, a disaster recovery program, and an archives program. Familiarity on a practical level with the requirements of implementing these programs in a corporate setting is required.

Part V: Equipment, Supplies, and Technology The applicant must be knowledgeable about office filing equipment and supplies, as well as the equipment and supplies used in all standard records operations: micrographics, telecommunications, reprographics, word processing, and data processing. The applicant should also be familiar with ergonomics and media preservation. (*Ergonomics* is the science of the workplace; the objective of ergonomics is to integrate the physical, physiological, and psychological factors involved in creating work to maximize productivity.) Knowledge of other technologies such as image systems, integrated workstations, and computer-assisted design is also required. The applicant is expected to know the standards for equipment and technology and how they impact records management.

Part VI: Case Studies The last part of the examination involves problems that interrelate all of the previously described elements of records management.

The first five parts of the examination may be taken in any sequence, but the last part (Case Studies) cannot be taken until the candidate has passed the first five sections. In addition, the applicant must meet all of the educational and experience requirements before sitting for the examination. ARMA and its local chapters prepare members to pass the examination by offering workshops and publications. *Preparing for the CRM Examination: A Handbook* is available from ARMA headquarters.

Summary

The field of records management is expanding to include all areas of records and information resources. Consequently, most records management positions require a combination of education and experience. A variety of career opportunities exist in the field of records and information management. Entry-level positions require a high school diploma and often post-secondary courses or a bachelor's degree. Generally, management positions require several years of experience in the field and a bachelor's degree in library science, business administration, administrative information systems, or a closely related area.

The Association of Records Managers and Administrators (ARMA), The National Association of Government Archives and Records Administrators (NAGARA), the Society of American Archivists (SAA), and the Association for Information and Image Management (AIIM) are the professional associations for records personnel. They offer a variety of benefits for their members, including training opportunities and job placement assistance.

The Institute of Certified Records Managers (ICRM) administers the ICRM program and the Certified Records Manager (CRM) examination. As one requirement for certification, the CRM examination tests applicants' knowledge in all areas of records management.

List of Terms

chief information officer
records analyst
Association of Records Managers and Administrators (ARMA)
Industry Action Committee
National Association of Government Archives and Records Administrators (NAGARA)
Society for American Archivists (SAA)
Association for Information and Image Management (AIIM)
Institute of Certified Records Managers (ICRM)
Certified Records Manager (CRM)
Association of Records Executives and Administrators (AREA)
ergonomics

Discussion Questions

1. What are some of the benefits of joining a professional records management organization?
2. What are the educational and experience requirements for entry-level positions in records management?
3. What are five positions in the records management field. Describe the qualifications and duties of each position.
4. What are the duties of a records analyst? How do those responsibilities differ from those of a records manager? center supervisor?
5. Why do records management positions at all levels require more technical skills than they have in the past?

6. How does belonging to a professional organization help an individual advance in his or her job?
7. What is the Institute of Certified Records Managers and what does it do?
8. What areas of knowledge are required to pass the Certified Records Manager examination?

Activities

1. Write to ARMA International and obtain information on student membership. Present a short oral report to your class on the requirements for and benefits of student membership in ARMA. Supplement your report with your opinion of the general benefits of joining professional organizations.
2. Attend a local chapter meeting of one of the records management professional associations. Prepare a written or oral report of the meeting.
3. Survey the newspaper and job placement agencies in your area. Find what records management positions are available and the qualifications they require. Make a listing of those positions and some information about them or cut out the actual ads and compile them in a notebook for distribution to your classmates.
4. Choose a business or organization that has a full-time records manager and interview the manager to find out the career path the manager followed to reach his or her present position. Prepare a written or oral report on this information.
5. Obtain recent copies of the journals of one of the professional records management organizations from the library or by writing the organization (ARMA, AIIM, and so forth) and prepare a report summarizing the contents of the journal.

References

Association of Records Managers and Administrators, Inc. (ARMA) 4200 Somerset Drive, Suite 215, Prairie Village, Kansas 66208 (brochures 1987–1988).

ARMA International Annual Report, 1987.

ARMA International. "News, Notes & Quotes." 1986–87 issues.

ARMA, Utah—Salt Lake Chapter. "Connection." 1986–87 issues.

Goodman, David G., and Arlene Motz. "CRM Exam Review." *Proceedings of the ARMA International 32nd Annual Conference*. Anaheim, California, October 19–22, 1987, pp. 3–31.

Chapter 11 Highlight

Making a Career in Records Management

College students sometimes think that to get into a records management career, they must have a career plan from the moment they enter college. While it would be efficient to major in records management from the beginning, that particular major may not be available—then what? Fortunately, many academic areas can provide a foundation for a career in records management. Gwen Moore is presently the education coordinator for ARMA. She was formerly the records management training coordinator for the Bureau of Records Analysis of the Utah State Archives, a position she held from 1985 to 1988. Previously, she served in several records management positions including archivist, special projects clerk, records clerk, and library technician. She holds a masters of business administration degree and a bachelor of arts degree in history with an emphasis in archival administration. Gwen explains:

> *I became interested in archival administration during my last year of college. I was preparing my schedule and one of my professors suggested a directed study in archival administration. He explained what it would entail, and I thought it sounded interesting and agreed. That year was one of my favorite [years] and it also hooked me. . . . [Going] to work at the Utah State Archives, however, was not what I had originally planned. I had fully intended to go into the archival end of things, but instead the position [I obtained] was in records management. I had to gain vision in a slightly colored light. Whereas at school we [had been] interested in saving things, in records management we [were] weighing all criteria first. Some things [were] maintained, but we also wanted to destroy things that weren't needed. I think now I am very happy that I got into the records management side because there is more action. In an archives, the archivist is pretty much stuck in a building with the records, whereas in records management we are out there with the records keepers working shoulder-to-shoulder with them and their records.*

Gwen is also a Certified Records Manager and has received several awards for her work in the records management field, including "Chapter Member of the Year." In her former job as records management training coordinator, she directed colleagues in records management training programs for government agencies; planned, coordinated, and conducted records management training sessions; designed training materials, supervised other records management employees, consulted with public agencies to define information systems problems and recommend solutions, and assisted in writing policies and procedures.

Although many people with a college degree who pursue a career in records management have majored in business, Gwen Moore's background is not unusual. Students with majors in history, liberal arts, library science, and similar fields can find challenging and satisfying positions in records management.

Chapter 12 Small Business, Local Government, and State Government Applications

Learning Goals

1. To learn the types of records commonly found in small professional business offices.
2. To become familiar with records management systems in a medical clinic.
3. To become familiar with records management systems in local and state government.
4. To understand how records management is coordinated between state government and its local related offices.

Introduction

The records in a very small business that has no connection to a corporate home office often can be maintained entirely in a simple alphabetic or numeric file folder system. However, the size of the business (at a single location) actually has less impact on the records management systems used by the business than one might expect. What will affect the records management system is the range or scope of the business operations in which the company engages. For example, a single store in a national franchise operation may have a sophisticated (and often computerized) records system that is used by many other stores and maintained in a home office. A small chain of three or four stores, on the other hand, may have entirely independent and relatively unsophisticated records management operations. Finally, the single-location small business very likely will deal primarily with a paper, manual record system.

In the first part of this chapter, we will focus on records management applications in single-location businesses that have no affiliation with a larger organization. In the last half of the chapter, we will look at local government applications, some of which have a relationship to state government records management (although essentially local government offices manage their records in much the same way as single-location businesses). We will also examine some of the records management operations in state government.

The applications in this chapter will help you see how the information in previous chapters is applied in specific, practical situations. These applications can serve as a guide for setting up records management systems in similar professional and government offices.

Professional Office Records

Small businesses universally keep certain records that pertain to the customers they serve; for example, client or customer files, accounts receivable, and records of daily business operations. Small businesses, too, keep records pertaining to the companies who serve them such as accounts receivable, catalogs, and supplier files. Of course, the methods used to manage the records will vary and the business will have many records specific to its own operations.

Professional offices are those that provide medical, legal, financial, or other professional services to clients. The records management system in a professional office is said to be *client-based*; that is, the primary and vital records of the business are client records. All professional offices provide services to their clients; therefore, it is essential for offices to keep accurate records of their clients and of the services being provided to them. It is also important to maintain records security and to keep track of each individual practitioner's clients. For example, when doctors or lawyers leave a firm or clinic to open their own offices, they may take their client files with them. To avoid problems in the records system, the professional office needs an exit procedure for situations in which the practitioner leaves with client files. The following sections explain and illustrate the overall records operations in a small medical clinic and the exit procedure used in a law firm.

Records Management in a Medical Clinic

The Budge Clinic in Logan, Utah, is a small medical facility that houses eighteen physicians who practice in a variety of specialties. The clinic estimates that it serves over 300 patients per day, of whom about 25 are new patients. The clinic is located in a two-story building, which incorporates a pharmacy (see Figure 12.1), and operates a separate women's clinic in another building.

The laboratory and x-ray facilities, as well as the administrative and accounting functions for clinic staff and patients, are centralized. All patient records, which are the primary records kept, are maintained in a records center on the bottom level of the clinic. In 1987, the clinic managed between 60,000 to 100,000 patient files and related records. The Budge Clinic has three full-time and two or three part-time employees in their records department. The clinic always employs a records supervisor, but the number of records clerks varies depending on the operations that are planned. For example, extra staff are hired when the office plans to purge its files.

Current patient records are kept in the records area, a well-lighted, furnished and finished portion of the basement floor of the building in which some doctors' offices, a reception area, and the insurance offices are also located. The current patient records are stored in file folders on metal shelving in a terminal-digit system.

Figure 12.1 The Budge Clinic

Source Courtesy of The Budge Clinic, Logan, Utah.

Patient files are retrieved at night for appointments the following day and retrieved during each day as needed by doctors. The estimated daily activity in the center is 300 files pulled for appointments and another 250 pulled for analysis or other reasons.

Current Patient Records System

The current patient file folders are on open shelves in a lateral file arrangement. The clinic has used a terminal-digit system since 1970. The folders used in the system are prenumbered by the company that makes the folders. Therefore, an accession file for recording the last number used is not needed; the number on the folder is assigned to the next new patient. A rotary file system for keeping track of patient names and their assigned numbers is used.

Rotary Patient File The large rotary strip file shown in Figure 12.3 is used to record patients' names and their assigned numbers. The patient's name, DOB (date of birth), city, phone, and file number are recorded on the strip, and the strips are arranged alphabetically by last name. The strips slide so they can be easily rearranged to accommodate new patient names. In other words, the rotary file acts as an index or pointer to the actual terminal-digit system. Of course, it is absolutely imperative that the correspondence between the rotary file and the actual terminal-digit files be kept as close to 100 percent as possible.

Actually, two systems provide information to retrieve patient files: the rotary patient file and the computer billing system. Patients make appointments directly with their doctors. Each doctor's nurse then supplies a written list of appointments for the next day to the records center, and the records clerk writes in the patient's number. If the patient does not have a file, a new folder is made up when the patient arrives for his appointment. The new file is prepared in

Figure 12.2 Records Center Files

Source Courtesy of The Budge Clinic, Logan, Utah.

Figure 12.3 Rotary Patient File

Source Courtesy of The Budge Clinic, Logan, Utah.

the reception area at the new patients desk. The lists are then sent to the computer operators, who enter the information into the computer for billing purposes. At the end of the day, the computer operator generates the list of patients who will be seen the next day in the form of two 2-×-3-inch stickers for each patient. The stickers contain the patient's name, file number, physician, and so forth. One set of stickers is given to a night operator who retrieves all the patient files for the next day. The other set of stickers is attached to a billing sheet. (The billing process is described on page 184 under "Related Nonmedical Records.")

Patient Medical Records The file folders for patient medical records provide two types of information: (1) patient medical records within the folder and (2) identifying information on the outside of the folder. Within the folder, the patient information sheet is first (see Figure 12.4) followed by the continuation form (doctor's notes), lab reports with the most recent on top, x-ray reports with the most recent on top, hospital reports, referrals, and the patient's history.

As seen in Figure 12.5, the front of the folder provides additional information about the patient. A box (listing years) is printed there. The most recent year the patient was seen is marked in the box; this information is useful when files are being purged. The doctors also place a sticker (provided by drug companies) on the front of the folder if the patient is receiving a particular medication that must be known. In addition, large colored dots are placed on the front of the folder to designate unusual credit status. For example, a blue dot may mean that the patient is in arrears, a red dot may signify that the patient should not be granted credit, and a fluorescent orange dot may mean that the person has filed bankruptcy.

Medical files are sent up to doctors' offices in a dumb waiter. In order to keep the various folders for each doctor separated, the medical files are inserted into another folder labeled with the doctor's initials. When the doctor is finished with the patient's file, the file is placed in a designated holder on the wall near the doctor's office. The folders are picked up three times a day by the records staff and refiled.

Out Card When patient medical files are retrieved from the records center, an out card is put in place of the file. (The Budge Clinic refers to its out guides as out cards.) The out card, shown in Figure 12.6 and diagramed in Figure 12.7, is red plastic with clear plastic jackets for inserts. One of the jackets holds the computer slip that is printed out for the daily appointments. This slip is inserted by the night clerk when the files are pulled for the following day's appointments. The sec-

Figure 12.4 Patient Information Form

ACCOUNT NUMBER B

THE BUDGE CLINIC
LOGAN, UTAH

Telephone

Birth Date
Referred by

History No.
Register Date

NAME ______ Surname First Second
SPOUSE

AGE SEX ADDRESS

FAMILY HISTORY

Occupation

Father ______ Name Age Health

Mother ______ Name Age Health

Sibs (Ages & Health

FAMILY ILLNESSES

Allergy	Heart	Diabetes
Skin	G. I.	Thyroid
EENT	CNS	Blood
Bronchial	Kidney-Bladder	Chromosomal
Lung	Muscular-Ortho	Other

PAST HISTORY

Pregnancy, Labor, Delivery, Neonatal
Birth Wt.
(Include Blood Type, Rh, VDRL, Drugs, Illnesses)

Feeding, Allergy

Growth, Development

Accidents, Hospitalizations, Injuries

Sickness

Previous Immunizations

Miscellaneous (Water Supply, milk, habits, drugs)

SYSTEM REVIEW

Allergy
HEENT
Skin
Resp.
CV
G. I.
GU
CNS
Thyroid
Diabetes
Blood
Psych.
Musculo-Skeletal

Date ______ Age ______ Sex ______

Chief Complaint ______

Present Illness ______

Physical Exam. Weight ______ Height ______ O. F. C. ______ C. C ______

Temp. ______ Pulse ______ Resp. ______ B. P. ______

Gen. ______

Skin ______

Breasts ______

Head ______

EENT ______

Neck & Nodes ______

Heart ______

Chest & Lungs ______

Abdomen ______

Genit. & Rectal ______

Extrem. & Back ______

Neurol. ______

Extra ______

Diagnosis ______

Treatment ______

Source Courtesy of The Budge Clinic, Logan, Utah.

Figure 12.5 Patient File

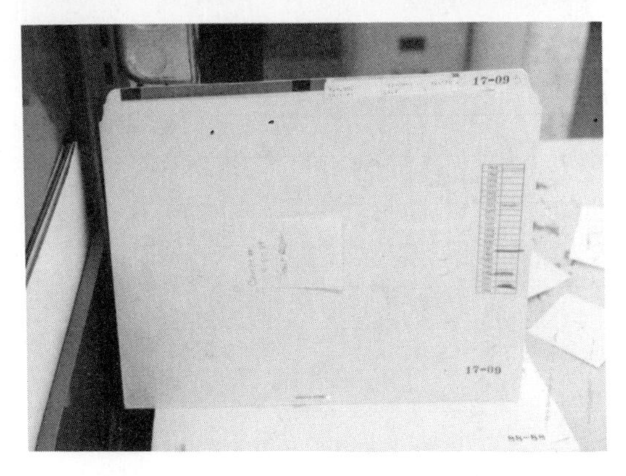

Source Courtesy of The Budge Clinic, Logan, Utah.

Figure 12.6 Out Card for Patient Files

Source Courtesy of The Budge Clinic, Logan, Utah.

Figure 12.7 Diagram of an Out Card

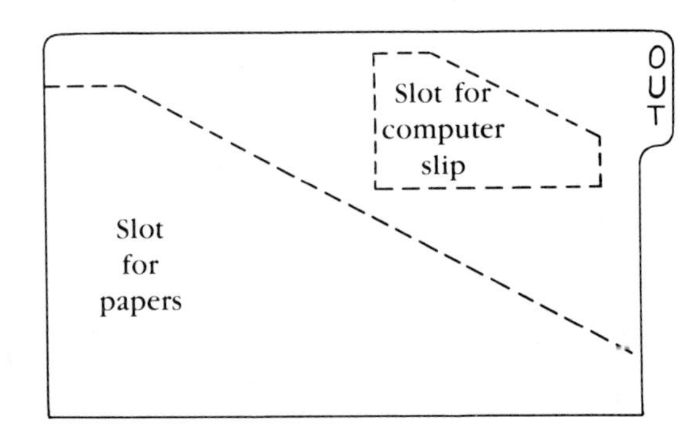

ond slot is used to insert papers that come in while the file is out.

Inactive Patient Records System (Microfilm Jacket)

On about an annual basis, the records staff purges patient medical files that are five years old with no activity during that five years. The contents of those files are microfilmed, hard copies are shredded, and the file folder (and number) is used again. The microfilm is cut into strips and inserted into microfilm jackets, which constitute the inactive patient files. Each day when the records department receives the lists of appointments, if a patient does not have a file, the patient's name is checked against the microfilm jacket files to see if inactive records already exist. If so, the microfilm records are copied and put in the patient's new folder.

The jackets are filed alphabetically by last name in a *notch and color system.* In other words, notches along the top color-coded edge of each jacket designate how the jackets are filed in trays.

A code is used to designate the arrangement of notches for each letter of the alphabet (two notches are used for each letter).

For example, assuming there are forty spaces across the top of the jacket that could be notched, A = notches in the third and eighth spaces, B = notches in the fifth and tenth spaces, and so forth. The strip of color across the top of the jacket is used to code the first letter of the patient's first name with a predetermined color (for example, red = A, B, C; green = D, E, F, and so forth). The microfilm jacket for Dan Sampson would appear as follows:

> S (Sampson) = notches in 25th and 39th spaces at top of jacket; D (Dan) = green strip across top of microfilm jacket. The operator chooses a jacket with a green strip across the top and uses the notching machine to notch it for the last name (Sampson). The jacket is then filed alphabetically by last name within each color set; for example, Sampson, Dan; Simmons, David; Smith, Denise, and so forth.

With this type of system, the notches will ensure that all last names beginning with a certain letter are filed together. The color-coded edge will ensure that all first names beginning with a certain letter are filed together within a particular notched section of the file. However, within each color-coded section, the jackets are filed first by surname and then, if the surnames are the same, by first name. As illustrated in Figure 12.8, the jackets for all four individuals are notched for S in the same locations. "Dan Sampson" is filed before "Dora Sampson," and both jackets have green strips because the first names start with D. The surname "Slick" follows "Sampson," but the strip on that jacket is also green (for "Dixie"). The surnames "Speck" and "Stine" follow "Sampson" and "Slick" in alphabetical order, but the strips on those jackets are red (for C—"Clem" and "Carol"). The code for the file must be kept available for clerks to refer to it, and retrieval takes a little time; but this file is accessed infrequently.

Figure 12.8 Notch and Color System

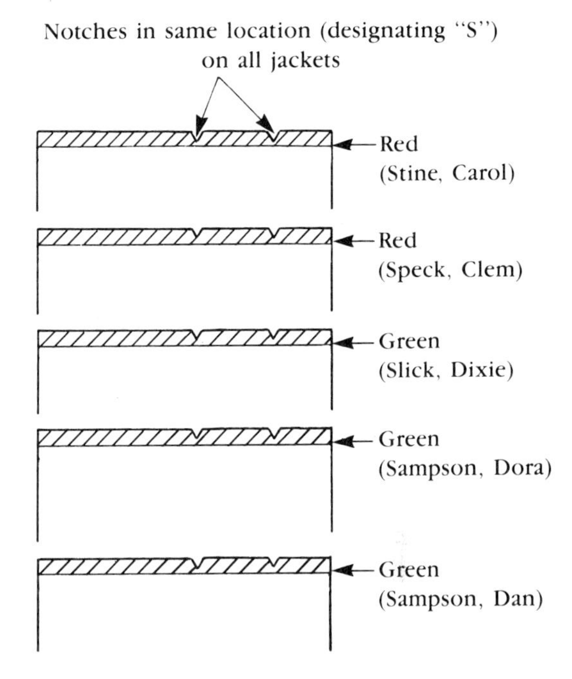

Related Medical Records

Several other types of medical records supplement the records system.

Transient Patient File Physicians often see patients who do not live in the area and are not likely to return. Although records for these *transient patients* must be kept, it is impractical to incorporate them into the current patient record system. Therefore, in The Budge Clinic, these files are kept in folders in a vertical file cabinet in alphabetical order by last name. The name of the transient patient is also kept on the rotary patient file.

Deceased Patient Files When a patient dies, his or her folder is removed from active patient medical files and placed in this file, where the folders are filed alphabetically by last name.

Miscellaneous Medical Records Another category of medical records are those for patients who see a clinic doctor in the hospital but not at the clinic. Doctors take turns serving in the hospital emergency room and may treat people who are not their regular patients. These folders also are kept in a vertical file cabinet alphabetically by last name. Because reference to miscellaneous patient (hospital) files is not on the rotary patient file, these folders, too, are checked when a new patient medical folder is created. If the patient has hospital records, the records are moved to their clinic folder. When hospital records come into the clinic, the active and inactive medical records are checked to see if the patient has an existing file.

X-Ray Envelopes Every x-ray is numbered sequentially on the film itself and the film is stored in an envelope. The film number is recorded on a patient card. Based on the x-ray(s), an x-ray report is sent to Records for the patient medical folders. The latest two years of x-ray envelopes, along with the patient x-ray card file, are kept in the x-ray department both for security and convenience. Older films are arranged by the film number on shelving in a separate location.

Card File A card file of patient records that are very old (prior to 1970) is kept. These cards have only the dates that the patient was seen plus doctor's notes. The cards are filed alphabetically by last name of patient.

Related Nonmedical Records

In addition to medical records, two other kinds of records are needed.

Charge Forms When a patient comes to the clinic, he or she picks up a charge form at the reception desk. One of the patient stickers generated by the computer is put on the form; the form itself has hundreds of services listed. The form is taken to the doctor's office (or lab) where the services provided are noted by the nurse. The form is then sent to data entry where the charges are inserted. The charge form is the entry data for the computer billing system.

Insurance Records The Insurance Department adjoins the records section in the clinic. Insurance records for patients are kept in a separate color-coded system. Alphabetical file guides divide the file, and folders are filed alphabetically by the last name. In this system, the color of the file folder indicates the first letter of the first name. Each folder has letters down the side. On the folder, the first letter of the patient's last name is covered with a black marker and all As, Bs, and so forth are in the separate sections designated by file guides. Because the folders are arranged laterally (with side tabs), a black mark in the wrong location is visible immediately, so misfiles are easy to see. The filing procedure is similar to the notch and color system used in the microfilm jacket system.

Exit Procedure in a Legal Office

Law offices also have a client-based records system and need to maintain the integrity and security of client files. Toward this end, the records manager implements a plan called the *exit procedure*. The following information is the exit procedure used at Butler and Binion, a Houston, Texas, law firm; it could be applicable in any law office with more than one attorney (Franklin, 1987). The general procedure can apply to any office in which clients are seen by individual practitioners, and the integrity of client files must be maintained when a practitioner leaves the firm.

Ownership of firm records is the first consideration when establishing exit procedures. This includes all records—client records, reading files, billing files, pencil or working files, and personnel and management records. The firm must decide if records created by a representative of the firm can be considered to be personal and under what circumstances those records can be released.

As soon as the records department is notified of the departure of an attorney, the records manager should meet with that person and review the firm's requirements for the removal of any records the lawyer wishes to take. At Butler and Binion, a computer printout of all open records for which that attorney is responsible is prepared. Each item is reviewed by the section head. Then, it is the departing attorney's responsibility to make the records department aware of the disposition of every record on that inventory.

Because the departure of partners usually involves complex procedures and negotiations, the records manager should work closely with the management committee of the partnership on each case to determine the procedures for the release of firm records. All records that are to remain at the firm are identified for disposition by the records department. As soon as it is known who the responsible new attorneys will be, the records are either delivered to those attorneys or closed and sent to off-site storage. Efficient disposition of the exit records is very important from the standpoint of malpractice, since about 50 percent of all law-related malpractice claims stem from poor law office and records management operations and consist mostly of missed procedural deadlines.

When client records are released, one decision to be made is what records are considered the property of the client and what records are considered *firm-privileged* and should not be released. Firm-privileged records can include attorney notes, research, drafts, and internal memoranda. Those portions of the record should be removed before releasing them. Because attorney working files contain confidential client information, the firm policy on ownership should be very clear on the requirements necessary for their release. The attorney should guarantee that the records contain no original documents and should agree to make any portion of the record available upon request.

Documentation for the release approval should contain the client's written request for release and a designated partner's authorization to the records manager to release the records. The records department's internal records are then noted to include date of release, recipient, and authorizing partner. Before records are actually released, all accounts receivable should be cleared.

A formal exit procedure will facilitate the exiting process. Therefore, an exit checklist (shown in Figure 12.9) circulated to administrative managers ensures that no step has been overlooked. The records department maintains a separate checklist of the exit procedure that documents the completion of the exit process (shown in Figure 12.10).

In the interview with the departing attorney, the records manager should give the attorney a copy of the firm's policy on the release of records, along with a step-by-step explanation of the release procedure. The computer printout, which will detail the transfer of active records, should be delivered and discussed. At Butler & Binion, the procedure is to pull the closed files from off-site storage, review and remove firm-privileged records, review closed personal files, give departing attorneys a list of their files, and ask them to make arrangements to have the files transferred to the new site or the files will be destroyed in ninety days.

Communication is one of the primary keys in an exit procedure. Departure can be a very emotional situation. It is part of the records manager's responsibility to be sensitive to that situation and to carry out the exit procedures to the best of his or her ability and in the best interest of the firm.

Figure 12.9 Exit Checklist for Managers

Butler & Binion Exit Checklist

Please initial and date the appropriate space to signify that each item has been processed. When all items have been completed, please return this form to the Director of Administration.

Date: ________ Name: ________________ Last Working Date: ________

_____ Determine status of accounts receivable and unbilled time

_____ Determine reassignment of client matters

_____ Check status of American Express, telephone charges, personal account *$__________

_____ Determine status of outstanding travel advances *$__________

_____ Determine status of club memberships

_____ Determine status of time sheets through last date

_____ Reassign secretary

_____ Remove name from building, telephone and legal directories

_____ Collect parking card

_____ Inform switchboard operator and mailroom

_____ Check return of portable dictation unit

_____ Remove library books from office

_____ Cancel Lexis identification number

_____ Determine location and reassignment of open files

_____ Retrieve and return closed files

_____ Determine disposition of closed files

*Please indicate if outstanding amount should be deducted from paycheck

Comments: ____

____

____

Source LaVerne Franklin, Butler & Binion, Houston, Texas.

Records Management in Local Government

City and county offices that deal with licensing, law enforcement, utilities, and hundreds of other public services constitute local government. The larger the city, the more the records management system begins to resemble that of a multinational corporation. However, thousands of small local government offices perform daily services for their citizens with a minimum of complexity.

Figure 12.10 Exit Checklist for Records Department

Records Department Exit Checklist

Name: ______________________ Date: ____________

Section: ______________ Last Working Day: ____________

_____ Policy on release of records discussed

_____ Computer printout of active records delivered and discussed

_____ Review and remove firm-privileged records

_____ Review closed personal files procedures

_____ Update Records Department Records

    _____ Client File (computer)

    _____ Docket Inventory

    _____ Docket Calendar

    _____ Conflict-of-Interest

Comments ____

Source LaVerne Franklin, Butler & Binion, Houston, Texas.

These offices use manual systems for many of their records management operations and probably will continue to do so for many years.

Records management in local government is most concerned with keeping track of registrations, licenses, cases, addresses, incidents, and other records of that nature. Some of these records provide the information needed to assign services and accurately tax citizens. In some locales, protection of records is a major concern, and local government must provide for the eventuality of disasters. The following sections describe two particular records applications: (1) practical methods of disaster recovery, and (2) the records management procedures in a small police department.

Disaster Recovery in Orange County

The following information is excerpted from *Records Management Systems for County and Municipal Governments: Case Studies* (Swift, Browne, and Nissenson, 1987) and describes practical procedures for disaster recovery.

Because California has no comprehensive statutes governing county and municipal records, and the state offers no practical assistance to local records officials, a direct obligation has been placed on counties and municipalities to organize and preserve their own records. Orange County, the largest county in California and the seventh most populous county in the United States, is in the process of developing a Vital Records and Disaster Recovery Program by identifying the county's most important records and providing a system of protection from loss due to natural and man-made disasters such as fire, flood, and earthquake.

The Orange County program is significantly different from virtually all others because of its capability to cope with the salvage of damaged paper records (usually water-soaked records), even after a major regional disaster of a magnitude that could destroy the normal supply and support systems that are generally available after a localized disaster. This capability was developed as a direct result of original laboratory research conducted by Orange County records personnel.

The Major Threats in Orange County

The conventional methods of salvage are totally inadequate to deal with the major disasters that are likely to occur in Orange County. Conventional methods dictate that ideally all important records should be protected through the maintenance of a duplicate copy stored off-site; but a complete protection system may not be in place. In an isolated disaster such as one affecting a single building, the objective of the salvage operation would be to dry the paper as quickly as possible to avoid mold growth (which can occur within forty-eight hours) or when drying is not possible, to prevent mold growth by freezing the records until resources can be found to dry them. Drying techniques include interleaving paper towels or other absorbent paper between the sheets of wet paper, simple air drying, or obtaining the services of a firm that can dry the records in a vacuum chamber.

The threat of large regional disasters in Orange County, such as earthquake or flood, could be so devastating to the entire region that there would be no support system to carry out salvage operations. Orange County could not depend on the availability of freezer space at cold storage plants, access to a vacuum chamber, or even sufficient paid or volunteer staff to dry the records at the disaster site.

First, there is the threat of earthquake along either the San Andreas or Newport-Inglewood Faults. According to experts, a major earthquake along either fault will almost certainly strike the area sometime in the next few decades. When it hits, Orange County can expect a major or total disruption of electrical power and telephone service for weeks or even months. Transportation will be severely disrupted as a result of the collapse of freeway and railroad overpasses, landslides and debris from buildings. A recent study predicts that fire storms will destroy entire neighborhoods, and thousands of homes and businesses that survive the initial earthquake will be lost. In Orange County alone, 50,000 people could be homeless, 100,000 injured, and several thousand dead.

Also, in 1970, the Army Corps of Engineers found that the threat of a major flood along the Santa Ana River was much greater than previously assumed. Currently, the Santa Ana River, which runs through the heart of Orange County, is viewed as the greatest flood threat in the western United States. Over one million people live or work in the vicinity of the river's path. In view of these threats, the Orange County records management personnel decided to conduct its own laboratory tests to determine what practical steps could be taken to preserve records.

Wet Paper and Mold Growth Tests

Shortly after the laboratory was established, the department heard that the "printing" on a photocopy would probably dissolve in water and the information would be lost. Immediately, a photocopy was placed in a pan of water to test this assertion. A week later, the printing was still fine and the paper had not even begun to disintegrate. Subsequently, a variety of paper records were submerged in water for up to six weeks without major damage to the paper or inks. Some paper, in fact, was kept damp for a year without major deterioration.

The discovery that wet paper did not distintegrate even after long periods of time led to further investigation on another serious problem that occurs when paper is wet for long periods of time—mold growth. If the growth of mold on wet paper could be prevented, it would not be necessary to rush records to a freezer or dry them within a few days. One of the tests in controlling mold growth was to spray fungicide (which was mixed with denatured alcohol in accordance with instructions in the literature) on the outside surface of a stack of wet records (mold typically grows on the outside first) to kill any existing mold or spores. Because the fungicide has limited residual action, the records were sealed immediately in a plastic bag to avoid further contamination from the spores normally found in the air. The method appeared to be successful, but later tests showed that alcohol alone would serve as a disinfectant and kill (or inhibit the growth of) the mold and spores. Both isopropyl (rubbing) and denatured (industrial) alcohols were effective.

A Practical Procedure for Stopping Mold Growth

Tentative instruction for using the alcohol method in an actual disaster involves using approximately 1 to 2 ounces of alcohol per cubic foot of records. All six sides of the stack of records (top, bottom, and sides) must be thoroughly sprayed. The inside of the plastic bag must also be sprayed prior to inserting the records. Clear plastic bags are best because the condition of the records can be viewed easily. Occasionally, a second spraying may be necessary if mold begins to grow after a few weeks. When using alcohol, precautions must be taken to avoid prolonged exposure to skin or breathing of the spray mist. Because alcohol is flammable, it must not be used near a source of ignition such as pilot lights, open flames, or electric motors. This seems to be an excellent solution to the problem of dealing with wet records after a major areawide disaster (assuming that several gallons of alcohol can be safely stockpiled). The records could be kept in the bags for weeks or months, until resources became available to dry them.

Paper Acidity Tests

Mold grows best in slightly acidic conditions; therefore, the acidity of various paper samples was tested, followed by an attempt to grow mold on the paper. This test showed that the paper with the highest acid content supported mold growth well, whereas those samples with less acid (pH of 5 or higher) were poor growth mediums for the mold. This was recognized as an important discovery, since it is possible to alter the acid level of paper using "deacidification solutions."

Archivists sometimes use these solutions to "deacidify" or neutralize the acid in paper and thereby increase the life of the document. Therefore, a stack of paper was soaked in water. Half the stack was sprayed with a deacidification solution (on the outside only) and half was not. After two weeks in a warm, humid environment (in a plastic bag in a warm room), mold had nearly covered the untreated portion, but the treated half was virtually mold free.

A Practical Method for Deacidifying Paper

Because it would be difficult to obtain the usual deacidification solutions after a major disaster, as a practical alternative, ordinary baking soda (sodium bicarbonate) and water was tested. It was found that a solution of 3 to 5 tablespoons of baking soda in a quart of water was fairly effective in preventing mold growth on wet paper (there is no need to seal the records in bags with this technique). The advantages of using the baking soda solution is that it is inexpensive, readily available, and absolutely harmless to the persons applying it. The one disadvantage of using the solution (as explained by a member of the staff of the Library of Congress Research and Testing Office) is that the sodium ions in the baking soda may eventually contribute to the breakdown of the paper over a period of time. However, if there is no alternative available and if the records are scheduled for destruction in a few years anyway, or if the records could be copied (microfilmed or photocopied) after being dried, the baking soda treatment should be considered as a potential salvage method. On the other hand, the deacidification solutions used by archivists, if available, would not contribute to the eventual breakdown of the paper and would actually increase the life of the paper.

In both the alcohol and deacidification (including baking soda solution) techniques, the objective is to stabilize the wet records until resources are available to dry them. One objection to these methods is that when records are kept wet for long periods of time, the inks may diffuse or bleed until they are no longer readable. The next procedure, therefore, tested this theory.

Ink Dissolution Test

When records personnel tested ink for dissolution, they found that water-soluble inks tend to diffuse very rapidly and often nearly disappear within a few days. After that, the inks that are left (presumably nonwater-soluble inks) diffuse very slowly. It was found that there was very little difference, as a rule, in the condition of the insoluble ink from the end of day one through day fourteen when the test was stopped. Since most salvage efforts do not get started for at least a day or two after the disaster, it would appear that, in general, the completely water-soluble inks will usually be lost no matter what technique is used. But there may not be a major problem with the legibility of insoluble ink records, even if they are wet for a long period of time.

Because the salvage methods used by Orange County records personnel have never been used in an actual emergency, they must be considered experimental and should be reserved for those situations in which conventional methods cannot be used.

Records Management in a City Police Department

The Police Department of the city of Logan, Utah, is typical of a local government operations in a small city (pop. 35,000). The department has thirty-three police officers and eleven additional staff including clerks, crosswalk guards, animal control personnel, and office staff. The department's major records management activity is the system for dealing with criminal activity and traffic enforcement. The police department also handles li-

Figure 12.11 Logan Police Department

Source Courtesy of City of Logan, Utah, Police Department.

censing for bicycles and animals. Because the department shares information with other local, county, and state agencies, some of its records are sent to or received from other offices both manually and via computer.

The Logan Police Department is housed in a one-story and basement building near other city offices (see Figure 12.11). A reception area and the administrative offices are located on the ground floor, along with the offices of the chief of police and captain. The booking area, squad room, roll call room, evidence room, holding cells, and detective offices are located in the basement level. The department does not have a jail, so prisoners are kept in holding cells until they can be transported to other incarceration facilities.

The primary records of the police department are incident reports and arrest records. Incident reports are extremely important because they constitute the information for estimating criminal activity, and are the basis for criminal investigation. Arrest records are equally important because they provide a chronology of activity for legal purposes. The criminal process system is a complex interaction of citizens, suspects, police officers, lawyers, and courts. Eventually, an incident may involve all of these elements, or it may start and stop solely with the involvement of the police. In either case, one must understand the basic process to understand the records management system.

Incident and Arrest System

The process begins with a personal complaint to the police department or a complaint that comes through a dispatcher by phone and computer. The dispatcher is a county sheriff employee and is located in a separate building across the street from the Logan police station. If the dispatcher determines that an incident falls within the jurisdiction of the Logan city police, the complaint information is sent to a computer terminal at the Logan police department.

Figure 12.12 Incident Report Form

INCIDENT REPORT **LOGAN CITY POLICE**

Victim (Business)
Victim (Person)
Address of Victim

CASE NUMBER

Date	
Time	Day

Reported By Address Telephone

Nature of Incident	
Location of Occurrence	Area No.

Date	
Time	Day

Received By	Officer Assigned	Time Assigned
Time on Location	Time Clear	Arrest No.

Victim Home Ph.	Business Phone	Crime Code	Property Code
			Property Amount

HOW INCIDENT WAS REPORTED

☐ phone ☐ in view ☐ letter ☐ twx

☐ person ☐ radio ☐ telegram ☐ other ____________

DETAILS OF INCIDENT:

OFFICER'S INVESTIGATION:

☐ cleared ☐ active

☐ unfounded ☐ suspended

☐ no further action

X ______________________ __/__/__

Investigating Officer Date

THIS REPORT MUST BE COMPLETED BY END OF SHIFT

Source Courtesy of City of Logan, Utah, Police Department.

Figure 12.13 Pickup Baskets for Reports

Source Courtesy of City of Logan, Utah, Police Department.

The complaint information is investigated and may result in a filed incident report or an arrest and its related records.

Incident Report An *incident report* (shown in Figure 12.12) is prepared by the dispatcher and transmitted to the police department by computer. Police officers are dispatched to the scene of the incident. The printout of the incident report received by the department is transferred to the top portion of a three-part form. The form is numbered by year and then sequentially (for example, 87-0001), and this number becomes the case number.

The entire form is placed in a basket (see Figure 12.13) to be picked up by an investigating officer, who fills out the bottom portion of the form after he or she has investigated the incident. Then the parts of the form are distributed. Information concerning the investigation is entered into the computer; next, one part (white) is filed in a vertical file using a numeric system. The files are categorized by 100s. A second part (yellow) is placed on one of several clipboards labeled by type of incident (crime). The clipboards are hung on a wall to be referred to by officers (see Figure 12.14). The last part (card) is kept only if the incident is one that will require follow-up. These cards are arranged in a card file by subject (crime) and alphabetically by victim's name within each subject section. The cards are purged every

Figure 12.14 Wall-mounted Clipboards

Source Courtesy of City of Logan, Utah, Police Department.

five years, but the incident information on the computer is never purged.

Simple though they may be, items such as baskets and clipboards are practical, inexpensive, and efficient methods of keeping records that will be picked up or need to be referred to frequently.

Arrest Report People who have been picked up as suspects in the commission of a crime are kept in holding cells until they are booked. The booking process includes filling out arrest slips and fingerprinting. The arrest information is first prepared by hand by the arresting officer. This handwritten slip is then typed onto a three-part form. (The arrest report form is shown in Figure 12.15.) A white copy of the arrest report is kept in an arrest book filed by number in ascending order with the most recent number on top. The number is assigned sequentially using the same procedure as that for incident reports. A second copy (yellow) is sent to the city or county attorney. The last copy (pink) goes back to the arresting officer.

Arrest Cards and Fingerprint Cards The arrest card is typed at the same time that the arrest report is prepared. The information on the arrest card includes the name of the arrested person, crime, arresting officer, and so forth. If an arrest card already exists, the new information is added to it. Arrest cards are filed alphabetically by last name of the arrested person. The information on the arrest card is always checked against the arrest report for accuracy and typed into the computer records. Arrest cards are not purged unless the record of arrest is expunged by legal proceedings. Fingerprint cards, if prepared, are sent to the Federal Bureau of Investigation (FBI) or to the Bureau of Criminal Investigation (BCI), depending on the type of crime.

Accident Reports and Issued Licenses

When the police department is notified of an accident, an officer responds. If an accident has occurred, the officer then calls the department to get a number for the accident report. These reports are numbered and filed sequentially, and the number provided to the officer is determined from an accession book. The handwritten copy of the accident report is brought to the office and, if the accident was minor, only the handwritten copy is kept and the information is entered into the computer. If the accident is major, the report is typed on an accident report form and entered into the computer records.

Dog licenses are provided by the police department, and, for this, prenumbered forms and tags are used. A copy of the form and its associated tag are given to the owner; the original of the form is sent to the city offices where the information is entered and kept on computer.

Bicycle licenses are handled similarly. The form and the license itself have the same number. The owner of the bicycle is given the license; the department keeps the two-part form filed by name of owner and by license number.

Records Management in State Government

No universal system of records management exists for state governments, although all state government agencies are guided by federal records legislation and requirements. Each state devises its own system for managing the records of state offices and, in some cases, for local government offices, as well. The following information on the Bureau of Records Analysis of the Utah State Division of Archives and Records Service provides insight into the records management operations within a state government system.

The organization chart for the Department of Administrative Services for the State of Utah, of which the Utah State Archives is a part, is shown in Figure 12.16.

The Utah State Archives retains government records only, both state and local, and some historical records. Therefore, in this

Figure 12.15 Arrest Report Form

CITY OF LOGAN
POLICE
RECORD OF ARREST

INCIDENT NUMBER ______

ARREST NUMBER ______

NAME: LAST	FIRST	MIDDLE	JUVENILE CUSTODY INFORMATION		
ALIASES: LAST	FIRST	MIDDLE	FATHER	ADDRESS	PHONE
RESIDENCE:			MOTHER	ADDRESS	PHONE
AGE	DOB	PLACE OF BIRTH	GUARDIAN	ADDRESS	PHONE

SEX	HGT	WGT	EYES	HAIR	RACE	HISPANIC ☐ NON-HISPANIC ☐	SCHOOL	GRADE	DROPOUT YES ☐ NO ☐

SCARS, MARKS, TATTOOS, ETC.	SS NUMBER	OTHER JUVENILES INVOLVED
OCCUPATION / EMPLOYER	DRIVERS LICENSE NUMBER	RELEASED TO / REASON FOR DETENTION
RELATIVE	CITY, STATE, PHONE	PARENTS NOTIFIED YES ☐ NO ☐ / REASON FOR NOT NOTIFYING
DATE OF OFFENSE / TIME	PLACE	CHILD LIVING WITH: BOTH PARENTS ☐ FATHER ☐ MOTHER ☐ GUARDIAN ☐ OTHER ☐
DATE OF ARREST / TIME	PLACE	ARRESTING OFFICER: NO.
OFFENDERS VEHICLE / MAKE	MODEL / YEAR / LIC. NO.	STATE / COLOR

CHG.	STATUTE CITATION	INITIAL CHARGE AND CLASSIFICATION	DISPOSITION	NCIC CODE	DUI TIMES
					FIRST OBSERVED
1					STOP MADE
2					FIELD TEST
3					ARRESTED
4					BAKER RULE
5					TEST RAN

DESCRIPTION OF OFFENSE(S):

EXHIBITS OR DOCUMENTARY EVIDENCE AND DISPOSITION:

WITNESS 1	ADDRESS	PHONE	AGE	INVOLVEMENT
WITNESS 2	ADDRESS	PHONE	AGE	INVOLVEMENT
WITNESS 3	ADDRESS	PHONE	AGE	INVOLVEMENT
WITNESS 4	ADDRESS	PHONE	AGE	INVOLVEMENT
WITNESS 5	ADDRESS	PHONE	AGE	INVOLVEMENT
WITNESS 6	ADDRESS	PHONE	AGE	INVOLVEMENT
VICTIM 1	ADDRESS	PHONE	AGE	DISCIP. AND AMOUNT OF LOSS
VICTIM 2	ADDRESS	PHONE	AGE	DISCIP. AND AMOUNT OF LOSS

ANY PRIOR ARRESTS	YES ☐ NO ☐	NCIC CHECKED	YES ☐ NO ☐	LOCAL FILES CHECKED	YES ☐ NO ☐	ARREST CARD MADE ☐
INCARCERATED YES ☐ NO ☐	BAILED $	DATE	TIME	TO APPEAR	DATE / TIME	PHOTO NO.

WHITE - ORIGINAL CANARY - ATTORNEY PINK - PRESS and OFFICER

ARREST NUMBER ______

Source Courtesy of City of Logan, Utah, Police Department.

Figure 12.16 Organization Chart

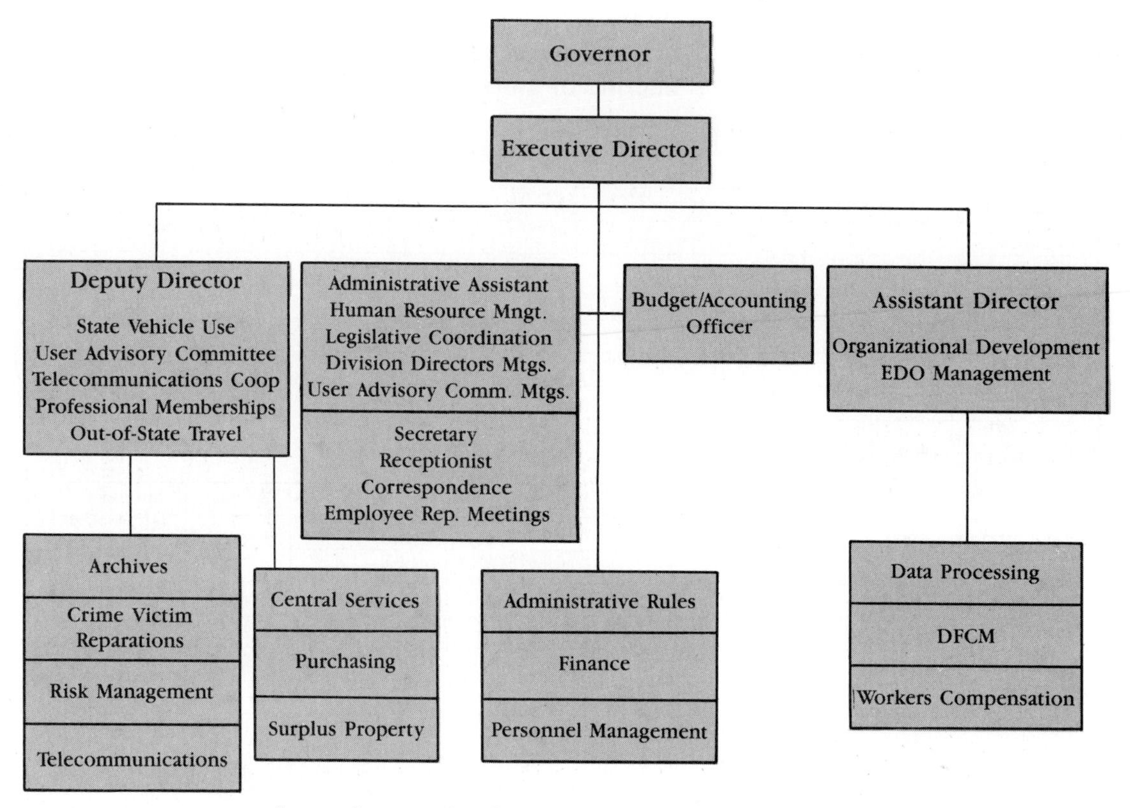

Source Courtesy of Utah State Archives.

case, the term "archives" refers to a larger category of records than just historical records. In fact, very few historical records are kept in the Utah State Archives. The primary function of the archives is to maintain and store the records of the executive branch of the state government. Records are maintained in two locations: the basement of the capitol building and in a branch office. The Utah State Archives offers a useful service to state agencies and local government offices through the Bureau of Records Analysis by providing records analysts to assist with records management. Analysts normally spend four days in the agency office and one day in the home office (archives). This service helps the state agencies and local offices coordinate their records management systems with those of the Utah State Archives, particularly in the storage of government records. In this way, the archives significantly reduces the chances that its records personnel will have to deal with incompatible records systems.

The Utah State Archives microfilms records (if it is determined that there is a need to do so), stores records in a records center (in hard copy), and provides records for research purposes. As a part of the previously described service to state and local government agencies, the Utah State Archives also provides records management training through a records management training coordinator (see the highlight following Chapter 11).

The records center and microfilming

Figure 12.17 Inventory Worksheet

Utah State Archives
Inventory Worksheet

Department or Office	Date

Division	Bureau

Address

Responsible Authority and Title

Records Officer	Phone
Person Filling Out Inventory (if other than records officer)	Phone

Records Series Information

Records Series

Varying Title(s)

Location (specify room number, building, etc.)	Inclusive Dates

Arrangement of Files ☐ alphabetical ☐ numerical ☐ alphanumerical
☐ Other (specify) ______

Filed by (e.g., invoice #)	Annual Volume Accumulation

Purpose

Description (types of forms and information included)

Format: ☐ paper ☐ microform ☐ automated data system ☐ audio tapes
☐ video tapes ☐ other (specify) ______

Quantity/Volume:		Size:
no. of letter drawers	______	
no. of legal drawers	______	
no. of cartons	______	length ____ width ____ height ____
no. of volumes (books)	______	length ____ width ____ height ____
no. of card drawers	______	length ____ width ____ height ____
no. of map drawers	______	length ____ width ____ height ____
no. of shelves	______	length ____ width ____ height ____

other ______

Agency Code	Records Series no.	Date

continued

Figure 12.17 continued

Records Series Information, Continued

Does the record you have described contain any information on individuals?
☐ yes ☐ no

If yes, please indicate which types of data by checking the boxes below

☐ age
☐ alcohol/drug addiction
☐ appearance
☐ assets/debts
☐ birthplace
☐ brothers/sisters
☐ checking/savings accts.
☐ civil/criminal court
☐ credit rating
☐ current/past address
☐ date of birth
☐ dental history
☐ driver license number
☐ educational level
☐ employer
☐ employment history
☐ expenditures
☐ family history
☐ finger prints
☐ food purchase/ consumption
☐ GPA/class standing
☐ home ownership
☐ job position information
☐ living conditions
☐ marital status
☐ medical information
☐ membership in groups
☐ military service
☐ mortgage information
☐ motor vehicle ownership
☐ name
☐ national origin
☐ next of kin
☐ number of children
☐ occupation
☐ occupational licenses
☐ occupational preferences
☐ parent's birth information
☐ personality inventory
☐ physical characteristics
☐ physical disabilities
☐ police record
☐ political affiliations
☐ property ownership
☐ psychiatric information
☐ public housing occupancy
☐ race/ethnic group
☐ references
☐ religious preferences
☐ salary/income
☐ salary withholdings
☐ security/investigation
☐ sex
☐ signature
☐ social security number
☐ tax information
☐ telephone number
☐ victim information

other unique identifiers
☐ ________

Is this the record copy? ☐ yes ☐ no.
If this is not the record copy, where is the record copy located? ________

Is this record duplicated in another office?
☐ yes ☐ no. If this record is duplicated in another office, which one(s)? ________

Does your office receive federal funds to support the function these records serve?
☐ yes ☐ no

Cite related federal and state statutes as well as rules which may apply to these records

How many times do you refer to these records during one month per filing cabinet drawer? ________

Recommended Retention and Disposition

Total Retention ________
In Office ________
In Records Center ________
Final Disposition
☐ Transfer to the state archives with authority to weed
☐ Microfilm and destroy the original (If this box is checked, the microfilm must also be scheduled)
☐ Destroy/erase
☐ Other (specify) ________

Reason(s) for recommended retention and disposition?

General schedule citation ________

Source Courtesy of Utah State Archives.

Figure 12.18 Implementation Schedule

RECORDS MANAGEMENT IMPLEMENTATION SCHEDULE

BUREAU OF RECORDS ANALYSIS
UTAH STATE ARCHIVES AND RECORDS SERVICE
ARCHIVES BUILDING/STATE CAPITOL
SALT LAKE CITY, UTAH 84114
533-5250

ANALYST: ____

DEPARTMENT: ____
DIRECTOR: ____
ADDRESS: ____
RECORDS OFFICER: ____

ACTIVITY	DATE
Read statutes	
Obtain organization chart	
Read section of current budget report and other relevant publications about department	
Write other states for their schedules for this department	
Check Federal Guidelines	
Check records analysis agency file	
Check Taking Stock II for agency data processing equipment	
Introduction letter to administrator	
Meet with administrator	
Meet with management	
Select records officer and/or note on local system agency file	
Outline records officers responsibilities	
Negotiate implementation schedule	

ACTIVITY	DIVISION 1	DIVISION 2	DIVISION 3	DIVISION 4	DIVISION 5	DIVISION 6	DIVISION 7	DIVISION 8
Inventory records (DATE)								
Analyze records (DATE)								
Submit records series to the SRC (DATE)								
Provide instruction in:								
Files management								
Records retention scheduling								
Semi-active records								
Office automation								
Historically valuable records								
Information Practices Act								
Classify records & complete IPA worksheets								
Assist with implementing schedule								

Source Courtesy of Utah State Archives.

operations of the Utah State Archives are similar to those described elsewhere in this book, so we will focus on another important function, records analysis.

Records analysis in state and local agencies begins with a records inventory. The forms used by the Bureau of Records Analysis to inventory the records and determine what records series are in use are shown in Figure 12.17. A records management implementation schedule (see Figure 12.18) helps the analyst coordinate the necessary activities for the agency to set up a records management system.

Figure 12.19 Information Practices Act Worksheet

DEPARTMENT:	DIVISION:
NAME OF INDIVIDUAL PREPARING REPORT:	**CLASSIFICATION:** □ PUBLIC □ PRIVATE □ CONFIDENTIAL
RECORDS SERIES TITLE:	
VARYING TITLE:	

INSTRUCTIONS: PLEASE PRINT. PLEASE CHECK ALL THE BOXES THAT APPLY IN EACH SECTION. THESE CATEGORIES OF INDIVIDUALS ARE VERY GENERAL. PLEASE ADD ANY THAT YOU FEEL ARE MORE DESCRIPTIVE. ALL AGENCY HEADS ARE REQUIRED BY LAW TO PROVIDE THIS INFORMATION. THIS IN ACCORDANCE WITH UCA 63-2-85.1 THRU 63-2-85.4.

WHY IS DATA COLLECTED? (UCA 63-2-85.2)

a □ TO SUPPORT CLIENT / STUDENT CASE MANAGEMENT
b □ TO MANAGE FINANCIAL / AUDIT RECORDS
c □ TO SUPPORT PERSONNEL / EVALUATION / PROMOTION ACTIONS
d □ TO RECORD MEDICAL / DIAGNOSIS / DISEASE CONTROL INFORMATION
e □ FOR ADMINISTRATION AND PROGRAM MANAGEMENT
f □ TO MEET FEDERAL OR STATE LAW REQUIREMENTS
g □ TO SUBSTANTIATE CITIZENS' RIGHTS AND CLAIMS
h □ TO DETERMINE AND / OR DOCUMENT ELEGIBILITY
i □ TO PROVIDE STATISTICAL / SUMMARY STUDIES / RESEARCH INFORMATION
j □ TO SUPPORT ADMINISTRATION OF JUSTICE AND PUBLIC SAFETY
k □ TO SUPPORT REGULATORY / CERTIFICATION / LICENSING FUNCTIONS
l □ OTHER (Specify) ____________________

WHAT METHODS ARE USED TO MAINTAIN THE INTEGRITY OF THE FILE? (UCA 63-2-85.2)

a □ FILE GROUP SECURITY INCLUDING LOCKED CABINETS OR PLACED IN THE STATE RECORDS CENTER OR ARCHIVES
b □ OFFICE PERIMETER SECURITY INCLUDING ONE OR MORE OF THE FOLLOWING: RESTRICTED OFFICE AREA, LOCKED
c □ OFFICE, ALARM SYSTEM, ARMED GUARD, SECURE STORAGE VAULT PROTECTED THROUGH DATA PROCESSING SECURITY PROCEDURES

HOW CAN INDIVIDUALS FIND OUT IF THEY ARE THE SUBJECTS OF DATA COLLECTED BY YOUR AGENCY? (UCA 63-2-85.4)

a □ CITIZEN ASKS AGENCY
b □ OTHER (Specify) ____________________

WHAT METHOD CAN A PERSON USE TO GAIN ACCESS TO THE DATA? (UCA 63-2-85.2)

a □ ORAL REQUEST TO THE AGENCY
b □ WRITTEN REQUEST TO THE AGENCY
c □ REQUEST BY PROFESSIONAL REPRESENTATIVE
d □ COURT ORDER
e □ OTHER (Specify) ____________________

WHAT METEHOD CAN A INDIVIDUAL USE TO CONTEST THE ACCURACY, COMPLETENESS AND PERTINENCE OF THE DATA AND THE NECESSITY FOR RETAINING IT? (UCA 63-2-85.4)

a □ CITIZEN CONTACTS AGENCY
b □ COURT ACTION
c □ OTHER (Specify) ____________________

OVER

FROM WHAT SOURCES WAS THIS DATA COLLECTED ? (UCA 63-2-85.2)

a ☐ THE INDIVIDUAL ABOUT WHOM THE RECORD PERTAINS
b ☐ THE GUARDIAN OR PARENT OF THE INDIVIDUAL
c ☐ ANOTHER AGENCY (Specify)
d ☐ INVESTIGATION PROCESS
e ☐ EMPLOYER
f ☐ EDUCATORS
g ☐ PROFESSIONAL CLIENT RELATIONS--COUNSELORS, DOCTORS, LAWYERS
h ☐ REGULATED CORPORATIONS
i ☐ OTHER (Specify) ______

WHAT INDIVIDUALS ARE COVERED BY THE DATA ? (UCA 63-2-85.2)

a ☐ INDIVIDUALS PARTICIPATING IN PROGRAMS ADMINISTERED BY YOUR AGENCY
b ☐ INDIVIDUALS APPLYING FOR OR RECEIVING ASSISTANCE FROM THE STATE THROUGH YOUR AGENCY
c ☐ INDIVIDUALS APPLYING FOR OR LICENSED BY THE AGENCY TO PERFORM CERTAIN FUNCTIONS OR PARTICIPATE IN SPECIFIC ACTIVITIES
d ☐ INDIVIDUALS APPLYING FOR STATE EMPLOYMENT OR ARE EMPLOYED OR HAVE BEEN EMPLOYED IN STATE SERVICE
e ☐ INDIVIDUALS UNDER INVESTIGATION
f ☐ TAX PAYERS
g ☐ INDIVIDUALS WHO HAVE FILED A COMPLAINT OR OTHERWISE CONTACTED THE AGENCY
h ☐ INDIVIDUALS NAMED IN A COMPLAINT
i ☐ INDIVIDUALS ON MAILING OR SUBSCRIPTION LIST
j ☐ INDIVIDUALS APPLYING FOR OR RECEIVING BENEFITS OR COMPENSATION
k ☐ INDIVIDUALS DONATING GOODS OR SERVICES
l ☐ OTHER (Specify) ______

WHAT CATEGORIES OF INDIVIDUALS WILL HAVE ACCESS TO THE PERSONAL DATA IN THE EXERCISE OF THEIR DUTIES ? (UCA 63-2-85.2)

a ☐ THIS DIVISION
b ☐ OTHER STATE AGENCIES (Specify) ______
______
c ☐ PRIVATE SECTOR GROUPS (Specify) ______
d ☐ OTHER (Specify) ______
______

COMMENTS:

SIGNATURE OF INDIVIDUAL PREPARING REPORT:	DATE

• if more space is required, attach additional sheets — 001100 REV 10/87

Source Courtesy of Utah State Archives.

Figure 12.20 Inventory of Personal Data Elements

Department ______________________________

Division ______________________________

Bureau ______________________________

Inventory of Personal Data Elements This Office May Collect, Use, or Maintain

Which of the following personal identifiers are found in records in your office?

- ☐ age
- ☐ alcohol or drug addiction
- ☐ appearance
- ☐ assets/debts
- ☐ birthplace
- ☐ brothers and sisters
- ☐ checking and savings accounts
- ☐ civil/criminal court involvement
- ☐ condition of living quarters
- ☐ credit rating
- ☐ current and past addresses
- ☐ date of birth
- ☐ dental history
- ☐ driver's license number
- ☐ educational level
- ☐ employer
- ☐ employment history
- ☐ ethnic group
- ☐ expenditures
- ☐ family history
- ☐ finger prints
- ☐ food purchase and consumption
- ☐ grade average or class standing
- ☐ home ownership
- ☐ income
- ☐ job position information (e.g., grade/step, etc.)
- ☐ marital status
- ☐ medical information
- ☐ membership in groups
- ☐ military service
- ☐ mortgage information
- ☐ motor vehicle ownership
- ☐ name
- ☐ national origin
- ☐ next of kin
- ☐ number of children
- ☐ occupation
- ☐ occupational licenses
- ☐ occupational preferences
- ☐ parent's birth information
- ☐ personality inventory
- ☐ physical characteristics
- ☐ physical disabilities
- ☐ police record
- ☐ political affiliations
- ☐ property ownership
- ☐ psychiatric information
- ☐ public housing occupancy
- ☐ race
- ☐ references
- ☐ religious preference
- ☐ salary
- ☐ salary withholdings
- ☐ security/other investigation
- ☐ sex
- ☐ signature
- ☐ social security number
- ☐ tax information (specify) ______________________________ ______________________________
- ☐ telephone number
- ☐ victim information

other unique identifiers

- ☐ ______________________________
- ☐ ______________________________
- ☐ ______________________________
- ☐ ______________________________

Source Courtesy of Utah State Archives.

Records that can and should be microfilmed are identified and the analyst conducts a feasibility study to determine the costs of microfilming. The Utah State Archives also monitors its agencies for compliance with the Information Practices Act, which deals with privacy and confidentiality of records. For this purpose, the records analyst uses the Information Practices Act Worksheet shown in Figure 12.19 and the Inventory of Personal Data Elements shown in Figure 12.20. These forms help the records analyst determine what records management system the local agency should use and what data is sensitive and may require special handling.

Each of these procedures and accompanying forms provides the agency with the information necessary to set up a records management system that is efficient and that is compatible with the system used in the state archives.

Summary

Small, single-location businesses often use paper, manual systems for their records. Chapter 12 has described specific, existing applications of records management in professional offices and government offices.

In professional offices, the records are client-based. These records are required for the daily operations, which provide services to clients. When practitioners leave a professional office, the related client records must be handled efficiently through exit procedures to avoid problems of security and problems related to provision of services to the clients.

There are many government offices that operate relatively independently in terms of their records. The records systems are often manual and involve keeping track of events and people in their jurisdiction. Disaster recovery procedures may follow conventional methods, but plans for disaster recovery under circumstances in which conventional methods cannot be used should be considered. Practical experience has revealed that several "nonconventional" methods may be feasible.

State government has the responsibility for maintaining government records and, in some cases, may coordinate its records system with that of its local agencies. This coordination requires cooperation between records personnel in state and local government agencies. In the case of the Utah State Archives, records analysis provides the basis for a system of coordination between that entity and its state and local agencies.

List of Terms

professional office
client-based record
notch and color system
transient patient
exit procedure
firm-privileged record
incident report

Discussion Questions

1. Under what circumstances would the major records in a professional office be considered client-based?
2. What documents typically are found in a patient's medical file?
3. How is a patient-name file used to find the patient's folder in a terminal-digit filing system?
4. Using the notch and color system described in this chapter, what is the order for the following names: Mary Jones, David Jones, Beth Jansen, Mark James?
5. Why is an exit procedure important in a professional office?
6. What are some of the major records management concerns of local government offices if a major disaster occurs?

7. What are two practical approaches that can be used to salvage paper records in case of a disaster?
8. How is an incident report similar to a client-based record?
9. What records would a police department be likely to obtain from a state office? What records would it send to the state office?
10. What forms and procedures are needed in a state records agency that assists local agencies with records management?

Activities

1. Visit the police department in your city, or any local government office. Determine what major records are kept and what systems are used for maintaining them. Make a flowchart of each records system.
2. In terms of the description of records management in a medical clinic in this chapter, describe what would be required if a section of the rotary index file were destroyed.
3. Visit a law firm or medical office and obtain copies of the forms they use. Analyze the forms in terms of their efficiency and present your findings to the class. (Refer to Chapter 4 for information on forms design.)
4. Prepare a set of disaster recovery procedures for a hypothetical (or real) small business whose records are primarily paper and client-based. The major consideration will be the availability of backup records and how to make them available.
5. Design a color-coded system for microfilm jackets that would work well for keeping *active* medical records. You may incorporate notches, but try to design a system that allows faster retrieval than the one described in this chapter.

References

Franklin, LaVerne. "Exit Procedures for a Lawyer Leaving a Law Firm or Legal Department." Unpublished manuscript, Butler & Binion, 1340 Allied Bank Plaza, Houston, Texas 77002, 1987.

Swift, Pamela S., Jeri Ann Browne, and Len Nissenson. "Records Management Systems for County and Municipal Governments: Case Studies." *Proceedings of the ARMA International 32d Annual Conference*, Anaheim, California, October 19–22, 1987, published by Association of Records Managers and Administrators, Inc., 343–353.

Chapter 12 Highlight

Get a Microcomputer

Many of the regular tasks of a records manager are repetitive in the sense that they require standard input and output. Generally, the tasks will involve text documents that require updating, analysis, and distribution. Other tasks involve internal records, scheduling, and tickler notes. Given this situation, any company that needs a records manager needs a microcomputer for the records manager.

Of course, almost any task can be accomplished without a microcomputer. The point is that the tasks can be accomplished more efficiently with one. In addition, the greatest benefits of using a microcomputer are often the least expected, as new and more efficient methods of dealing with responsibilities are discovered.

The following potential areas of use should be considered in a cost–benefit analysis to determine the feasibility of microcomputer use for records management. Unless otherwise indicated, all of the suggested uses can be accomplished with a word processing software program. Excellent word processing software for microcomputers sells in the \$20–\$300 range.

1. Use a time scheduler for to-do lists, tickler notes, meetings, and as a way to organize your activities.
2. Keep listings of goals, objectives, and the role of the records manager on the microcomputer.
3. Consider training packages that use the microcomputer for training records personnel. Use the microcomputer to create training materials.
4. Use the microcomputer to create the forms used for correspondence, reports, and forms management. Do forms design, analysis, and creation on the microcomputer with desktop publishing applications.

5. Keep the records management manual on digital media. It will be easy to review, update, and print out changes.
6. Do performance evaluations on the microcomputer. Use a spreadsheet for budgets.

Also, use good records management for the microcomputer media. We suggest organizing your disks by subject. For example, keep each section of the records management manual in its own computer file and all of the files on their own disk. Always be sure to have at least one backup of each disk. Archive the disks on a regular basis. Completely copy each disk, date it, and store it in an archives area.

Chapter 13

Corporate Records Centers and Computerized Applications

Learning Goals

1. To recognize the characteristics of computerized corporate records management applications.
2. To understand records center operations in a corporate environment.
3. To become familiar with distributed and virtual central records management.
4. To learn how a bank uses an optical disk system for document-image processing.

Introduction

This chapter describes and illustrates some practical applications of records management systems in corporations. The Hughes Aircraft Company records center provides an excellent example of practical applications in a corporate records center. Other applications described here focus on computerized records systems that deal with distributed records management and virtual central records (see Chapter 3).

The computer can be an efficient tool for managing records distributed throughout the many branches of a large corporation. Through telecommunications and computer technology, records in different geographic locations become virtually centralized. The result is a system of distributed records management and virtual central records. The Marriott guest reservation system is an example of distributed records management. The computerized records management of a hypothetical retail store, linked to the home office of its parent company, also is described here as an example of virtual central records. Finally, the use of a computer optical disk document-image system in a banking environment is described to illustrate how an optical disk system increases the flow of information while reducing the need for paper records.

Records Center Operations: Hughes Aircraft Company

Hughes Aircraft Company, a subsidiary of General Motors Company, specializes in the design and production of high-technology electronics for military, scientific, and commercial use. The company's activities span more than 1,700 projects and include over 12,000 separate products, ranging from air defense systems to radar-based avionics, from missiles to space satellites, from communications to displays, and from optics to microelectronics. Although most of the company's 78,000 employees are located in southern California, a major missile manufacturing facility is located in Tucson, Arizona; and smaller plants, subsidiaries, and offices are distributed across the United States and in eighteen foreign countries. The corporate headquarters for Hughes Aircraft Company is in Los Angeles, California.

All records management at Hughes is coordinated through company policies, and generally records operations are centralized in southern California. The Corporate Records and Information Resource Management (CRIRM) office is located in the Los Angeles corporate offices. A records manager heads the CRIRM and administers the records and information resource management program for the Hughes organization. The records manager ensures that Hughes Aircraft Company complies with the laws and regulations that apply to large private-sector organizations. For example, records series must be retained according to state and federal regulations. Also, because Hughes Aircraft has many military contracts, the associated records series must satisfy the audit regulations of the United States Department of Defense.

A records manager in a complex organization often is a member of an information systems project team. Because the records manager knows where major information subsystems are and how information flows throughout the organization, the manager's input allows the team to structure the project records correctly for audit purposes, for litigation support, and to meet regulations. This role as supporting project team member is the primary one for the records manager at Hughes Aircraft.

Many of the Hughes Aircraft divisions and groups send their inactive records to the Company Records Center located in Hawthorne, California. Some small divisions use commercial center storage for small quantities of records if it is more practical and convenient to do so. The Company Records Center (CRC), which covers 75,000 square feet with a capacity of about 300,000 cubic feet of records, is managed by a supervisor. The center has several administrative offices, micrographics facilities, and a large warehouse area with shelving for cartons. Twenty-five people work directly in the records center or are designated as records management staff; about twenty-five others are records coordinators in other departments who act as liaisons with the records management staff. The CRC has a computer system for tracking records, making space assignments, and providing activity reports. The following descriptions and applications focus on the security systems, storage procedures, retrieval operations, records disposal system, and the computer tracking and report system used in the center.

Security Systems

Because many of the activities at Hughes Aircraft deal with government contracts, it is important for the CRC to maintain a high level of security. Therefore, only authorized personnel are allowed in the records center building. Visitors coming into the building must sign in and be accompanied by Company Records Center staff.

The records storage area has an intrusion detection system which consists of a series of light beams focused throughout the interior, and doors and windows are equipped with contact/motion detectors. After regular work hours, the security system is activated. If someone invades the protected space, an alarm goes off and the Security Systems office is notified.

Other security devices include sprinklers and smoke detectors to protect against fire damage. Water damage is monitored by water flow detection devices tied in with the intrusion detection system. Cartons are treated to be fire retardant and the entire records storage area is fumigated monthly.

Figure 13.1 Interior of Records Center Warehouse

Source Courtesy of Hughes Aircraft Company.

Storage Procedures

The CRC has a shipping and receiving dock where about 300 cartons of records are processed each day. The cartons used are one-piece cubic foot boxes (lid and carton are connected) that are assembled in office areas as needed. The predominant shelving used in the CRC is the *high-rise unit,* steel uprights with pressboard shelving that rise several tiers. A secondary type of shelving is *stacks-on-steel,* stacked cardboard drawers supported by a steel framework. The stacks-on-steel are being phased out and are no longer used for incoming records.

In the warehouse area (see Figure13.1) where cartons are stored, a *bank-and-space numbering system* is used; that is, cartons are stored two deep, two high, and five wide on back-to-back shelving units, so that each row of shelving consists of two banks, back-to-back, approximately ten shelves high. Space is assigned by the CRC computer as records cartons arrive in a manner similar to the numbering procedure used in the row-unit-shelf (RUS) system as described in Chapter 10. Even-numbered spaces are on the outside, odd-numbered spaces are on the inside.

Union contracts require that warehouse people take clerks up to levels above the second shelf and retrieve and replace boxes for the clerks. Figure 13.2 shows the lift truck machine that is used in the records center to move boxes and lift operators up to higher shelves to get boxes.

The storage process starts when a division of Hughes decides to send inactive records to the center. First, a Records Transfer Authorization (RTA) form (see Figure 13.3) must be prepared by the depositing division. The RTA contains a decription of the records and the depositor (the department or individual who sends the records). A records center clerk reviews the RTA and enters the retention period. (The RTA is a four-copy form with accompanying instructions.) The records center retains the original (shown in Figure 13.3), a second copy goes to records administration, the depositor department receives the third copy, and the depositor recieves the last copy. The records are placed in standard center-approved boxes and shipped to the CRC.

Figure 13.2 Lift Machine

Source Courtesy of Hughes Aircraft Company.

When the records are received by the records center, the boxes are compared to the Record Transfer Authorization to ensure that the proper records have been received. The boxes are checked to verify that each has the correct RTA number written on the front of the box along with other descriptive information. The cartons are then moved to the computer-assigned spaces.

Storage and protection of certain unique records series is accomplished by providing the depositor with special cabinets for "dedicated" use. These cabinets are located in the records center vault. The department installs its own locking bar on the cabinet and maintains access and control over it. A records center staff member verifies that individuals accessing the cabinets are authorized to do so.

Vault Storage

Within CRC is a large, high-security vault, which is used for vital records storage. The vault has motorized, mobile shelving units, as well as fixed shelving. The vital records are primarily on microfilm cartridges and machine-readable magnetic tapes. The film/tape cartridges are numerically labeled and colorcoded by the depositing department to identify the information content. Each space on the shelf also has a number that is the space assignment number used by the records center. Because some cartridges are stored for only a short time, the original department numeric and color codes are kept on them.

Retrieval Operations

When a division needs to access records that have been sent to the center, a Request for Records form is needed (see Figure 13.4). The Request for Records describes, as completely as possible, the needed records. Requests can be made by mail, telephone, or in person.

Record retrieval is done on both a carton and a single document basis. However, retrieving single documents is limited by available staff time. Therefore, if many single documents are requested, the requestor is asked to come to the records center to pull the documents from the retrieved cartons him- or herself. For a single whole carton request, the center will retrieve and ship the carton within twenty-four hours.

Records Disposal

Based on the retention data from the RTAs, the computer system automatically generates a disposal authorization form (see Fig-

Figure 13.3 Records Transfer Authorization

HUGHES

PREPARED BY	PAGE OF
DATE	PHONE

RTA NO. 130010

RECORDS TRANSFER AUTHORIZATION

DEPOSITOR	ORG. CODE	ORGANIZATION NAME	LOC.	BLDG.	M/S	PHONE	TRANS. DOC. NO.	DATE RECORDS REC'D.

DEP. BOX NO.	MEDIA	CODE	RECORDS DESCRIPTION *Important: see instructions attached*	CONTAINER	TYPE CODE	BEGINNING & ENDING DATES OF RECORDS MO./YR.	MO./YR.	SECURITY	CODE	CONTRACT CODE, HAC REFERENCE OR GLA NUMBER(S)	V	A	RETENTION PERIOD	BANK	BOX	EXPAND

DEPOSITOR'S SIGNATURE

DATE

CLASSIFIED RECORDS LISTED HEREIN HAVE BEEN MARKED FOR AUTOMATIC DECLASSIFICATION.

CHECK IF APPLICABLE ☐

ACCESS TO RECORDS RESTRICTED TO (CHECK BELOW)

A. ____ DIV. MGR.
B. ____ DEPT. MGR.
C. ____ SECT. HEAD
D. ____ SUPERVISOR
E. ____ DEPT. STAFF
F. ____ FOLLOWING NAMES:

TRANSFER TO RECORDS CENTER

☐ APPROVED ☐ NOT APPROVED

REASON:

BY: COORDINATOR DATE

7001 CS FEB 84

DISTRIBUTION: 1. White—RECORDS CENTER; 2. Blue—RECORDS ADMINISTRATION; 3. Green—DEPT FILE; 4. Canary—DEPOSITOR INTERIM RECEIPT

Source Courtesy of Hughes Aircraft Company.

ures 13.5 and 13.6, pages 213 and 214) when the records are ready for destruction. The form is sent to the depositor department that originally sent the records to the center. On the form, the records designated for destruction are described and the depositor must indicate on the form if the records can be destroyed or if they should be kept longer.

Figure 13.5 shows the first form sent to the despositor. Second and final notices (see Figure 13.6) are sent if necessary. If the depositor wishes records to be kept beyond the original destruction date, that extension must be approved by the records manager.

After disposal authorization by the depositor department, the actual destruction of the records also must be authorized by the records manager. Then a listing of those cartons that are to be destroyed is generated by computer along with the space assignment code, and the boxes are pulled by the warehouse people. The cartons are stacked together for removal and destruction by a commercial destruction firm.

Figure 13.4 Request for Records

NO. 054230

REQUEST FOR RECORDS

HUGHES

TO: **COMPANY RECORDS CENTER**
Loc. CR, Building C4, M/S 1
PHONE: **973-3604**

DATE

REQUESTED BY:	ORG. CODE	LOC.	BLDG.	M/S	ROOM	PHONE

DESCRIPTION OF RECORDS

□ TEMP. OUT	□ PERM. OUT	□ REHIRE
□ SEARCHES	□ RETURNS	
□ INFO	□ M/F □ COPY	□ UTL

□ MAIL	□ TRANSP. NO.
RELEASED TO	DATE
CHECKED & MAILED BY	DATE

1364 CO JUL 84 DISTRIBUTION: 1. White—ACCOUNTABILITY; 2. Yellow—FILE; 3. Pink—REQUESTER.

Source Courtesy of Hughes Aircraft Company.

Computer Tracking and Report System

The records center's computer generates a monthly Activity Report of about twenty pages of summary statistics on records center operations such as the number of cartons received in the center, the number destroyed, general requests that have come into the center, the number of retrievals, searches, and the monthly Record Transfer Authorization (RTA) activity. The RTA activity lists the number of cartons that come in at one time from any one depositor. The computer can produce listings of all holdings for a particular group or division for a particular time period. Of course, the computer can search for boxes by RTA number or description. The computer is also used to keep information about employees such as time worked and vacations.

The costs of the records center were originally assigned on a proportional head count basis. That is, if a department had 10,000 employees, then the department was assigned one-eighth of the costs (that is, a percentage of the total number of employees in the company). The costing was converted to a *fee-for-service* basis, meaning that a department pays costs based on the services performed.

At Hughes Aircraft Company, the records center provides the central records storage facility for the corporation, and the computer is used to manage the storage and retrieval of records. Situations in which the records actually are stored on computer are described in the following sections.

Figure 13.5 Authorization to Dispose of Records

COMPANY RECORDS CENTER
AUTHORIZATION TO DISPOSE OF RECORDS

RTA # 290
PAGE: 1

Date: 10/20/87

AUTHORIZER INFORMATION

Name: ____________

Title: ____________

Telephone: ____________ Date: ____________

Org: ________ Org Name: ____________

Location: ____ Bldg: ______ MS: ____________

DEPOSITOR INFORMATION

Name: P. ROB

Org: 20/03/01 Org Name: RS

Location: RE Bldg: R8 MS: 668

RECORDS MANAGEMENT APPROVALS

____

Date: ____________

DEPOSITOR AUTHORIZATION

The CRC is authorized to dispose of all records listed below except those for which I have requested an extension by circling the box number and stating the period and reason required.

Signature: ____________

DEP. BOX NO.	REQUEST FOR EXTENSION		PRE EXT
	PERIOD (mos or yrs)	REASON	
1			
1A			
2			
2A			
3			
3A			
4			
4A			

Source Courtesy of Hughes Aircraft Company.

Distributed Records Management: The Marriott Reservation System

The difference between a paper-based manual system and a computerized records system are astounding. Probably the first thing that strikes the eye is the physical difference in the workplace. In the computerized system, the total records area is small and dominated by computer workstations and a printer or two. The entire work area for all the records staff is just a modest-sized room. The work activity is concentrated at workstations with little movement by the records personnel. Compare this to the traditional paper files system, where there are racks and racks of paper files occupying a great deal of space, and records clerks continually scurry among the racks. The Marriott Corporation reservation system clearly illustrates this difference.

Marriott Corporation was founded in 1927, beginning as a small root beer stand in Washington, D.C. Today the company has over 210,000 employees, serves over 5 million meals a day, and develops over $1 billion in real estate each year. The major components include lodging, which is comprised of

Figure 13.6 Second and Final Notices of Disposal Authorization

SECOND NOTICE

DISPOSAL AUTHORIZATION FOR RECORDS IN THE COMPANY RECORDS CENTER
RTA NO.

To:
OR Current manager of:
Org: Org name:
Location: Bldg: MS:

Date:
From: Records & Information Resource Management
Org:
Location: Bldg: MS:
Telephone:

The Company Records Center (CRC) sent you an AUTHORIZATION TO DISPOSE OF RECORDS for records deposited by your organization on the above Records Transfer Authorization (RTA). You were asked to authorize disposal of the records listed on the AUTHORIZATION. We have not received your response.

Your prompt response is vital to the effective and efficient control of Company records. Please complete the AUTHORIZATION and return it to the above address within five (5) working days.

If you have responded, please disregard this notice. If you did not receive the letter and AUTHORIZATION or have misplaced it, please contact the Company Records Center (CRC).

Thank you for your cooperation.

COMPANY RECORDS CENTER — PHONE 973-3604

19654A CO SEP 86

FINAL NOTICE

DISPOSAL AUTHORIZATION FOR RECORDS IN THE COMPANY RECORDS CENTER
RTA NO.

To:
OR Current manager of:
Org: Org name:
Location: Bldg: MS:

Date:
From: Records & Information Resource Management
Org:
Location: Bldg: MS:
Telephone:

The Company Records Center (CRC) has not yet received the AUTHORIZATION TO DISPOSE OF RECORDS form which was sent to you for the above RTA. This is the third and final request for your response.

If we do not receive your response within ten (10) working days, we will proceed with disposal of the records listed on the AUTHORIZATION. You must respond now if you wish to retain these records. The records will be disposed of after the expiration of ten (10) working days.

If your organization is no longer responsible for these records, notify the CRC immediately. If you have responded, please contact the CRC. We have no record of your response.

Thank you for your cooperation.

COMPANY RECORDS CENTER — PHONE 973-3604

19654B CO SEP 86

Source Courtesy of Hughes Aircraft Company.

Marriott Hotels and Resorts, Marriott Suites, Residence Inns by Marriott, Courtyards by Marriott, and Fairfield Inn; contract services, including food service management, airline catering service, and airport restaurants and shops; and restaurants, including Big Boy, Roy Rodgers, Hot Shoppes, and highway locations. At the beginning of 1988, Marriott's lodging operations encompassed 361 hotels with a total of approximately 103,000 rooms. This line of business represented 41 percent of sales and 51 percent of operating income (Marriott, 1987).

Features of MARSHA

All major hotels today have some sort of computerized reservation system. Marriott's reservation system is called MARSHA (Marriott's Automated Reservation System for Hotel Accommodations). MARSHA is derived from the IBM system called PARS (Programmed Airline Reservations System). Generally, any room reservation system keeps track of all of the rooms in a hotel by occupancy.

The reservations in the MARSHA system are called Guest Name Records or GNRs. The GNR contains two categories of information: guest information and room information. (Figure 13.7 shows the paper reservation form.) Guest information consists of the guest name, address, phone number, the calling party (who is making the reservation), and similar data. The room information consists of room type (single, double, and so forth), number of persons, rate, and special requests.

MARSHA will allow agents at Central Reservations offices to create Guest Name Records (GNRs) in a free-form manner. For example, while on the phone, the agent can skip around the display screen entering information as it is obtained and querying the calling party as required. The agent, not the computer, controls the conversation with the guest.

In order to make reservations, MARSHA must contain the hotel room information such as number of rooms available, as well as the room types and rates. In fact, MARSHA contains this information for all of the Marriott lodging operations and can display and quote actual rates for any Marriott hotel.

The MARSHA system allows reservations personnel to build a GNR by using the client file records of travel agents, Club Marquis members, and Preference Plus members (the latter two groups describe the status of people who frequently stay in Marriott hotels). Other functions of the MARSHA system allow agents to display and modify any GNRs, using either a confirmation number, a cancellation number, a hotel code, an arrival date, or a guest name.

The primary function of MARSHA is to make reservations. Extremely useful secondary functions made possible by the computer allow hotels to use MARSHA to control inventory of the authorized number of rooms, to set restrictions for certain time periods, and to protect rooms for special groups or conventions. In addition, the report functions of MARSHA allow the hotel to display room availability, number of rooms sold or authorized, rooms that are not available, percentage of occupancy, and history of inventory modifications. By using list options, reservations agents can review GNRs with common data to obtain summary reports. The hotel reservations manager uses MARSHA to prepare weekly reports that summarize and forecast the hotel's weekly reservation activity. For special requests, MARSHA has a query facility that can obtain reservations data by criteria, such as how many reservations were made on a specific date or between two dates.

The actual mainframe computer hardware is transparent (unseen and physically separate) to the operators. The mainframe hardware and software are located in Frederick, Maryland, but can be located anywhere. Each hotel's workstations are linked

Figure 13.7 Reservation Form

CODE ________ ARD ________________ DPD ________________ 6 PM GTD
NAME: ____
CO. ____________________ CC# ________________ X. ____
ADDRESS ____________________ TA ____________________
____________________ ADDRESS ____________________
____________________ ____________________
____________________ CONVENTION: ____________________
SHARING WITH: ________________ RESV. CHG: WAS: ________________
PH. # ____________________ NOW: ____________________
PERS. MAKING RESV. ____________

SINGLE	DOUBLE	DOUBLE/ DOUBLE	PARLOR/SUITE	# RMS.	# PEOPLE

SPECIAL REQUESTS

____
____
____
____
____
____

AGENT ACCEPTING ____ TIME: ______ DATE TAKEN: ____________

Source Courtesy of Marriott Hotel, Salt Lake City, Utah.

to the mainframe hardware and software through telecommunications. The records reservation personnel work in an office that is virtually paper free. During those infrequent times when the computer is down, the operators take information on the paper forms (see Figure 13.7). When normal operations resume, the information is entered into MARSHA.

Features of PMS

In addition to MARSHA, each Marriott hotel has a version of the PMS (Property Management System) that also operates through transparent mainframe hardware and software. PMS takes care of the room inventory, accounting, personnel, and other subsystems unique to the hotel. The MARSHA and PMS systems are physically distinct so that each system has its own workstation. In Figure 13.8, the two terminal workstations shown are a PMS and a MARSHA station.

Clearly, the PMS data must coincide with the MARSHA data. In fact, as MARSHA operates, it exchanges data with PMS to keep both systems up to date. When MARSHA reservations are not accepted by PMS, an exceptions file is created which must be reconciled. An exceptions file consists of

Figure 13.8 Reservations Clerk

Source Courtesy of Marriott Hotel, Salt Lake City, Utah.

items that need special attention. Reservations agents regularly access the exceptions file and complete, correct, or properly deal with the information to make it acceptable to PMS.

Both PMS and MARSHA keep their records on-line for three months. After that time, the records are taken off the systems and stored in a variety of forms as inactive records.

Training for MARSHA and PMS is available on the computer system in the form of self-paced tutorial lessons. The lessons available cover both MARSHA and PMS operations. The lessons to train Marriott reservations clerks are listed in Figure 13.9 (CBT is an acronym for Computer-Based Training).

Virtual Central Records: Subsidiary–Parent Records Management

In this section, we will describe a *virtual central records system.* This is a hypothetical computerized records management system used by multiple retail outlets of a parent company, but it is based on one in actual use. The parent company is TIRECO, a large tire company with headquarters in the United States. The products of the company include automobile accessories and services, as well as petrochemicals. Of the retail outlets that market its goods and services, TIRECO owns approximately 2,000. It also has hun-

Figure 13.9 PMS/CBT Courses

Introduction Module

INTROCBT	Introduction to Computer-Based Training
INTROPMS	Introduction to PMS Lessons
HARDWARE	Property Management System Hardware

Registration Module

STATCODE	Registration/Reservation Status Codes
ROOMCODE	PMS Room Status Codes
SEARCH1	Guest Name Searches Part-1
SEARCH2	Guest Name Searches Part-2
SCREEN1	Reservation/Registration Screen I.D. Part-1
SCREEN2	Reservation/Registration Screen I.D. Part-2
CHECKIN1	PMS Registration Part-1
CHECKIN2	PMS Registration Part-2
CHECKIN3	PMS Registration Part-3
SHARES	PMS Registration of Shared Accounts
RMAVAIL	Room Availability Displays
TYPEINV	Type Inventory Displays

Accounting Module

GSTACCT1	PMS Guest Accounting Part-1
GSTACCT2	PMS Guest Accounting Part-2
GSTACCT3	PMS Guest Accounting Part-3
GSTACCT4	PMS Guest Accounting Part-4
BATCHPST	Batch Charge Posting
CHRGROUT	Guest Charge Routing
SHFTCLS1	Shift Closing Report Part-1

Reports Module

HSECOUNT	PMS House County Display

PMS/MARSHA Interface

TWOWAY1	Introduction to the 2-Way Interface

Source Courtesy of Marriott Corporation.

dreds of other retail outlets that are independently owned that carry its products. We will look here at the retail outlet, Little Tire, which is independently owned; but the description of the records management system could apply to both company and independent stores.

Little Tire, a TIRECO tire center, is representative of the independently owned TIRECO retail stores that primarily market tires and automobile services. There is a showroom for tires and related products and a service area for mounting tires, doing wheel alignments, tune-ups, and other automobile maintenance and repair.

The store uses a computer program—we will call this program the TIRECO Computer Business Management System (TCS, for short). The system is designed for use by all TIRECO stores whether company owned or independent. The independents, like Little Tire, lease the system from TIRECO. Leasing includes full maintenance and support via a toll-free phone number that accesses a home office.

TCS is designed around a national account program that acts like a credit card for the retail store. Using this program, the retail store can order and charge merchandise from the home store, receive credit for sales commissions, or accept other vendors' charges against the store's account. At the end of the month, the program does a billing for the retail store.

A comprehensive manual is included with TCS that serves mainly as a reference. The manual leads the user through all of the applications showing the appropriate display information. The manual illustrates each of the operations with examples and contains an index and glossary. TCS is a menu-driven program, so the user normally can determine what to do simply by reading the screen. (Figure 13.10 shows typical computer screens for the TIRECO system.) The system starts from a MAIN MENU where the major options are selected.

The system is usually left on twenty-four hours a day. This allows the telecommunications exchange between the retail store and the home office. Enhancements to TCS to extend the scope of the system are made regularly in addition to program alterations to correct problems. These changes originate in the home office and are telecommunicated to the retail stores. To avoid interference with daily activities, telecommunication changes typically are done on a Sunday or at other times when the retail stores are closed. Hard copy of changes made to the computer system are mailed to the stores to update the TCS manual.

Applications of TCS

The major applications are point-of-sale, inventory management, accounts receivable, accounts payable, general ledger, and payroll. These functions are standard business procedures that have been computerized by the TCS program. The following section describes the point-of-sale (POS) application.

The primary purpose of the POS application is to prepare invoices for products and services purchased by customers. If necessary, new customer information is added to the history files by CUSTOMER (name, address, . . . , phone) and VEHICLE (year, make, model, color, license, state). POS will prepare the customer work order, with type of service, costs, mechanic, salesperson, and similar information. This work order information is added to system files and can be recalled as a customer's vehicle history. While using POS, the salesperson can access the Sales Aid screen to select service types and to check inventory. POS can be used to create a sales quote (valid for a certain period of time) by merchandise and/or by customer. For existing customers, search characters are entered (first characters from customer's last name) to access the existing customer's record with CUSTOMER and VEHICLE information. If everything proceeds normally, the customer eventually picks up the vehicle, the work has been satisfactorily performed, and POS produces the invoice bill, which the customer pays.

Administrative Functions of TCS

The administrative functions of TCS include editing names assigned to service or inventory codes, merchandise, advertising (for example, mailing labels), generating statistics for sales and/or service by employee, providing location profile (store hours, sales tax rates, etc.), sending messages to the home office, doing journal tickets to transfer funds from one account code to another, printing out reports that are sent from the home office, and other miscellaneous operations. The reports produced include an Inventory Summary (produced in various forms), Weekly Tire Order, and Inventory forms.

Figure 13.10 Initial and Main Menu for a Computer Business Management System

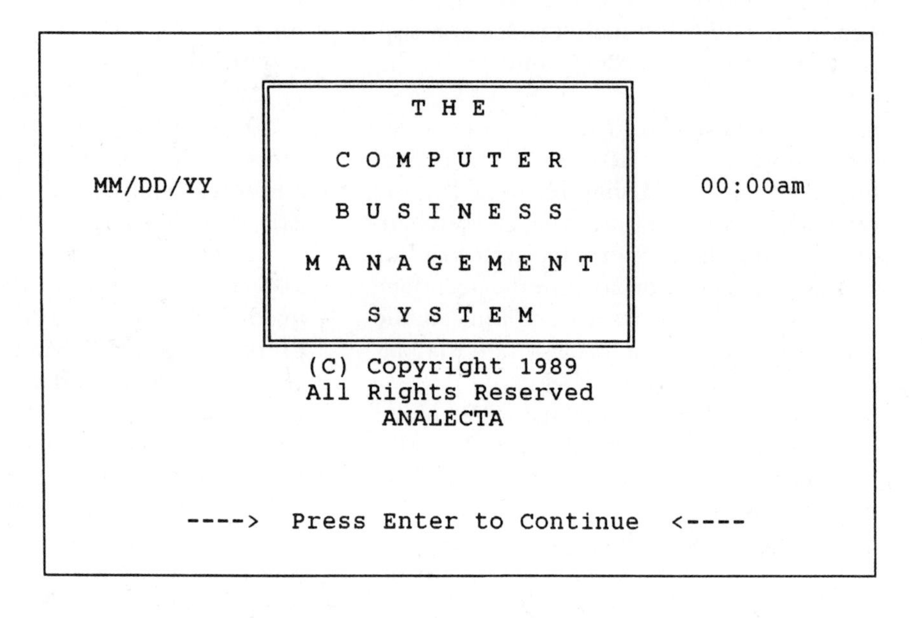


```
Computer Business Management System

                 M A I N   M E N U

F1   Point of Sale             F6   Sales Reports
F2   Cash Receipts             F7   Inventory Stats
F3   Accts Receivable          F8   Administration
F4   Payables                  F9   End of Day
F5   Personnel                 F10  Quit CBMS

MM/DD/YY          Store # 9999          00:00am
```

Customer or Vendor Reports also can be produced.

A computerized system such as the one we have been describing effectively removes nearly all paper records from the store. The remaining paper records deal with exceptions not normally processed. The standard four-drawer vertical file will sit unused except for nonrecord items. In one sense, this kind of computerized system puts the user in more direct control and contact with the store's records, but the gain in speed and accuracy may be at the expense of flexibility and understanding. The owner of Little Tire may have no idea of internals such as the programming, actual hardware specifics, retention periods, record formats, number of files, and so forth; and the manual provided to this hypothetical retail store by the home office may not provide this information. Nevertheless, virtual central records management via telecommunications is the trend of the future. The process eliminates many paper records and speeds the transmission of information through a geographically dispersed organization.

Optical Disk Processing: Security Pacific National Bank

Computer technology is especially useful in dealing with the enormous volume of documents processed by banks. In this section, we will describe the optical disk document-image system used by Security Pacific National Bank (FileNet, 1987). The key element in this application is the use of a computerized system to deal with massive amounts of paper records.

Security Pacific Corporation, a diversified financial services company with assets of over $46 billion, is headquartered in Los Angeles, California. In 1987, Security Pacific had over 640 banking offices in California and over 500 financial service offices in 46 states and in 28 other countries. Security Pacific Corporation's largest subsidiary is Security Pacific National Bank. With assets of $40 billion, Security Pacific is the second largest commercial bank in its home state of California and the seventh largest bank in the United States.

Security Pacific National Bank is a leader among financial institutions in the use of electronic banking and high-technology information management techniques. At one point, the bank found that its International Banking Group's Money Transfer Department was getting bogged down because of the large quantities of paper the department had to process every day. Like all financial institutions, its international payment transactions were dependent on documentation stored on paper, microfilm, and microfiche. When information was required, it had to be retrieved by hand or with the aid of a computer and then routed manually through the department.

To reduce the time spent handling its transactions and to increase departmental productivity, Security Pacific installed an *optical disk-based document-image* processor, manufactured by FileNet Corporation. The International Money Transfer Department now stores documents on high-density optical disks, and then routes that information electronically to the appropriate people. In the past, letters of correspondence and signed authorizations for fund transfers, as well as originals of wires, were stored in the Investigations Section in separate paper files and in chronological order. Original correspondence letters were logged by date, sequence number, remitting bank, dollar amount, and territory.

Computerizing a Manual Process

The International Money Transfer Department receives approximately 2,500 written and telephone inquiries monthly. Each day, approximately 1,250 are actively under investigation. Because most investigations take more than a day or two, the department was burdened with massive amounts of paper. All available information and records regarding any inquiry were placed in a paper file folder, and a supervisor sent the file to an investigator's desk for processing. Some inquiries could be completed in a single day; others took from two weeks to three months. Because documentation used in an investigation must be retained, it was essential that nothing be misplaced or lost during an assignment. As a result, all file folders were sent back to the supervisor's desk at the end of the day, regardless of their stage of processing. The next day, the supervisor redistributed the folders. When an investigation was completed, the documents were stored manually again. If new inquiries requiring the same records came in, the entire procedure was repeated.

With the optical disk system, Security Pacific automated the procedures throughout the investigation activity. In the optical disk system, when a document arrives, one staff member enters it into the system with a scanner (digitizer), where its image is digitized and captured permanently on optical disk. Another person indexes it by document class and subject so that the document image is assigned to an electronic file, just as the original papers and photocopies previously were put in file folders. Document images are electronically indexed by multiple-subject categories. Once the items are stored on optical disk, the document images can be retrieved in less than twenty seconds. To maintain control and avoid confusion, the department uses special software to define the path for the document images. The department supervisor uses the software to assign tasks to investigators, prioritize the work at an investigator's workstation, and assign a tickler date if a task must be postponed. If an investigator is out ill or on vacation, work can be directed to another workstation. Each investigator proceeds through a list of actions, and then chooses a function and completes the task. When he or she signs off, the software automatically sends the document back to the supervisor's workstation. From there it can be transmitted to the next person, completed, or filed.

Special Features

When the investigation requires accessing the mainframe computer, the document image processor's multi-function workstation provides a *window;* that is, a space on the computer screen "opens up" and overlays the text being worked on. Information can be brought into the window without disrupting the processing under way. If an investigator has a question about a document, he or she can retrieve it by entering one or more pieces of index information into the workstation. When the requested material is associated with other documentation, several pages appear, and the operator can browse through them. If a file folder is requested, it will appear on the workstation screen and can be scanned in the same manner as a paper file folder.

Security Pacific handles transactions using a variety of forms. To capture these transactions, special software with interactive graphics capability lets the user create forms on the workstation. If the operator, for example, wants to fill out a tracer document, the forms package is called up to generate the correct form. To fill out the forms, word processing is provided with the system. The completed forms can be filed with other document images on the optical disk or sent to the printing station, where a high quality printer quickly provides a hard copy.

Summary

The records operations in corporations employ traditional records centers, as well as computerized records management systems. Large, distributed records management systems are recognizing the value of the computer in efficient information mangement.

The Hughes Aircraft Company maintains a corporate records center and uses the computer for tracking records center operations; whereas the Marriott Corporation reservations system and that used by a retail outlet of a parent company are examples of distributed records systems and virtual central records systems, respectively. The optical disk system employed by Security Pacific National Bank illustrates ways in which the computer captures and distributes information from paper documents and eliminates the handling and storage of paper.

The trend of the future is to incorporate telecommunications and computerized records operations into records management, thereby removing the user from direct contact with paper records.

List of Terms

high-rise unit
stacks-on-steel
bank-and-space numbering system
fee-for-service cost system
virtual central records system
optical disk document-image system
window

Discussion Questions

1. What forms are needed for transferring records to a corporate records center?
2. What procedures are followed when records center documents are to be destroyed?
3. What is the major role of a manager who is in charge of the entire information management system in a corporation?
4. How does a computerized reservations system eliminate the need for paper records?
5. How does a system such as TCS aid small retail businesses with their transactions?
6. What are some of the devices and equipment used to maintain security in a corporate records center?
7. Why is it necessary to have records disposal authorized by more than one individual?
8. How does an optical disk system eliminate repeated transfer of paper files?

Activities

1. Visit a hotel/motel chain in your city and determine how it handles its reservation system. You should be particularly interested in how reservations are made from outside agencies, such as travel agencies and other hotel/motels.
2. Many large corporations attempt to keep all records permanently. Visit a branch office of a retail chain and report on their method of records storage. Comment on the records management principle that "storage space available tends to determine records disposition."
3. Some states are contemplating converting their driver's license records to a computerized system that would allow links to the license plate division, insurance companies, and police agencies (for traffic violations). List the advantages and disadvantages of such a change.

4. Because of the continuing and growing need for secure storage for inactive records, some experts suggest that the government provide regional records centers as a national service. What do you see as the benefits and drawbacks in federal records centers?

References

Esposito, John J. *Moody's Handbook of Common Stocks* (Fall 1987).

FileNet Corporation. "User Profile: Security Pacific National Bank Puts Optical Disk Document-Image Processor to Work." *AIIM Conference Daily* (Tuesday, April 28, 1987): 69–70.

Marriott Corporation. *Annual Report 1986.* Marriott Drive, Washington, D.C. 20058, 1987.

Chapter 14

Records Management in the Data Processing Center

Learning Goals

1. To identify the role of records management in data processing.
2. To become familiar with specific records management operations in a data processing center.
3. To differentiate between computer physical media and digital records.
4. To learn how to construct a naming convention.
5. To understand the tree-structured directory concept.
6. To become familiar with the elements of disaster recovery planning.

Introduction

In business, the data processing center performs the regular processing operations that use computer facilities. Regular processing operations usually include accounting activities such as general ledger, accounts payable and receivable, inventory, and billing. Other processing includes personnel procedures such as payroll, word processing, and other similar business operations. The computer hardware can range from the mainframe level with enormous processing capabilities to the single, standalone microcomputer level. Prior to 1980, the microcomputer was not available for general business processing, so virtually all *data processing* (DP) *centers* used mainframe or minicomputer hardware. Today, a DP center may include any combination of mainframe, minicomputer, or microcomputer hardware linked in a variety of configurations.

The process of records management applies to all business records, including those in the data processing center such as client records or personnel files. However, the data processing center requires software, procedures, and documentation to process the business data, and those processes, software, and documentation can be considered as a set of records unique to the data processing center that require management for efficient operations. This chapter will examine the application of records management principles to the business data processed in the DP center, the software programs and procedures used to process the data, and the other records involved in data processing.

DP centers store information in a digital format on physical media such as magnetic tapes. Both the physical media and the digital content of that media require management. The following sections differentiate between the media types and point out those areas in the data processing center in which records management can be applied.

Computer Physical Media

By *physical media*, we mean the actual physical (and tangible) devices on which information is stored. For example, a phonograph record contains information such as music that is retrieved through a special device, a phonograph player. But the phonograph record itself and its album cover are the actual media that we handle, store, classify, and retrieve. Some people may store their record albums by major category (classical, rock, country), and then by artist within the categories. Retail stores that sell a large number of phonograph records, radio stations, and other large-scale phonograph record users are concerned with efficient management of the physical media, with no real concern for the substance or contents of the media. In this context, we distinguish two major types of computer physical files: *paper media* and media containing digital information (*digital physical media*).

Paper Media

Not too long ago, most computer systems used cards for many input and output operations, with paper output for reports. Business data and computer programs were on these cards of heavy stock, approximately 3¼ × 7⅜ inches in size. Considerable space and resources were required to store, manipulate, and retrieve these cards. A large program or data set might consist of thousands of sequentially ordered cards—and woe to the operator who dropped a box of them! Today, the cards have virtually disappeared in favor of digital data on magnetic media. Left-over cards are now sold as cute memo cards.

In the card days, most programs were on cards; but paper listings, or hard copy, of the cards regularly were produced, stored, and used as reference material. This remains true today, even though videotext (displayed digital media) has largely replaced cards. For a large data processing center, thousands of programs and their associated hard copy must be managed. The classification system usually is the program name according to a naming convention. A major problem is maintaining correspondence between the paper records and the videotext records. Too often, if a change is made to the videotext, the paper copy is not updated. As a practical matter, a data processing center with substantial activity in its videotext records may find that the paper/hard copies should not be maintained, stored, or retrieved.

Other paper records in a data processing center will include the documentation associated with the creation, analysis, design, testing, and implementation of business computer applications. This documentation can be invaluable for maintenance to existing applications and should be managed carefully to allow for efficient storage and retrieval. Another sizable mass of paper consists of the operating and applications program documentation and their regular updates. For example, a mainframe system using COBOL will accumulate an amazing amount of paper documentation on COBOL along with regular updates. Similarly, a microcomputer system that uses DOS (Disk Operating System) will have substantial documentation describing DOS along with regular updates.

Together, the paper records of a data processing center are often called the *DP Library*. Since these records rarely are managed professionally, the storage, use, and retrieval of the information often is very inefficient. Too many data processing centers are reinventing the wheel by developing procedures for their paper libraries that have been in use in records management for years. This is unfortunate, especially because the company's own records center could provide the knowledge and skills to manage the DP files effectively.

Digital Physical Media

There are two major types of computer digital media amenable to records management: magnetic or optical disks, and tapes. The procedures and equipment for managing disks and tapes as records are no different from those used for paper records. (We described some of the possibilities for records management of these media in Chapter 6.)

However, the management of disks and tapes is more than simply a matter of storage and retrieval. A complete program of records management—from an accurate inventory to prudent retention scheduling and, eventually, to disaster planning—will provide significant gains in the use of the media. In fact, DP centers can benefit from the experience of records management in these matters rather than attempting to develop these procedures anew.

Managing Digital Records

In a computer environment, many of the records are in a digital format stored on suitable media. The media encompasses floppy disks, optical disks, magnetic tapes, *DASD* (direct access storage devices), and other media that are capable of storing and retrieving data in a digital format.

Some types of digital records are not open to media management because they are marketed as a complete package with the management processes included. This may be due to the nature of the media (extremely difficult to alter) or the inflexibility of the surrounding system. For example, an optical disk system may include the records of interest along with the software for storage and retrieval. The optical disk may be capable of additions, but not alterations, and no hardware has been included to change the system in any significant way. The system can only be used to add, delete, and edit data within very prescribed limits. In other words, no meaningful records management can be applied to this type of system—it is already in place.

Another example is the computer's operating system, which accompanies the computer hardware. The operating system rarely is altered, and such changes normally are discouraged by the vendor. The management procedures are well defined and accompany the equipment. But there remain many opportunities for the management of digital media, and the introduction of microcomputers into the business world is increasing the need for records management in the DP center.

The principles of records management can be applied in the management of digital records in the areas of naming conventions, structured directories, and operation libraries. In this section, we will examine each of these areas in terms of their application to digital data in the data processing center. (The related topics of COM and CIM [computer output/input microfilm] were covered in Chapter 8.)

Naming Conventions

Computers store groups of digital data as files, for example, reports, letters, programs, data, and other material. The computer accesses the files by their *filename*, just as file folders are accessed by their name or label. A computer allows a maximum number of characters to name a file. A name can be composed of one or more groups of characters called *nodes*. Nodes are separated by a unique symbol such as a "." (dot) or a "\" (back slash).

A popular mainframe naming system defines all nodes as eight or fewer characters with a limit of forty-four total characters. The most popular microcomputer name type is the eight-character dot three character format (XXXXXXXX.YYY). The Xs and Ys can stand for any alphabetic character or number. Most nonalphanumeric characters are avoided in names because they may have special meanings such as the "." (dot) and "\" (back slash). Spaces or blanks in names are universally prohibited because a space is defined in computer systems as a *delimiter*. A delimiter is used to end a name or command, so a space in a name would make the name invalid.

Suppose you are starting a new computer system. You are creating and storing computer files in digital format on magnetic media such as floppy disks. With only a few files and a few disks, you would have no problem remembering what each file contains. However, as the number of files grows, naming them in a unique way and remembering what each name means becomes more difficult. Eventually, you may use the same name for two different files, accidentally replacing an old file with a new one. Also, you may spend too much time examining the contents of your files because you can't remember what each name means. These problems become overwhelming as the number of files grows into the hundreds and thousands. These difficulties can be avoided by using a standard procedure called a *naming convention* for naming files. (This procedure, similar to subject classification for paper records, was discussed briefly in Chapter 6.)

Figure 14.1 shows how an author might name the files for books he or she is writing. The files are stored as digital data on a computer system.

A naming convention would itself be a file on the computer that would be updated as changes, additions, and deletions occur, and a printed copy of it would be kept available for reference. If the files were backed up or archived, the convention would be stored with copies of the files both as a computer file and as a printed copy. Having a copy of the naming convention available for the archived materials is essential.

A naming convention should be structured according to a general organizing topic with a number of related subsets. In Figure 14.1, the general organizing topic is an author's books, with subsets of elements of book parts and version numbers. Following the example, the author might have another, separate naming convention for her business correspondence, and perhaps a third naming convention for her reference material and notes.

Computers use the filename for operations that list files, delete files, copy files, compare files, look at the contents of files, and do other procedures. These operations are part of the computer's operating system and often are accessible from applications programs. These file operations are extremely useful for managing computer files. For these procedures, all computer operating systems allow the use of *global filename characters*, which greatly extend the range and flexibility of file operations. Virtually all

Figure 14.1 Computer Naming Convention Example

BOOKS Naming Convention	Last Update MM/DD/YY
X X X X Y Y Y N	Description
- - - - - - - -	
X X X X	Book Name OAKS = Wind in the Oaks LOLO = Love Lost WILD = The Wild City
Y Y Y	Part of Book INT = Introduction CHn = Chapter n, n = 1, 2, . . . APn = Appendix n, n = 1, 2, . . . BIB = Bibliography
N	Version Number, 0–9

Explanation and Examples

This is an 8-alphanumeric-character naming convention with three major types indicated by X, Y, and N.

OAKSINT0	Introduction to Wind in the Oaks, version 0
OAKSCH21	Chapter 2 of Wind in the Oaks, version 1
WILDBIB3	Bibliography of The Wild City, version 3

Alterations or Additions

The Name of Book category (Xs) will expand as new books are added.

The Part of Book (Ys) should not change unless a new element is added.

The version number (N) is limited to the ten values 0–9. Changes will require a change in the entire naming convention.

computer systems allow the use of the special characters "?" and "*".

The character "?" in a filename means that any valid character can occupy that position. For example, the filename ABC?DE refers to any file that starts with ABC and ends with DE, such as ABCXDE, ABCYDE, or ABC1DE. In this way, the computer can process groups of similar files using the "?" global filename character. More generally, the "*" character indicates that any character can occupy that position and all the remaining positions in the node. For example, in an eight-character node system, the filename SYSTM* could refer to SYSTM01, SYSTEMBAK, or SYSTM.

The use of global filename characters to process groups of files can be remarkably productive if the naming convention has been developed to take advantage of group processing. This means that the position of the characters in the naming convention must be standardized. As shown in the example in Figure 14.1, each group of characters must be completely defined and the names must conform by position to the convention specifications. A final consideration is that each filename must be unique and, hopefully, somewhat meaningful.

Note that date/time information is not used in most naming conventions because it is universally available in the computer operating system through a directory command. Other information that virtually all computer systems automatically provide is the size of the file and how much room is left on the physical media for files.

Structured Directories

A data processing center may contain hundreds, thousands, even tens of thousands of files, each with a unique name following a good naming convention. If we know the name of a particular file, or can determine the name from the naming convention, then we can retrieve the file. For straightforward storage and retrieval, almost any computer system is adequate. However, if we are seeking information from the files that may or may not exist and/or the computer operating system is relatively slow and unsophisticated, then we need a more efficient way of organizing or structuring the files to enhance our retrieval capabilities.

For example, suppose we are looking for all correspondence involving the XYZ Corporation, and the naming convention suggests that we should search for all files that match the global filename xyz.* to obtain our answer. If there are thousands of files, such a search may turn up far more information than we need and may take an excessive amount of time. But if we could just search those groups of files that are candidates, the search would be faster and more productive. This leads to the idea of *structured directories* in which major groupings of files are given a name (the directory) and subgroupings in directories are given names (*subdirectories*).

Most computer systems have the capability of using structured directories and subdirectories to improve file retrievals. Directories and subdirectories can be conceptualized as names for the storage areas of collections of files. For example, in a microcomputer system, we might store floppy disks in fifty-disk containers and keep ten container groups together in file drawers. Each file drawer could be named as the directories, and the fifty-disk containers would be named as the subdirectories. In the same sense, directories can be considered as the first node of a filename. For example, we could have all of our files on direct access storage devices and have four major directories named HIST, WORK, TEST, and PROD. A file in the WORK directory might be named ACTG001.TBL indicating a table of accounting values. The complete file specification would be WORK.ACTG001.TBL indicating the directory as the first node.

Figure 14.2 illustrates a *tree-structured directory* sample. Because the shape of the diagram is in the shape of the roots of a tree, directory structures are called trees. Many computer operating systems have a command, for example TREE, that tells the computer to show the directory structure of a specified storage device. In Figure 14.2, WIDGETDV (the WIDGET Division) is the main or *root directory*. There are three subdirectories of WIDGETDV: ACCNTG (Accounting), SALES (Marketing and Sales), and PERSNL (Personnel and Payroll). The subdirectory SALES has two subdirectories of its own, JOHN and LINDA, indicating the owners of the files. Finally, LINDA has two more subdirectories, MEMOS and REPORTS. The actual groups of files named FILE01, FILE02, . . . , FILE99 indicate any number of files, not more subdirectories.

To access files in a tree-structured directory, the complete specification including all directories is used. From Figure 14.2, to access the file named FILE54 in the JOHN subdirectory, we would ask for WIDGETDV.SALES.JOHN.FILE54. (On a microcomputer, back slashes are used instead of dots.) This is called the complete file specification or *path name*. The term path indicates the trail followed from the root directory to get to the file. Most computer systems allow the user to specify the paths to be used and contain commands to create, delete, and change (sub)directories.

The primary advantage of a system that

Figure 14.2 A Tree-Structured Directory

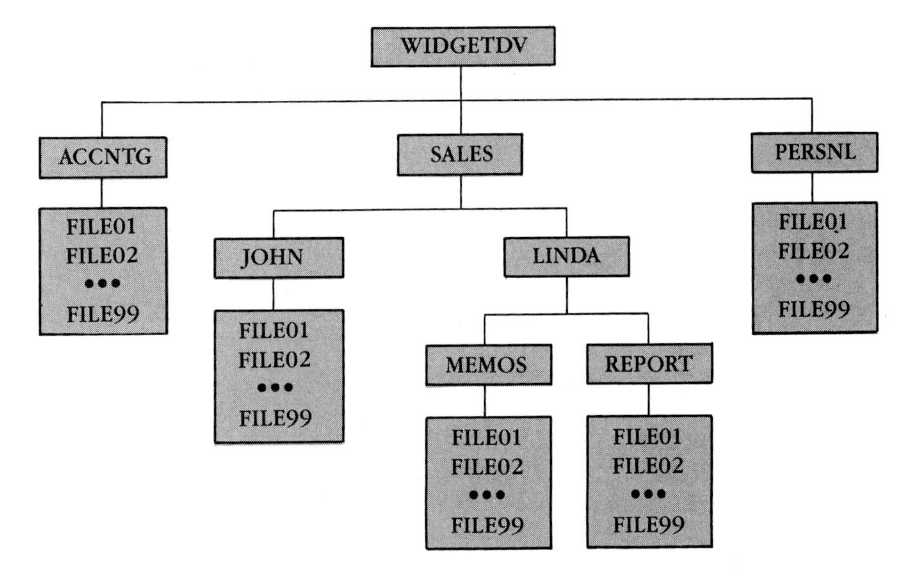

uses a tree-structured directory is that searches and subsequent retrievals can be made from a specific directory or subdirectory rather than having to access all of the files for every operation. A careful and meaningful categorization of files into a tree-structured directory can significantly increase productivity in a data processing center. Unfortunately, a directory structure in an active, rapidly growing data processing center is often left to grow without management. The result is a substantial amount of inefficiency that could be corrected with the proper management of the directory system.

Libraries

Surveys in data processing centers of all sizes show that the main activity is maintenance of the existing processing systems. In mainframe environments, maintenance activities consume between two-thirds and three-fourths of the personnel, hardware, and software resources. A never-ending stream of alterations seems to be required in order to keep present systems working efficiently and up to date. Moreover, data processing centers are constantly requested to add enhancements and new systems to those already present.

Maintenance changes and enhancements will require alterations to application programs, tables, and other types of software. Collectively, these pieces of software are called *modules*. A module is a distinctive "chunk" of software that may stand alone, or more likely, be part of one or more applications being processed by the DP center. A *library* is defined as a collection of similar modules. For example, professional programmers refer to program libraries that contain standard, tested modules that can be used as building blocks to create application programs.

Obviously, the idea of libraries should be linked to structured directories. To facilitate file storage and retrieval, the different directories and subdirectories should represent or be equivalent to libraries. This is the case in most DP centers. A tree-structured directory is developed with references to the conceptual libraries, and conversely, directories come to represent libraries. But the use of these libraries is interactive and the use of files from different files must be managed.

When alterations are made to modules, they must be tested and, when accepted, moved into production status. Therefore, three different module versions can exist in the system, all with the same name. In order to follow a standardized procedure, which minimizes confusion between the versions, each version is stored in a different library. In a tree-structured directory, there might be libraries (subdirectories) named WORK, TEST, and PROD to reflect the respective areas of (1) working on a module, (2) testing a module, and (3) using the module in regular production.

If the modules are on separable media—for example, floppy disks—then the disks might be labeled WORK, TEST, and PROD. If the modules are all contained on direct access storage devices, then they might be separated by prefacing their names with the qualifiers WORK, TEST, or PROD. The different versions all will have the same name, but they are accessed by their respective library designation.

This situation can cause chronic problems in a large, rapidly changing data processing center where there may be hundreds of modules undergoing alterations. When a module is involved in two or more distinct alterations, care must be taken so that changes occur in the correct order to the correct version. For example, if there is a module in the TEST library, then it should not be accessible to the WORK library until it has passed back to the PROD library. Some mainframe environments have special software just to deal with this problem.

Of course, there may be libraries for specific types of data: the operating system, the electronic mail, word processing files, and others. A common library often found in DP centers is a history subdirectory. This library, often named HIST or HISTORY, is used to keep a record of the changes that have been made to modules. Of course, if a change is made in a software module, it is expected that the appropriate notes and comments will be placed in the software. But notes in the modules are not sufficient when five, ten, or fifty modules are affected, and an overview of the changes is required to understand what was done, when it was done, and who did it. This is the function of the HIST library.

Disaster Recovery Planning

The idea of *disaster recovery* often becomes meaningful in the wake of a disaster. There is nothing quite like a near disaster to prompt planning. An oft-quoted statistic is that two-thirds of all businesses that suffer a major disaster go out of business—they never recover. Because of its concentration of data and operations, the data processing center is a candidate for disaster recovery planning. Although disaster planning should include the entire business, the focus of such planning will be the DP center.

Data processing disasters include power failures, operator errors, systems and applications program errors, equipment malfunction, natural disasters (fire, flood, earthquake, tornado), and sabotage or theft. In general, the more complex the DP center's hardware and software, the greater the chance for disaster, and the greater will be the difficulty of planning for disasters.

The primary purpose of a disaster recovery plan is to guarantee business operations in the face of a major disaster. Insurance companies and regulatory agencies are extremely interested in promoting, if not requiring, that the companies they service have disaster recovery plans to place to reduce the probability of failure. However, there are a number of other advantages to disaster recovery planning:

1. the clarification and streamlining of internal controls

2. security for operations and data that may involve a legal liability
3. possible reductions in premium rates
4. availability of data for research.

Disaster recovery planning seemingly has sufficient advantages to be pursued. But disaster planning involves trade-offs, and the most common trade-off is convenience for security. For example, we can physically restrict access to files to maximize security, but the convenience of accessing those files will be severely restricted. A gain in security will always be balanced by a loss in convenience. The financial trade-off is that of cost versus budget. The basic question is how much to budget for an event that may not happen. If a disaster does not occur, then it may be difficult to justify the incurred expense of disaster recovery planning. The fact is disasters do occur, and disaster planning should be thought of as insurance.

Experts in the area suggest that the broad area of disaster recovery planning be broken down into the three components of data, processing, and planning (Smith, 1987). The first two elements, data and processing, are concerned with security and recovery of the operations. The planning element involves the procedures to follow for the development of a plan.

Data Security and Recovery

The data component in disaster recovery is concerned with ensuring the security of the data. In almost every case, the data can be secured through a regular program of backups that are stored in a secure off-site location. The data is in digital format, often as magnetic media, therefore this is the format for the backup computer data. The most cost-effective means is to create the backups on computer tape, which are then rotated through secure off-site storage. These backups are known as *rotational data* and include both business data in the data processing systems and applications programs. Backing up vital data on a daily basis is tedious at best, essentially unproductive, and always costly. At the microcomputer level, the resources required may seem excessive, but the bottom line is to back up all data, especially hard disks (Wilcox, 1987).

Processing Security and Recovery

The processing component is concerned with guaranteeing that essential data processing could continue during a disaster recovery. Of course, we assume that the data is available from the secure off-site location. The options for alternate processing include returning to manual operations, reciprocal agreements with sister companies, and contracts with service bureaus. Too many mainframe data processing centers are incapable of returning to manual operations, even if the processing is curtailed to absolute minimal levels, because of the sheer quantity of operations involved and the unavailability of the data in the proper format. Reciprocal agreements with sister companies require that the sister company have sufficient processing power to handle the additional load. Because this requirement is not always feasible, contracts with service bureaus become an attractive option. The service bureaus can spread the processing loads among multiple clients, thus acting as processing insurers.

The Planning Operation

The planning component consists of the creation of a *disaster plan* for the data processing center and a backup *emergency plan*. Of course, the DP plans should be integrated with any existing disaster plans developed in other departments. Figure 14.3, "The Elements of a Disaster Plan," is based on expert advice in disaster contingency planning (Balon and Gardner, 1987).

Figure 14.3 The Elements of a Disaster Plan

Risk Assessment
- ☐ Estimate disaster probabilities
- ☐ Assess protection costs
- ☐ Determine allowable losses
- ☐ Figure recovery costs

Prevention
- ☐ Vital records protection program
- ☐ Physical prevention devices
- ☐ Logical prevention plans
- ☐ An ounce of prevention . . .

Preliminary System Development
- ☐ Interim plan development
- ☐ Suggest equipment and procedures
- ☐ Explanation of recovery costs
- ☐ Outline of the complete plan

Final System Design
- ☐ Refine preliminary plan
- ☐ Locate and secure all agreements
- ☐ Specify all equipment and procedures
- ☐ Prepare comprehensive documentation

Testing
- ☐ As feasible, do a dry run
- ☐ Record results for comparisons
- ☐ Verify plan operations
- ☐ Amend plan to minimize problems

Approval
- ☐ Gain approval at all stages
- ☐ Involve management at major phases
- ☐ Distribute plan and approvals
- ☐ Annually repeat approvals

Figure 14.3 shows the steps to be followed in the development of a disaster recovery plan. These steps are risk assessment, prevention, preliminary system development, final system design, testing, and approval. Important factors are listed in the boxes below each step. They will minimize the work involved in the development of the plan and maximize the acceptance of the plan in the business organization.

Any disaster plan should consider the inclusion of not only the plan of action after the emergency, but also an emergency plan for those times when a disaster is imminent; that is, when there is a warning of a disaster. This is most appropriate when environmental conditions have produced a pattern of disaster situations such as flooding or hurricane. Although these disasters cannot be predicted with any certainty to occur on a specific date, some warning usually is possible. The disaster plan should specify the steps to be taken in a warning situation.

A disaster recovery plan will alert required staff, specify and control the disaster situation, and indicate restoration procedures. In the development of a complete plan, appropriate sources should be reviewed for information that is specific to the business situation. Murray (1987) has compiled over 200 sources of information on aspects of disaster recovery.

Summary

The data processing center performs the regular computer processing operations of the business. Records management applies to all business records, including those in the data processing center. DP center records include business data records as well as the software, procedures, and documentation necessary to process the data. The three areas in the data processing center that benefit from records management include (1) the management of the computer physical media, (2) management of the digital records, and (3) disaster recovery planning.

Computer physical media include paper, floppy disks, and tapes. The physical media requires management in the same sense as active records. The digital contents have unique aspects which require naming conventions, structured directories, and management of the module libraries.

The purpose of a disaster recovery plan is to guarantee business operations in the face of a major disaster. It is often difficult to justify the commitment of resources for an event that is unlikely to occur. Disaster recovery planning involves plans for data security and recovery, as well as processing operations security and recovery. A complete disaster plan also specifies who will control the disaster situation and provides recovery procedures.

List of Terms

data processing center
physical media
paper media
digital physical media
data processing (DP) library
DASD
filename
node
delimiter
naming convention
global filename character
structured directory
subdirectory
tree-structured directory
root directory
path name
module
library
disaster recovery
data security and recovery
rotational data
processing security
disaster plan
emergency plan

Discussion Questions

1. What is the difference between digital physical media and digital records?
2. What would you name the computer file that contains the naming convention itself, such as the one in Figure 14.1?
3. What is the feasibility of using a three-character group in a naming convention representing the file owner's initials? How many people could be accommodated? Does everyone have three initials?
4. What should the relationship be between module libraries and tree-structured directories?
5. What are the advantages and disadvantages of disaster recovery planning?
6. What steps should be followed in the preparation of a disaster recovery plan?

Activities

1. Visit a data processing center and find out the extent and management of its physical media, especially the paper files. Prepare a brief report (four to five pages) on your findings.
2. Visit a data processing center and survey the use of retention scheduling for its files, particularly with respect to the digital physical media

such as magnetic tapes and (floppy) disks. Prepare a retention schedule based on this information. If the center already has a retention schedule, obtain a copy and prepare a report explaining the various items in the schedule.

3. Develop a naming convention for use with microcomputer word-processing correspondence files using the "eight-dot-three" format (XXXXXXXX.YYY). Consider the initiator of the correspondence, the type of correspondence (letters, memos, directives, etc.), and the word processing operator who actually creates the file.
4. Visit a data processing center and determine the naming convention in use for the digital data.
5. Visit any business and prepare a report on its disaster recovery plan. If the business doesn't have one, then talk to at least three people in the business and report on what they hope to do about the records they are responsible for in a disaster.
6. It has been said that data processing managers always have a five-page disaster plan. The first page is their letter of resignation and the last four pages is their résumé. Visit a data processing center and assess the validity of this type of "disaster plan."

References

Balon, Brett J., and H. Wayne Gardner. "Disaster Contingency Planning: The Basic Elements." *Records Management Quarterly* 21, no. 1 (January 1987): 14–16.

Murray, Toby. "Bibliography on Disaster Preparedness and Disaster Recovery." *Records Management Quarterly* 21, no. 2 (April 1987): 18–41.

Smith, Stephen J. "Disaster Recovery Planning: Myth or Reality?" *Proceedings of the ARMA International 32nd Annual Conference*, Anaheim, California, October 19–22, 1987, pp. 319–27.

Wilcox, Art. "Backing Up Is Hard to Do." *PC World* 5, no. 3 (March 1987): 210–17.

Chapter 15

Computer-Based Records Management

Learning Goals

1. To become familiar with the concept of computer-based records management systems (CBRMS).
2. To be able to differentiate between database management and records management.
3. To explain the information and processing requirements for a computer-based records management system.
4. To be aware of the systems life cycle approach.
5. To be knowledgeable about security in a CBRMS.

Introduction

Traditional methods of records management are becoming difficult to use adequately with the sheer mass of today's records governed by literally hundreds of statutes determining their retention (Heite, 1984). Stating the problem is simple—How can a business keep track of its records?—solving it is complex. In order to deal effectively with this problem, businesses are turning to the computer. The computer offers a cost-effective method for tracking records more efficiently and accurately than manual alternatives. Computer systems also allow searching and tracking functions that are not feasible in manual systems. The advantages of computer systems for records management have led industry observers to predict that the use of electronic file cabinets will increase significantly (Sample, 1982). This trend follows the general integration of the computer into office information systems.

This chapter explains the principles of a computer-based records management system (CBRMS). A CBRMS does not store records on a computer. The computer is used to track records through the record cycle, provide appropriate reports, and allow queries of the records. Because the records themselves are not stored on the computer, the hardware and software requirements for a CBRMS usually can be met by a microcomputer package, as long as the system can track a record through the record cycle, provide appropriate reports, and allow queries of the records. The typical capacity should allow for tracking 1,000 to 10,000 records.

A computer-based records management system is a type of database management. A *database* is any collection of business data organized in a way that it can be accessed for multiple purposes (Behling, 1986: 479). A *database management system* (DBMS) is a series of integrated programs designed to create, access, and manage a database (Behling, 1986: 483). Therefore, when the database being managed is a set of records and when a computer is used to track the records (as is always the case in a DBMS), then the system is a computer-based records management system.

Related to the concepts and hardware of a computer-based records management system is the *computer-assisted retrieval system* (CARS), which is based on micrographic film techniques for storage and the computer for retrieval. (Computer-assisted retrieval systems were described in Chapter 8.) In comparison, the CBRMS uses the computer to manage existing records but does not alter the format or storage of the records.

The Goals of a Computer-Based Records System

A computer-based records management system (CBRMS) should fulfill two goals: (1) the production of system reports and (2) immediate response to system queries.

System Reports

An efficient records management system should be able to describe accurately the status of its records in terms of their location and characteristics. The system should also contain action prompts that tell when to purge, transfer, and alter the status of records. To fulfill these requirements, the system should be able to produce the following types of *system reports*.

Records by Retention Status This report includes both the eventual status and the date of the status change. For example, one section of the report might show a group of records that should be kept active until a certain date, at which time they should be destroyed.

Records by Type This report shows the records by their type such as vital, active, inactive, archival, and so forth. It also shows if a record has been requested, is out (to whom), or is in its normal location.

Records by Location This report is a listing of the records by their physical location; for example, the building, file cabinet, or drawer.

Records by Security This report shows which records can be accessed by which people. For example, highly sensitive records may only be accessed by high-clearance people.

Records to Be Moved Based on retention status, this regular report indicates which records are to be purged, moved to inactive storage, archived, and so forth.

Records Update This is a report of records that were added, altered, deleted, or changed in status during a given period and is very useful in tracking the operation of the system. Many parts of this report could require a user sign-off. A summary over time of the report would allow attention to the growth and changes in the system.

Labels This report is a listing that provides labels for paper record files, file cabinets, boxes, and so forth.

Equipment Location This report provides a listing of the types of equipment by location and the capacity available and utilized. If the equipment in a given location reached near full capacity, perhaps 95-percent or greater utilization, the report would issue a warning.

Utility Report This report lists system characteristics; for example, a listing of the retention status codes or number of codes used to describe records.

In the sample (partial) report shown in Figure 15.1, the BLDG, ROOM, and FILE are standard codes for those locations. The CODE and the RECORD-NAME are general classification names for a general group of records that are filed by date within the group. The PURGE CRITERIA lists the criteria, usually the date, after which the files are to be destroyed. A more comprehensive purge report might contain a heading describing the type of purge such as incinerate, pulverize, or recycle.

The records reports would be produced on both a regular basis and when needed in a specific situation. The Figure 15.1 sample report would be produced on a regular basis, for example, monthly. Other reports would only be produced on request of a user.

Often, "on request" reports need to be just summaries rather than entire reports. For example, a user might want to check on the retention status assigned to a certain type of record, or a records auditor might want to know the ratio of record requests to active records. These information requests are called "queries."

System Queries

A *system query* is a request for specific information that is needed immediately but not likely to be requested on a regular basis. Queries are associated with computer-based systems because such systems can quickly provide more information than manual systems. Imagine trying to find out the volume of records to be destroyed over the next five years by month in a manual records system! A CBRMS should be able to provide that information.

If the report system is well designed, then the reports will supply the regular information needed. Queries will satisfy irregular needs, for example, the surprise audit.

Since information about each record is contained in the CBRMS, could one query the record itself as compared to information about the record? For example, could one obtain a listing of all records that relate to the minutes of the annual board meeting? or obtain a list of all records that pertain to the

Figure 15.1 Sample Records Purge List

BLDG	*ROOM*	*FILE*	*CODE*	*RECORD-NAME*	*PURGE CRITERIA*
C-12	407	19/3	EXAU	Expense Authorization	01/01/88
M-02	010	01/4	LMIN	Luncheon Minutes	all
F-01	100	03/3	GENL	General Ledger	01/01/75

Zellman Company over the last five years? To provide answers to these queries, the CBRMS must have information about the record's substance. Most CBRMSs contain some information about the record itself, such as the record's name, synonym, key words, and brief descriptive information.

Record Information Required for a CBRMS

For the CBRMS to produce reports and respond to queries, the system must contain information about each record. To produce accurate reports, the system requires information about the record's location, characteristics, and standing in the system. For answers to queries, the system needs additional information about the contents of the record.

Descriptive Record Information

It is difficult to specify precisely the information required for any records system because there are so many different types of records. However, some general categories typically apply to any records system. Figure 15.2 shows typical general categories and possible record information to be included in each category. It also describes the general elements that should apply to every record. Each record should be represented meaningfully in each element. The list is not meant to be exhaustive, since each records system has unique characteristics.

Query Elements

Probably the least familiar elements of record information are the DESCRIPTION items. These elements are the basis of the queries, and their primary purpose is a summarization of a record's information. They should provide a brief reminder to the user for easy storage and retrieval. The elements of DESCRIPTION are sometimes called *retrieval handles*.

The first DESCRIPTION item is a CODE. Every record should have a CODE, but it should not be unique. Typical codes are from three characters (shown in Figure 15.2, PPP, SSS, and TTT) to eight characters. The primary code is the main category; the secondary and tertiary codes are for further subdividing the categories. If more codes are needed, a fourth, fifth, or even a sixth code may be added. As a general rule, four codes should be the limit, with no more than fifteen possibilities for each code. This allows the system to distinguish 15*15*15*15 subcategories or over 50,000 types.

Figure 15.2 Typical Record Information for a CBRMS

General	*Possible elements to be included*
LOCATION	Building, room, file/shelf, drawer/box
MEDIA	Paper, card, aperture, film, magnetic disk
DESCRIPTION	
CODE	PPP.SSS.TTT for primary, secondary, tertiary codes
LINE	One, two, three
KEY WORDS	At least three key words (synonyms)
PRIORITY	Describing who has access to the record
DATES	Creation, check-out, updates
STATUS	Active, inactive, archival, destroyed, vital
RETENTION	Dates/periods of changing STATUS

Figure 15.3 Code Dictionary

PPP.SSS.TTT	*Description of parts*
FIN.	Financial Records
GEL.	General Ledger
PAY.	Payroll
BUD.	Budgets
DEP	Departmental
COR	Corporate
ACT.	Accounts
REC	Receivable
PAY	Payable

As codes are created and used, they should be organized into a standard format called a *code dictionary* (illustrated in Figure 15.3). The dictionary should be reviewed periodically for meaningfulness and for possible collapsing of categories.

The second type of DESCRIPTION is the LINE. Three lines is the recommended limit. The lines are each about thirty characters long and uniquely describe the record. Often, the first line is used, along with the CODE, to print the label for the record. It is not a coincidence that thirty characters fit nicely on third-cut file folder labels.

The last element of DESCRIPTION is the KEY WORDS item. As used in libraries, the *key word* is a word that is the focus of the record. For example, a record may be appropriately CODEd as a financial record, yet it concerns the Zellman Company exclusively. If it appears that this company affiliation may be important, then one key word should be assigned to "ZELLMAN." Unlike CODES, key words can be anything that seems relevant to the content of the record. The goal is to capture the essential content of the record. Key words do not have to fit a category and there may be no key words (rare), one, or more than one. Library systems have demonstrated that five key words should be the limit, with three being a practical number for most purposes.

Record Activity Information

A record's standing in the system refers to the characteristics that describe the record's activity. For example, a record's activity will be affected by its STATUS, and by when the status changes (RETENTION). In addition, it is important to know when a record was created or updated with alteration of information in the record. This is the DATES category. The most important element of activity will be the use of the record; that is, if a record has been checked out, when it was checked out, and how often it has been checked out. Finally, who can access the record is an important element of the activity record. The system should reveal who checked out the record (PRIORITY) and, perhaps, who attempted to check out the record without sufficient priority.

The amount of information about a record can be quite extensive. It is important to specify carefully the exact information needed for the records. Attention to the design at this point will go far toward avoiding changes and making the system efficient and useful.

Information Entry Format

The specific information about each record must be entered into the system to allow the generation of reports and to respond to queries. The conversion from a manual system to a CBRMS will involve entry of the information for each record. Essentially, a form is created to gather this information based on the categories shown in Figure 15.2. The form can be a standard paper form, or it may be a part of the CBRMS system.

Because the basis of the CBRMS is the form used to capture the record's information, careful design of the form to include the required information in a way that is easy to fill out, with few unknown possibilities, will help guarantee the efficiency and success of the system. A good methodology for developing the form is to do a trial run to see if it is capturing what is needed without too much trouble. Trouble spots are indicated when a place on the form is left blank because it is not clear what should be there. Similarly, if a record's information does not appear to be fully captured by the form, further analysis is indicated.

System Processing Requirements

A CBRMS will produce reports and allow queries about records. It is also important for the CBRMS to be capable of processing its own records. The processing requirements include the following types of activities.

System Activities

Creating Records Information This is used heavily when the system is installed and then as new records are added.

Editing Records Information There must be a provision to change the information about a record due to errors, new information, or for administrative reasons. Most changes will be on an individual case basis. Some involve mass changes, for example, when a retention category is changed.

Deleting Records Information This is not the usual method of record deletion, which would continue the record's existence, though marked as deleted. This rare event is to actually remove a record totally from the system.

System Operations These operations do not deal directly with the records but, rather, the way in which the CBRMS itself operates; for example, changing retention schedules, altering a report format, changing a screen's input layout, changing the frequency of input/output operations, and other system tasks.

Request Processing This activity is the dominant processing form—the retrieval function—and involves the usual operations of retrieval as shown in the flow in Figure 15.4.

Retrieval Processing

The flowchart in Figure 15.4 illustrates the careful design required for a CBRMS. It is important to completely specify all of the possible decisions that can occur in a situation because the computer can't think for itself. One must anticipate and plan for as many contingencies as seem reasonable.

Figure 15.4 starts with a user request for a record. The user may fill out a record request form, or perhaps make a direct request to an operator of the CBRMS using a computer. In either case, the next step is the CBRMS search for the record information in the system. If the record is found, then the retrieval continues; otherwise a report is forwarded to the user that the record as specified does not exist. The system also stores the fact that the retrieval failed for later printing in the record operations report.

If the record exists, its status is checked to see if (1) the record has already been retrieved (OUT) or (2) it has been requested but not yet physically checked out (SEARCH). If either of these conditions exists, then the condition is reported to the user and stored for later report. Otherwise, the status of the record is changed to SEARCH and a description of the record is produced and used for a physical search to access the record itself.

If the actual record cannot be located, then this information is stored for later report and also reported to the user. If the record is located, then the system is informed by changing the status to OUT and the record is delivered to the user. This completes the retrieval process.

The retrieval process in a CBRMS must

Figure 15.4 Retrieval Operations Flow

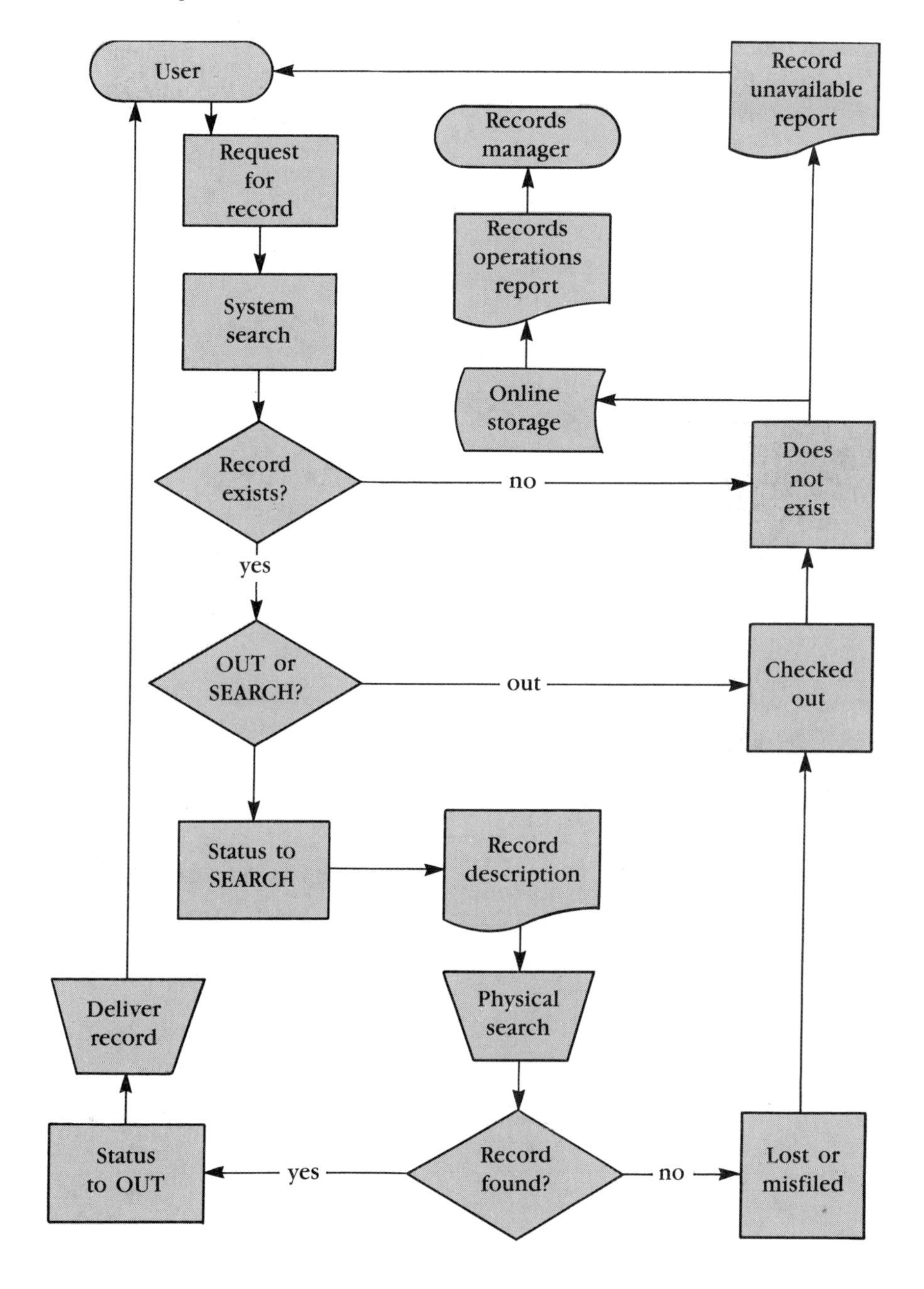

coordinate the information about the record in the system with the actual or physical record. The records unavailable report will provide information about the status of the retrieval operations and clearly show when records become lost to the computer system. Similarly, a report on the status of records will show which records are OUT or SEARCH, to whom they are checked out, when they are to be returned, and how long the records have had their current status. This type of report is the equivalent of a tickler file for checking the status of records.

Vendor CBRMS Versus Do-It-Yourself CBRMS

Not too long ago, no one would have suggested that a business attempt to develop its own CBRMS. Today, the increasing computer sophistication of businesses makes this a feasible alternative to purchasing a CBRMS from a vendor. The following section outlines the major issues to consider in deciding to purchase or to develop a CBRMS within the business. Because understanding the life cycle of a system is necessary in making the decision to develop or to purchase a CBRMS, the systems life cycle is described and briefly discussed. (We will return to the systems life cycle in Chapter 16 and discuss it from a slightly different perspective.)

The Systems Life Cycle

The steps involved in the development of a CBRMS follow those for any information system. The stages collectively are called the *systems life cycle* or systems development cycle. A general definition of the systems life cycle includes the stages of need identification, systems analysis, systems design, development, implementation, and maintenance (Behling, 1986: 72). The systems development cycle is used to organize our discussion of records management systems. A brief definition of the life cycle stages is shown in Figure 15.5.

The life cycle stages can be divided in different ways, but basically an information system follows a regular pattern from creation to regular use.

In the first part of this chapter, the need for a CBRMS was assumed and the systems analysis and design stages were described. The analysis and design concentrated on specifying the kinds of reports, queries, and systems processing that were expected. The following discussion finishes the design stage with the decision to make the system or buy the system.

Internal Development

While the cost of computer hardware continues to decline significantly, the cost of software development has increased. This

Figure 15.5 The Systems Development Life Cycle

Stage	*Activities*
Need identification	Initial evaluation and feasibility review
Systems analysis	Development of specifications for the proposed system
Systems design	Selecting procedures, equipment, and programs for the system
Development	Putting the design elements together and making sure it all works
Implementation and maintenance	Implementing the new system and keeping it operational

Figure 15.6 CBRMS Microcomputer Design Alternatives

Design	*Functions*	*Software Type*
Electronic filing	Simple queries by search and sorts	Word processing
Numeric	Sums, counts, with simple reports	Spreadsheets
Assorted elements	Queries, aggregation, and some reports	Integrated packages
Simple	Queries, reports, limited processing	Database packages (nonprogramming)
Full CBRMS	All functions	Programmable database

factor, in combination with the inherent problems in producing quality programs, are strong arguments against the creation of software for a CBRMS. Instead, a feasible alternative is to use existing software packages and perhaps some minimal in-house programming in a high-level language.

A CBRMS can be designed and developed on existing software applications without the problems involved in the creation of new software. The growing maturity of the software industry is reflected in quality applications in the areas of word processing, database management, spreadsheets, and other areas. These applications can range from quite simple to very complex. Figure 15.6 indicates some of the possibilities within the range of modest microcomputer hardware and software.

There are a number of possibilities available for internal development, as shown in Figure 15.6. In general, the more functions that are desired, the more resources must be committed to learning the intricacies of the software. If time and resources are not available to develop a full CBRMS, then the vendor alternative can be considered. For example, if having employees learn the high-level language associated with a programmable database is not feasible, then a business should consider software developed by a vendor.

Vendor Systems

Vendor systems come in different degrees of completeness and with various options. Due to the self-interest of the vendors, it is not always wise to let a vendor suggest what system is appropriate for a business. A productive approach is to prepare a *request for proposal* (RFP), which is a description of what the business wants the system to do, and let a number of vendors submit bids for systems that will satisfy the needs of the business. Figure 15.7 shows a sample RFP submitted to vendors by a financial business that is considering a CBRMS for its mortgage files. The RFP usually begins the systems analysis stage after the needs identification. An RFP would be accompanied by a cover letter describing the company's intent; for example, to install a CBRMS, the proposed schedules for bids, evaluation and decision, and the persons to be contacted. Prior to putting the RFP out to vendors, criteria should be established by which the bids will be evaluated. Of course, a primary consideration will be cost, but other considerations should include the flexibility of the proposed systems to accommodate changing conditions and requirements, and the degree of vendor support in the areas of documentation, installation, maintenance, and enhancements.

The RFP should include a description

Figure 15.7 Sample Request for Proposal

TO: Records Management Soft/Hardware Vendors

FROM: Terminal Financial Services

DATE: Month, Day, Year

SUBJECT: Request For Proposal (RFP)

We wish to install a computer-based records information system for our mortgage files which will enable the operator to retrieve the name of the file by the mortgage number.

Approximately 20,000 mortgage files are in the present manual, paper system and they are growing at the rate of about 100 per month.

We would like to obtain monthly reports that summarize the total files by mortgage amount, categories of mortgages, value by geographical area, due dates, and mortgage holders' demographics.

Please provide the prices and a description of the hardware, software, and other equipment or supplies to accomplish the above objectives.

Please include any environmental options you feel would be appropriate in your bid, for example, training, conversion aids, or maintenance.

of the quantity and type of records along with the reports and processing that are desired. The vendors probably will submit bids based on some options that were not considered in the RFP, though. Perhaps additional uses for the system were brought to light. Perhaps some vendors offer attractive leasing options that were not in the RFP. In any case, it is perfectly reasonable to do another RFP with more detailed specifications and allow the vendors to bid again.

When the bids are received, the previously established criteria can be applied to select the best proposal and to proceed to the systems design stage. At this point, an acceptable alternative is to determine that the proposal is not feasible. This might lead back to the beginning of the systems life cycle with a new evaluation and feasibility review. It can also lead to the conclusion that the entire project should be dropped. Most likely, a bid will be accepted, the project will mature, and the design stage will lead through development, implementation, and hopefully, a successful system.

Buying from a vendor can simplify the process of installing a CBRMS. The most complete systems are called *turnkey systems* because the vendor will do everything and the user need only "turn the key" on to make the system operational. Most vendors offer plain, or *vanilla systems*; adding options to a vanilla system, such as installation, testing, maintenance, training and customizing, leads to a complete turnkey system.

If a system is unique, a vendor may suggest that the degree of customizing necessary to fit the system is not cost effective. The vendor may suggest that the system be created through *contract programming*, which means that a system is custom developed by a vendor.

Complete vendor systems for large records systems are priced in the $5,000 to $10,000 range for the software. The software is written in a high-level language so that queries are possible, but a query will require some knowledge of the high-level language. The preferred hardware, not included in the above price, is an IBM® microcomputer or compatible.

Vendor systems can be single-user or multi-user systems with a local area network. The prices generally include minor program customizing, an operator's manual, training, consulting, and software maintenance for a period of one year. Keep in mind that these systems are CBRMSs because they do not store the records themselves but provide the means to track and manage the records.

Implementing the System

Implementation includes both installing and testing the system. The old (often manual) system is replaced by the new CBRMS and verified to ensure that all is working as expected. The conversion process will consist of entering the information about the records and then performing the major processes and producing the system reports.

Conversion Strategies

Time-frame strategies for implementation include the *weekend conversion* and the *from-this-point conversion*. In the weekend conversion, everything is stopped in the old system and the new system is started up after all the information is entered. This is a good strategy if there is time to stop the records system while the conversion takes place.

If time is at a premium and development of the system is problematic, a more suitable strategy would be the from-this-point conversion. The new system is installed, but information about the records is entered only as needed and in small batches. In this way, the system operates as a shell with all processes but without all the information. Normally, record information is entered as new storage and retrieval occurs.

Whatever conversion strategy is selected, record information will be entered into the system. It may be convenient to record this information on paper forms and then enter it into the system. However, a better approach is a *videotext* form, which is a form created on and stored in the computer. Using such a form can reduce data entry errors. Indeed, this feature could be considered as an integral part of the CBRMS.

Training

The CBRMS being described usually will replace a manual system, so little special training in the use of the system should be required. Because the system is relatively static in terms of the reports produced and the procedures followed, it should be constructed to be self-explanatory. The instructions and information provided by the system should be complete and user friendly.

Minimal training may not be realistic, however, when the query function is considered. Although the operation itself may not be difficult, the potential uses of the query may not be widely known or appreciated. In this case, training serves an advertising function as well as a teaching one. The query adds interesting new elements to the field of records management (more fully considered in Chapter 16).

Maintaining the System

A CBRMS will not operate indefinitely without maintenance. Although it may be difficult to see the need to allot time for maintenance activities, if time is not allowed, the system will degenerate and eventually can become a liability.

System Maintenance

General maintenance activities include fixing problems of correspondence between the physical records and the system information, altering retention periods, updating table information, changing report format and information, and other activities that keep the system up to date.

System maintenance activities refer to fixes applied to the system to keep it operating as it should. These are usually unscheduled, unanticipated, and unwanted, but they occur. Some time each month should always be allotted to removing system bugs.

The most important activity in a CBRMS is maintaining the correspondence (agreement) between the database and the records. A regular procedure must be in place for entering new record information and deleting and changing existing information. To have a regular procedure that would check the accuracy of the database would be useful. But, unfortunately, no one has yet devised a feasible method for doing so.

Of course, the system should also have some procedure for recovering from failure. One of the most straightforward approaches is to make sure that regular backups are made of the entire system. An automatic backup function would be a useful feature to specify in an RFP.

System Enhancements

A common error in CBRMS implementation is to consider the process finished after it has been successfully installed and tested. If a CBRMS is working well, with time allotted for regular maintenance, there would seem to be little reason to start changing it. However, a truly static, unchanging system is not compatible with the business world. The fact that the system goes through a life cycle indicates that the process is ongoing.

Enhancements are significant system additions that improve the quality of operations. They are not simple alterations, such as the addition of some information to a report or a change in report format. Enhancements can be the addition of a new report or system additions that allow a new query. Enhancements are not easily added to a CBRMS because they affect nearly all of the system operations and often require alterations to all of the existing information.

One of the first parts of a CBRMS targeted for enhancement is the reporting system. As soon as the system is operating smoothly and everyone sees how much useful information is produced—with apparent ease—there will be requests for more and different information. These requests are inevitable and should be well received because they verify the productivity of the CBRMS and promise that it will become even more productive in the future.

The second area of enhancement results from the query system. This area is slower to gain acceptance and use than the report system, but its potential is greater. As more regular use is made of the query system, users will see new applications and request more information. These requests are more difficult to evaluate in terms of productivity costs and benefits. For example, to satisfy a query request, it may be necessary to change nearly all of the record information and associated reports in a category of information. For a rarely used query, these changes may not be productive.

Generally, one should plan for enhancements. The more flexible the system for the incorporation of new processing or new reports, the less the long-run costs of system operation.

System Security

A CBRMS introduces security requirements and capabilities to check information that is not feasible in a manual system. So much information is so easily available in a CBRMS that one can check for system validity in a number of ways. But this ease of access is a double-edged sword, for it may allow unauthorized persons to access sensitive information. Thus security has two aspects: restricting access to information and validating information produced by the system.

Restricting Access

A popular method of restricting access is through the use of *passwords*. This method assigns levels of priorities to different types of information and procedures. For example, the records manager has the highest-level password and is allowed to access and change any information in the system, as well as obtain all reports and do all procedures. The lowest-level password(s) in the system allows a person to access just one or a few reports on the screen or do some simple queries.

Another method of restricting access to the system is to have all system changes routed to a transaction file for later processing. In this method, all record changes for the day are reported at the end of the day to the manager. If they all appear valid, the order is given to actually make the changes. This method is particularly useful if there is a great deal of user access to the system with little immediate physical control.

Another method of increasing security over system access is to create a transaction log for producing a security file to provide information on all uses of the system. All system users are informed regularly that a report of all system uses is produced and made available to the manager.

Validation of Information

A CBRMS easily can produce summary validity reports on a weekly or monthly basis for comparison of totals to see if everything looks reasonable. For example, a summary report of all records by current status should show a steadily increasing number of total records and about the same number of records in OUT or SEARCH status. With some ingenuity, the use of summary validity reports can point to problem areas. Reconciliation reports can check to see that total records in the system equal the last period's total plus new records (added in the current period) minus records deleted or purged. These reports check each other for a given time period.

Internal system checks during information entry can help reduce errors. For example, if only numeric or only alphabetic characters should be entered, then the system can check for the correct entry. Most systems have some capabilities for this kind of checking. It is often cost effective to do the checking here rather than finding and correcting a problem at a later, possibly inconvenient, time.

Summary

A computer-based records management system (CBRMS) involves computer hardware and software to track, report, and query records. The CBRMS needs detailed information about the records so that they can be processed and queried. A CBRMS can be created in-house or purchased from a vendor. Once a CBRMS is selected, then it must be implemented through converting the old system to the new CBRMS and delivering training as required. The installed system requires maintenance and consideration of enhancements throughout its life. A CBRMS brings with it an increased attention to security in terms of data access and checking that the information is accurate.

List of Terms

computer-based records management system (CBRMS)
database
database management system (DBMS)
computer-assisted retrieval system (CARS)
system report
system query
retrieval handle
code dictionary
key word
systems life cycle
request for proposal (RFP)
turnkey system
vanilla system
contract programming
weekend conversion
from-this-point conversion
videotext
system enhancement
password

Discussion Questions

1. What are the goals of a computer-based records management system?
2. Define the acronym CBRMS.
3. What information is required for a CBRMS?
4. What is the difference between a CARS, CBRMS, and DBMS?
5. What is meant by a "turnkey" system?
6. What are implementation strategies?
7. What maintenance is required for a CBRMS?
8. What are the two parts of system security in a CBRMS?

Activities

1. Contact a firm that markets a CBRMS and report on its system. Ask them to describe one of the RFPs they recently completed.
2. Interview a records manager or equivalent in an office that is considering a CBRMS. Describe the objectives of the CBRMS.
3. Follow the systems development life cycle to at least the design stage for a hypothetical (or real) records system.
4. Locate a business that is using a CBRMS. Describe the system enhancements it is interested in installing.
5. In Figure 15.4, "Retrieval Operations Flow," if a record has been checked out (OUT), or requested but not yet physically checked out (SEARCH), the user is notified and the process ends. Modify the flow to retry the retrieval if the record is OUT.
6. Describe a records management system that should *not* be converted to a CBRMS.

References

Behling, Robert. *Computers and Information Processing*. (Boston, Mass: Kent, 1986).

Heite, Ned. "Records Managers Face the Technology Explosion." *Interface Age* (February 1984): 54–57.

Sample, Robert L. "The Mathematics of Filing: Cabinets vs. Electronics." *Administrative Management* (January 1982): 38–42.

Chapter 16

Records Management as Database Management

Learning Goals

1. To become familiar with the concept of a database management system (DBMS) and how it differs from a CBRMS.

2. To understand the advantages of a DBMS for a records management system.

3. To become familiar with the structure and requirements for menu-based storage and retrieval systems.

4. To understand the phases of the systems life cycle and how they apply to the development of a records database management system.

5. To see the application of artificial intelligence and expert systems to storage and retrieval systems.

6. To become familiar with the features of an optical disk-based storage and retrieval system.

Introduction

In Chapter 15, we discussed how a computer can be used for managing a records system. Chapter 16 takes the next step and examines completely computerized systems in which the records are not only managed by the computer but also are stored on the computer in a database management system (DBMS). In a DBMS, the computer is used to track records through the record cycle, provide appropriate reports, and query the records, just as in a computer-based records management system (CBRMS). However, the added value of a DBMS for records management lies in its flexibility in the retrieval of information (Schroeder, 1987).

When records are accessible through traditional manual methods, searching for information is time-consuming and rarely financially feasible. This is particularly true when the search is undertaken with only partial or incomplete identifying information. With a DBMS, a search often can be successfully and economically conducted with imperfect information. We will look at the ways this can be done.

Since both the management procedures and the records are stored on a DBMS, the hardware and software requirements are significantly greater than those required for a CBRMS. The management of even a modest quantity of 5,000 records, for example, can be beyond the capabilities of a typical microcomputer system. The hardware requirements for a DBMS should be at least 640 KB RAM and a 20–30 megabyte hard disk—the upper limits for a microcomputer. The DBMS also requires a fast backup system. Similarly, the database software that was sufficient for a CBRMS probably would be too slow for feasible DBMS operation.

This chapter begins with a general overview of database management systems and the system life cycle of a DBMS. We then consider methods for sophisticated information retrieval, including menu-based storage and retrieval, structured query languages, artificial intelligence, and expert systems. We conclude with optical disk systems, a particular type of database management systems hardware.

Database Management Systems

The concept of a database is somewhat difficult to grasp because on the surface it is very much like any records management system. However, database management is different because everything that transpires with the record does so through the computer. For this reason also, the system requires procedures and organization that are unique to the computer and could not be accomplished manually. The procedures include establishing a project team to handle the database, devising and maintaining menu-based storage and retrieval, and using structured query languages.

Database Definition

A *database* is literally a base of data: a collection of data that forms the basis of an activity. (See also discussion on page 238.) The two elements essential to a database are coherence and organization.

Coherence means that the data are related to a specific activity or purpose. For example, a mail-order catalog is a database of items available for sale; a telephone directory is a database that provides telephone numbers; the card catalog in a library is intended to help locate library materials. Even if a database is coherent, however, it may not be useful. Consider a telephone directory in which the name, address, and phone number data are listed by order of phone number. This arrangement may be useful to some, but most people who use a telephone book need to have the information organized alphabetically by an individual's last name.

Organization means that the data are related in a meaningful way. In other words, if a database is organized, then it provides a way for people to meaningfully access parts of the database. Just as there are different ways in which people use a coherent set of data, so there are different ways to organize the data. Returning to the example of the telephone directory, there are at least three ways to organize the data in the directory—alphabetically by name, numerically by phone number, or locationally by street address.

Database Management

As with any records system, a DBMS requires procedures that allow the user to add, change, and delete the data easily, as well as to access the information. These procedures define the database management system (DBMS). A DBMS consists of the programs or software that allow the user to implement the storage, altering, and retrieval procedures.

Businesses often consider a DBMS in order to reduce the number of separate files they process, to improve the integrity of their data, and to allow efficient responses to user requests for information. The reasons for converting a records system to a DBMS, however, should focus on efficient storage and retrieval processes as well as management of the records.

Converting to Database Management Systems

Not all records systems are candidates for conversion to a database system. Factors to consider include the variety of existing classification systems, records media formats, and legal considerations. The major advantages of a DBMS for records management are space reduction, retrieval efficiency, incomplete information searches, and image enhancement.

If a paper records system is converted to a DBMS using digital methods of storage, the space savings can be considerable. A general guide would be a space reduction ratio on the order of 10,000 to 1. Of course, for such a reduction to be relevant, the paper records would have to be eliminated, and often this is not likely.

Retrieval efficiency in a DBMS can be amazing. If a user knows the name of the record to retrieve, a DBMS can get it in seconds. In addition, a DBMS can index the records on different attributes so that information can be located in different ways.

Incomplete information searches allow a user to query a DBMS to look for answers to general questions. For example, you might wish to ask a records DBMS how many times a record involving the ACME Company was accessed in March. The search would be a simple matter for a properly designed DBMS but a nearly impossible task for a manual records system. Another feature is that a DBMS can allow for ambiguous searches. For example, if you know the first three digits of the client's policy number and you think that the client's name is probably ANDERSON, then a DBMS can quickly and easily select all client records that satisfy the criteria and allow you to browse them to locate the correct client—all this in minutes, perhaps even seconds.

Because a DBMS is computer based, a display screen is usually available to view information and a scanner is usually available to "read" the information into the DBMS. A simple scanner or digitizer converts the image to a digital format so that it can be displayed and stored. More advanced scanners actually can read text and convert it to a format suitable for editing with word-processing software. These types of scanners often are called *OCR*s, or *optical character readers* (see page 123). If a document has had coffee spilled on it so that it is badly stained and very difficult to read, the user can specify the appropriate hardware and software in the DBMS to "remove" the stain—a process called *image enhancement*. Enhancing text documents is particularly appropriate for damaged records or for archival materials that are decomposing due to a high acid content.

Converting a traditional records system

to a database system requires considerable effort and preparation. Such a project benefits from systems life cycle methodology. This type of methodology is designed for the creation, development, and installation of computer-based systems.

The Systems Life Cycle

All systems go through a regular series of stages called the *systems life cycle*. The stages begin with the creation of the system and proceed through a regular series of events, which end with the new system in full operation. When the system no longer meets the needs of the organization, it "dies" and a new system is created. This creation–use–obsolescence sequence was discussed in Chapter 15. Here, we will look at the systems life cycle in terms of developing a DBMS.

Different books on systems analysis and design define the stages of the process in slightly different ways (Capron, 1986: 15–27). From the perspective of a DBMS as a possible system for records management, we can define four life cycle stages: (1) problem exploration and feasibility study, (2) analysis and design, (3) development and implementation, and (4) maintenance.

Problem Exploration and Feasibility Study

Problem exploration involves a preliminary investigation aimed at determining the scope and objectives of the system. The questions that should be answered include: What do we expect to accomplish? Do we really need a new system? Will the new system solve our problems?

If the problem exploration suggests that a DBMS for records management seems reasonable, the next step is to estimate the cost-effectiveness of the new system. Although a DBMS could improve an existing manual records management system, it may not be feasible to implement the DBMS within reasonable resource limitations. The *feasibility study* will make estimates of the costs involved compared to the expected benefits. A general rule of thumb is that the proposed system should pay for itself in estimated savings over a three- to five-year period.

Analysis and Design

If the problem exploration and feasibility study are acceptable, the next phase is the *analysis and design* of the new system. At this stage, a project team is formed to work on the system. The project team should consist minimally of a project manager, technicians, a records manager, and records users.

The role of the project manager is to order and coordinate the project. The project manager should be knowledgeable in both database systems and records management and should be a good "people" person. The technicians are those who will be responsible for the technical details of the system, for example, the hardware and software. The records manager also must be a good "team member" to allow the team access to the present system and to provide essential information about the records. Records users should be part of the team to ensure that the new system will be responsive to the users' needs.

The project team will carefully analyze the present system in order to establish the requirements for the new system. Analysis will answer questions such as: How many records are involved? How should the records be indexed? Exactly what do we want the system to do? The results of the analysis should be a carefully written list of the new system requirements.

The design of the system produces general and detailed plans. The preliminary design work reviews the system requirements and answers general system questions such as: What hardware and software will be needed? Can the system operate on existing equipment? How will the records be input into the system? What kinds of reports are desired? The detail design work gets down to the specific aspects of the system. This step would involve the design of input/output forms and screens, record formats, security controls, and the consideration of human factors.

The conclusion of the analysis and design stage often involves a presentation of the results by the project team to upper management and involved users. The purpose of the presentation is to communicate the present state of the project and to gain support for the coming stages. Unless there has been a major change in the project objectives or resource costs have unexpectedly changed, the next step is to get the new system ready and put it in place.

Development and Implementation

At the *development and implementation* stage, hardware, software, and procedures are developed to meet design requirements. If programs are required, programmers write and test them at this stage. Everything is readied for the new system to be operational.

During implementation, the switch is made to the new system. Within a planned time frame, the conversion will involve converting the old records to the new system, converting the old procedures to the new system, and training those who will use the system. After the initial conversion activities, an evaluation usually will reveal that minor adjustments need to be made to the new system. After these are performed, the implemented system often is evaluated by the users to determine if it actually does what was planned. If everything is satisfactory, the system goes into a long-term operational or maintenance stage.

Maintenance

The primary *maintenance* problem in a records DBMS is making sure that records are correctly entered into the system in a timely manner. Therefore, an integral part of the procedures for management must be regular and standardized entry procedures. Any hardware and/or software that facilitates record input procedures should be seriously considered. For example, using a scanner or optical character reader (OCR) for input is likely to solve many maintenance problems.

An associated problem is the validity of the input information. Care must be exercised continually to ensure that the information going into the system is accurate. Simply making sure that the information is correctly transferred from paper to computer system will not necessarily solve the problem because the initial information may have been incorrect! The solution is to verify all input information *before* it is stored into the DBMS. Information should be verified even if an OCR is used for input.

As a system is used, there should be regular maintenance of system features in addition to the usual equipment maintenance. To assess the operation of the system, it is important to check regularly the number of records in the system, the response time of routine operations, and the satisfaction of the users.

No matter how carefully a system is planned, designed, developed, and implemented, sooner or later changes will have to be made. New categories of information may be required or reports may need to be changed. These are called *system enhancements*. If the system increases significantly in quantity or expected quality of information, an enhancement may be insufficient to accommodate the changes. It is then time for a new problem exploration and feasibility study—the first stage of the life cycle—and a new life cycle commences.

Menu-Based Storage and Retrieval

Large-scale records DBMSs are becoming widely available. These large-capacity systems involving tens of thousands of records have generated a challenging problem: How can vast quantities of information be stored and retrieved efficiently by computer? One of the most popular methods of large-scale information storage and retrieval is the menu-based system.

Menu systems of storage and retrieval can be easy to use. A well-designed menu system can allow a person who is unfamiliar with the system to query it effectively. In a computer-based DBMS, the parameters of the storage/retrieval problem are set by the typical display screen: given a screen of eighty columns and twenty-four rows, what menu choices should be presented to the user to allow for efficient storage and retrieval? Usual parameters also restrict the row usage to every other row and require the process to operate on a naming convention.

The example in Figure 16.1 shows how a small corporation might structure a storage/retrieval process for its client files, which have a standard alphabetic name classification system embedded in a subject-type main menu. In this example, the operator is looking for the policy record for John Doyle.

Figure 16.1 shows a series of menus that would be displayed as the operator seeks the client record. Each menu allows a choice, for example, by moving the cursor to the desired location and then pressing the "enter" or "carriage return" key. Each choice results in the next menu, and the next menu, and so on until the actual client record is reached. This is called a *multiple menu system*. Even in a very large file, fewer than ten menus will be required to reach the record (client file).

In Figure 16.1, the choices the operator has chosen are shown by the arrow (→). The operator begins at the main menu with the category of "last name." If the main menu started with region, the next menu would present choices of the available regions. In this system, the NAME menus will be reached eventually regardless of the initial subject category. As the example shows, one continues choosing the appropriate category and moving through the menus toward more and more specific choices. Eventually, the last menu choice will lead directly to the policy record. Similar systems are used to access and/or store information by subject classifications, for example, in encyclopedia systems. However, a subject classification system probably will be ordered by logical categories rather than alphabetically. The first menu in a multiple menu system is also called the "master menu," because it allows the operator to choose which of the retrieval systems to use. For example, a library master menu might offer to start the retrieval process from either an author, subject, or title menu.

Figure 16.1 Multiple Menu for Storage/Retrieval

Main menu	*First menu*	*Second menu*	. . .	*Last menu*
Agent	A.	DA.		DOANE
Region	→ D.	DE.		DOBSON
Last name →	G.	DI		DOJO
Policy #	J	→ DO.		DOOLITTLE
. . .	. . .	. . .		. . .
Category	W.	DU.		→ DOYLE →

This type of storage and retrieval system offers the additional benefit of retrieval from incomplete information. For example, if the client's name is spelled incorrectly, it would not take much more time to locate the correct file. Multiple menu systems are often used to increase incomplete information retrieval efficiency. Another approach for increasing the efficiency of information retrieval is the use of structured query languages.

Structured Query Languages

A method in common use for data access in large-scale DBMSs is the *structured query language*, or SQL. SQLs are nonprocedural languages in that they specify the desired results rather than how to get the results. Programming languages such as Pascal or COBOL are procedural languages. SQLs are available for almost all types of computer hardware and system sizes, from mainframes to microcomputers. With an SQL, a user can query the database or perform the usual functions of updating, adding, or deleting information.

Many SQLs are nearly complete DBMSs in themselves, performing all of the DBMS functions, as well as having features that allow the easy creation of reports and input screens. SQLs are much more flexible than menus since they allow operators to formulate their own requests for information. The major disadvantage of SQLs is that a somewhat technical language must be learned to operate the system effectively.

All SQLs follow a similar format to access the database. There are commands to alter the database and commands to retrieve data. The retrieval function is usually the most common request and follows a SELECT/FROM/WHERE format. These basic SQL commands are described in Figure 16.2.

For example, we might use the following SQL command to achieve the same result as in the menu-based example:

Figure 16.2 Description of SQL Commands

Alter Database Commands

UPDATE to alter existing data
DELETE to remove information
INSERT to put new data in the database

Retrieval Command

SELECT data (by field name)
FROM the table(s) or relation(s)
WHERE conditions are met
using ANDs, ORs, and NOTs

```
SELECT policy#, name, address, type,
value, date
FROM policy-file
WHERE name = 'JOHN DOYLE'
```

These types of SQL commands can be saved and issued in a batch as a single request, or a series of them can be combined into a larger batch and executed on a regular basis to produce quick reports. A sophisticated SQL has literally hundreds of commands that allow the operator to do almost anything to the database. Some SQLs include a variety of procedural commands that allow the operator to write programs to tailor input and output to any specific requirements.

Artificial Intelligence and Expert Systems

Structured query languages still can be too restrictive and require too much time to be used effectively. A nonregular user may not wish to learn a query language just to make a simple information request. One solution to this problem has been the development of fourth generation languages that purport to use artificial intelligence.

Fourth-Generation Languages

A *fourth-generation language (4GL)* is one that allows the user to structure questions in English language form and seeks answers to vague or undefined parts of the question.

For example, suppose you want to query a database to determine the number of records that were actually retrieved in the last month. This would involve determining the number of records that had a status of OUT during a specific time period. Using a typical structured query language, we might use the following commands:

```
SELECT name, last-date, last-date-status
FROM active-files
WHERE last-date < 02ddyy
  AND last-date > 04ddyy
  AND last-date-status = 'OUT'
```

The structured query requests the record name and date information from the proper files with conditions that restrict the retrieval to a certain month (March).

On the other hand, a fourth-generation query language could allow the command:

> GET ME THE NUMBER OF RECORDS WITH A STATUS OF OUT DURING MARCH

If the command were unclear, for example, as to what year was involved, a fourth generation language might ask:

> IS THE YEAR yyyy? (YES/NO) ____

where yyyy is the present year. After answering "Yes" or "No," the query results would be displayed.

A fourth-generation query language is capable of tuning itself to the needs and definitions of specific users. For example, in the above query, the 4GL might ask:

> DOES "GET ME THE" = DISPLAY THE QUERY RESULTS ON THE DISPLAY SCREEN? (YES/NO) ____

The system appears to be "artificially intelligent" because it remembers the answers to questions and keeps this information available so the same questions are not asked again. Also, as a particular user asks questions and the 4GL remembers the style and syntax, it becomes "smarter."

Expert Systems

If a 4GL could not only learn the style and syntax of a user but also incorporate that user's knowledge, then it would be an *expert system*. Expert systems allow a user to query a database; if the answer is not in the database, the expert system will ask for, and incorporate, the answer into the database. Databases suitable for expert systems are those in which the database is expected to expand according to logical rules. Because a records DBMS usually expands by a simple accumulation of records, an expert system normally is not feasible.

Optical Disk Filing Systems

Imaging systems provide another means of storing and retrieving vast quantities of data. Optical disk filing systems, in particular, are emerging as a cost-effective means for large-scale records storage.

Optical Disks

An optical disk stores information digitally, similar to magnetic media, but the similarity ends there. Whereas magnetic media are written and read through the alignment of magnetized particles, optical media have a read/write process, which works by changing the optical characteristics of the media. A common method utilizes a laser, which burns or ablates a place on the disk. The burning or ablative process actually removes a tiny portion of the disk material, creating a depression; the presence or absence of a depression is then easily read. This is a permanent write procedure; in other words, when data is written to an optical disk, it cannot be altered at another time, as it can on magnetic disks. In consideration of the permanence of the writing process, most optical disks are referred to as *WORM* (*write-once-read-many*) devices. Another frequently used term is *CD-ROM*, or compact disk with read-only-memory, to indicate that optical disks are suitable for information that does not change. Although erasable optical media have been promised, no commercial versions are available.

A physical characteristic of optical disks is their potential to store information more compactly than other media, especially magnetic media. For the same size physical disk, optical media can store, in terms of magnitude, (ten times) more information than other media. For example, a commercially available optical disk can store 80,000 digitized documents or one million text pages or five *gigabytes* of data (1 gigabyte = 1 billion bytes). Such a disk would store letter-size documents equivalent to about fifty four-drawer vertical files. *Jukebox hardware* stores and accesses optical disks in a manner similar to the way that a jukebox stores and accesses phonograph records, and allows up to thirty-three disks to be resident. Such a system would allow the equivalent of over 1,500 four-drawer files to be stored in the space of an office desk.

In some circumstances, being able to write information only once can be a disadvantage. In this respect, optical disks are similar to micrographic recording on film. The associated advantage is that optical disks, once recorded or written, are not easily changed through accident or time. This characteristic makes optical disks suitable for the recording of vital records, archival material, and other records for long-term storage.

Optical Disk-Based Storage and Retrieval Systems

A system that utilizes optical disk technology for the storage and retrieval of records is called an *optical disk-based storage and retrieval system* (OSAR). The ideal OSAR inputs documents with an OCR, and after validation, automatically pulverizes the document. Storage and retrieval can be done with a multiple menu system, SQL, or with an expert system. If a hard copy is required, it can be generated in seconds on a built-in high-speed laser printer to original clarity. The display is at least page size or greater, and the clarity of the display is equivalent to the original paper document.

Commercially available OSARs can read and store a standard letter in five seconds. In multiple-disk jukebox hardware, retrieval time for the worst case (when the disk is not in the server) is about fifteen seconds. Compare that figure to manually searching the equivalent of 1,500 four-drawer files! Built-in indexing allows thousands of document categories with hundreds of index fields and characters per field, so one can use a menu-based system to locate files or use "wild cards" to locate files through key words.

The major advantage of an imaging system when the documents are stored on optical disk are:

1. virtually immediate retrieval
2. concurrent access
3. ability to transmit electronically
4. integration with other information through word-processing-like editing
5. improved control of documents (fewer lost records) and clerical productivity information.

Major manufacturers in the optical document management market include Eastman Kodak, Bell and Howell, Digital, Wang, Honeywell, TAB Products Co., 3M, and Prime. Sizes range from a modest capacity of 10 optical disks to larger systems containing 204 optical disks (2.6 billion bytes each = 2.6 gigabytes) for 530 total gigabytes of on-line storage. These systems can be interfaced with CAR, COM, CAD/CAM, electronic publishing systems, and all types of computer systems. Optional accessories include facsimile, and the systems can be multiple stationed and networked with other systems.

Will optical disk replace traditional micrographic systems such as CAR and COM microforms? Although they could in many applications, they probably will not for the following reasons. First, the large number of existing microfilm systems encourage continued micrographic use because the cost advantage of optical disk is insufficient to justify scrapping an existing microfilm system. Second, microfilm has proved to be viable as an archive storage medium and microfilm systems have been effectively interfaced with many other records management methods (Settanni, 1987).

Summary

Database management systems differ from computer-based management systems in that the records themselves are stored in the computer and are managed by procedures contained in the DBMS.

A database is a collection of data that forms the basis of an activity. Coherence and organization are essential to a database. Coherence means that the data are related to a specific activity or purpose. Organization means that the data are related in a meaningful way.

A DBMS requires procedures that allow the user to add or alter data easily and to access information. The major advantages of a DBMS for records management are space reduction, retrieval efficiency, incomplete information searches, and image enhancement.

Not all records systems should be converted to DBMSs. If a company chooses to convert its records system to DBMS, it should follow a systems life cycle methodology to do so. This methodology includes the following steps: (1) problem exploration and feasibility study, which involves a preliminary investigation and a feasibility study to determine cost-effectiveness; (2) analysis and design, which involves setting up a project team to produce general and detailed designs; (3) development and implementation, which involves acquiring necessary hardware and software and making the switch to the new system within a planned time frame; and (4) maintenance, which involves standardizing entry procedures, verifying the validity of input information, and performing regular maintenance of system features. The cycle is repeated as system enhancements are required.

Menu-based storage and retrieval, structured query languages, fourth-generation languages, expert systems, and optical disk filing systems all have contributed to the ease of managing vast quantities of data. A multiple menu system guides the user through the retrieval process by using a series of menus that are related to the particular records classification. A structured query language is a nonprocedural language that specifies desired results. A fourth-generation language seeks answers to vague questions. An expert system adds the aspect of "learning" and incorporating answers into the database. Finally, optical disk filing systems can provide permanent data storage of huge quantities of information with the advantages of almost instant retrieval, improved control of documents, and clerical productivity.

List of Terms

coherence
organization
image enhancement
problem exploration
feasibility study
analysis and design
development and implementation
maintenance
system enhancement
multiple menu system
structured query language (SQL)
artificial intelligence
fourth generation language (4GL)
expert system
WORM
CD-ROM
gigabyte
jukebox hardware
optical disk-based storage and retrieval (OSAR) system

Discussion Questions

1. What are the two essential requirements for a database management system?
2. How could a multiple menu system be used to retrieve a record?
3. Why are a series of menus necessary in a database management system?
4. What is the difference between a structured query language and a fourth-generation language?
5. What is meant by artificial intelligence?
6. When is an optical disk system a database management system?
7. What are the major advantages of a DBMS for records management?
8. What factors should be considered before converting a records system to a DBMS?

Activities

1. Contact two or more manufacturers of optical disk systems and request literature on their systems. Write a short report comparing the features of the optical disk systems, paying particular attention to the claimed advantages of each system.
2. You have been asked to create a storage/retrieval system for the Small University library and their newly purchased optical disk system. The university plans to transfer all feasible textual library materials to the optical disk system. There are presently in excess of 100,000 items including books, magazines, journals, and so on. The university wants to provide access to the information in an efficient, meaningful way. Prepare all appropriate menus and describe the operation of the system.
3. Expert systems and artificial intelligence do not seem to be realizing their potential in computer applications. Review the current literature on this topic. Is there really a future in records management for expert systems?

4. SQLs (structured query languages) appear to be the popular query language for mainframe database management systems. Prepare a report that describes the (relatively) simple features of SQL and its future for CBRMS applications.

References

Capron, H. L. *Systems Analysis and Design* (Menlo Park, Cal.: Benjamin/Cummings, Inc., 1986).

Schroeder, Chris. "Improved Information Access: The Next Challenge." *INFORM* 1, no. 4 (April 1987): 6, 55.

Settanni, Joseph Richard. "Micrographics Is Here to Stay." *IMC Journal* 23, no. 1 (January/February 1987): 50–53.

Chapter 16 Highlight

Digital Storage Capacities

Digitally stored information is associated with magnetic and optical media. Technically speaking, storing information in digital format means converting it to a numeric or digital form for storage. This means that a number is used to represent each character or symbol. Although the specific format may vary, a character or symbol is represented by a binary number composed of bits. Each bit can be a zero or a one. A group of eight bits is called a byte, and it is the byte that is used to represent characters and symbols.

One byte can represent an "A" or an "a" or "1" or any alphanumeric symbol. Early computers and storage devices could hold and operate on about 2,000 bytes. If we consider that 2,000 bytes is about equivalent to the number of characters on a typical page of a business record, then it is evident that early computers were not good candidates for storing or managing records.

The advances in computer technology have made available rapidly increasing amounts of storage. The following information is intended to help put storage amounts into perspective. The terms used in computer storage and the approximate number of bytes represented are shown in Figure 16.H1.

Figure 16.H1 Computer Terms and Associated Bytes

Term	*Symbol*	*Nominal bytes*	*Name*
Kilobytes	KB	1,000	thousand
Megabytes	MB	1,000,000	million
Gigabytes	GB	1,000,000,000	billion
Terabytes	TB	1,000,000,000,000	trillion
Petabytes	PT	1,000,000,000,000,000	quadrillion
Exabytes	EB	1,000,000,000,000,000,000	quintillion

Figure 16.H2 Typical Storage Capacities of Magnetic and Optical Media

This Device can Access About . . .	*Bytes*
A typical microcomputer	256 KB
A double-sided 5¼″ disk	360 KB
A double-sided 3½″ disk	720 KB
Microcomputer fixed disk	30 MB
Microcomputer optical disk	550 MB
Mainframe fixed disk unit	1 GB
Mainframe high capacity device	400 GB

The approximate or nominal bytes are representative of the true number. Actually, the number of bytes is a power of two. The kilobyte is really 2^{10} (two to the tenth power) or 1,024, the megabyte is 2^{20} or 1,048,576, and so on, with the exponent increasing by tens. The largest value shown above, the EB, is really 2^{60}, a number with nineteen digits! We really don't worry about the exact value, but instead concentrate on the nominal amount, which expresses the values in thousands. Each succeeding value is one thousand times greater than the preceding value.

Typical storage capacities of magnetic and optical media are shown in Figure 16.H2.

But what do the numbers in Figure 16.H2 mean? We need a perspective so that we can effectively judge the capacity of storage devices. Some approximations of storage capacities are:

In one second, you can see about . . .	20 bytes
You can handwrite in ten minutes about . . .	1 KB
One page is about 2,000 bytes . . .	2 KB
A typical Lotus worksheet is about . . .	8 KB
Input from a skilled operator per hour . . .	12 KB
You can read in about an hour . . .	75 KB
One book of about 250 pages . . .	500 KB
A college textbook of about 500 pages . . .	1 MB
Input from a skilled operator per month . . .	2 MB
An encyclopedia set . . .	50 MB
Input from a skilled operator per lifetime . . .	2 GB
A library of about 2 million books . . .	2 TB
The Harvard library of 10 million books . . .	10 TB
Theoretical capacity of the human brain . . .	35 TB
The Library of Congress has about . . .	1 PB
All recorded human text and records . . .	64 EB

Now we are in a position to judge if the storage capacity of a hardware system can reasonably accommodate the storage of a known group of records. If there are about 10,000 pages of records and we are considering installing them on a microcomputer system with a total fixed disk capacity of 10 MB, will they fit? Well, 10,000 pages are about 20,000 KB, or 20 MB. We would conclude that we are not even in the ball park and suggest device capacity should substantially exceed 20 MB for this system.

Appendix A

Standard Filing Rules and Examples

Filing rules are written for the purpose of making retrieval easy through consistency in filing. Another way to view this objective is that good filing rules allow anyone to store and retrieve files easily. Unique knowledge about the filing system is not required—knowledge of the filing rules is.

Organizing materials from A00000 to Z99999, or putting names in alphabetical order, may seem simple and, in a general sense, it is; yet detail and exceptions to the system can add significant complexities to the task. Appendix A will introduce the reader to standardized filing rules with special considerations given to computerized applications. All of the following material is completely consistent with the standard filing systems and rules as promoted by the Association of Records Managers and Administrators (ARMA, 1986).

Definitions

Filing rules apply to all materials, but they are more meaningful with alphabetic records because of the potentially greater complexities involved. For example, filing by terminal digit is straightforward and rarely involves exceptions. Alphabetic filing of personal and business names can be quite complicated, though, involving numbers, symbols, and bizarre names. In this appendix, we provide general classification system rules and examples for any type of filing.

Classification systems organize materials at different cumulative levels. Since this structure defines how all classification systems operate, it is important to define these levels and the terms presently in use carefully. As a rule, each level is composed of one or more of the objects in the preceding level.

Level	*Concept*	*Terms in use*
1	Single items	Letter, number, character
2	Item groups	Word, unit, field
3	Working part	Filing segment, record
4	Record type	Record series, file
5	All records	Database

For our discussion, we will use the last term at each level in the "Terms in Use" column (*character, field, record, file,* and *database*) because this constitutes present use in CBRMSs (computer-based records management systems). ARMA uses the letter/unit/filing segment terms.

A file is composed of one or more records which are composed of one or more fields that contain characters. Note that we are referring to the *names* of the files, records, and fields, whereas the *characters* compose the actual contents.

To illustrate these terms, consider a typical business with four characteristic files. We name the four files and indicate their fields using the convention: File(FIELD1, FIELD2, . . .).

Customer(ACCT_NO, NAME, ADDRESS, CITY, STATE, ZIP)
Employee(NAME, ADDRESS, CITY, STATE, ZIP)
Dealer(NAME, ADDRESS, CITY, STATE, ZIP)
Inventory(PART_NO, QUANTITY, RETAIL, WHOLESALE)

(Note that the underline in ACCT_NO is part of the fieldname.) The contents of ACCT_NO might be A134599, Z234554, or C234565, indicating a seven-character alphanumeric (composed of letters and numbers) field. Together, the four files compose a database.

All classification systems order records by either (1) the character-by-character method or (2) the field-by-field method. In the character-by-character method, materials are organized solely by the placement of the characters. For example, words in a dictionary, terms in an encyclopedia, or merchandise with a ten-digit code are ordered character-by-character. In the field-by-field (or unit-by-unit) method, materials are organized by the first field, then subsequent fields; each field is ordered character-by-character. This is the most common classification system used for alphabetic filing of personal, business, institution, and government names. We will assume the use of the field-by-field method in this appendix.

A term frequently seen in filing rules is *indexing*. In this context, indexing can be understood as just another way of classifying the materials. For example, in the Customer(ACCT_NO, NAME, ADDRESS, CITY, STATE, ZIP) file from above, we might file the records by the ACCT_NO or we might have them filed by the NAME using filing rules. In such a case, it would be appropriate to say the Customer file is indexed by either NAME or ACCT_NO. If the file were indexed by ACCT_NO, we might also keep a list (index) of the ACCT_NO and NAME ordered by NAME.

No matter how carefully we design our filing rules, cases will occur in which ambiguity cannot be resolved. Should it be filed as THIS or THAT?

The filing rules may not allow resolution of this dilemma. In such cases, the record is *cross-referenced.* Cross-referencing means filing the record according to the likely definition and placing a note or reference in other likely locations pointing to the actual file.

Filing Rules

Practical experience with filing and retrieval over many years has resulted in standard rules for alphabetic systems. For instance, ARMA (1986) has made available a forty-page booklet containing their simplified filing standard rules and numerous examples. Textbook references, professional organizations, and equipment suppliers provide similar rules and examples. Depending on the organization of the rules, the number of rules ranges from seven to fifty-two. A succinct version of the standardized rules is listed below. We assume that filing will proceed field-by-field.

Rule 1.1 If a personal name, use the last (surname) as the first field, the first name or initial is the second field, and subsequent names or initials as successive fields. If other than a personal name (business, institution, government, etc.), the first field should be the most commonly used reference.

a. Within each field, ascending order is: (blank, 0, 1, . . . , 9, I, II, III, IV, . . . , A, B, C, . . . , Z), or (blanks, arabic numbers, roman numerals, alphabetic letters).
b. Change all lowercase letters to uppercase.
c. Spell out all symbols (&, $, %, . . . refers to *a*mpersand, *d*ollar, *p*ercent).
d. Omit all punctuation (period, comma, apostrophe, dash, hyphen, etc.). Ignore a hyphen in a hyphenated word and treat its two elements as one field.

Again, the point of any set of rules is to provide consistency in filing and retrieving records. Rule 1.1 can be applied with consistency, but this may prove to be impossible under certain conditions. All filing rules contain ways to deal with exceptions and additional interpretations to ensure that the rules can be applied in all situations. The typical exception and interpretation rules follow, continuing with Rule 1.2.

Rule 1.2 Prefixes and suffixes can be included with the name, used as a separate field, or disregarded. The following table summarizes common practice.

Type	*Rule*	*Examples*
Prefix surname	Include with name, omit any space	D', Da, De la, Mc, St., Van
Suffixes	Separate field, ignore punctuation	II, Jr, CPA, MD, Maj, PhD
Pseudonyms, Royal titles, Religious titles	Separate field, as written	Dr Seuss, King George, Pope John Paul

Rule 1.3 Ambiguous names, foreign names, or nicknames should be filed as regular personal names if a surname field is identifiable; otherwise file as written. In any case, it would be wise to make all appropriate cross-references.

Rule 1.4 Place names or compass terms in business names should be treated as separate fields.

Rule 1.5 In general, ignore articles, conjunctions, and prepositions (the, a, for, of, and, &, etc.).

Rule 1.6 Acronyms or subsidiaries of businesses should be filed as written, with cross-references to parent companies if needed.

Rule 1.7 Following accepted practice (for example, in telephone books), governmental/political material is ordered by the name of the major entity followed by the distinctive name of the department, bureau, branch, etc.

Rule 1.8 Foreign governments are filed by their distinctive or official names as spelled in English.

The goal of the exception rules is to encourage consistency. The overall guide is to classify the record following standard use. For example, if a client signs his checks as "Doc John Rabben," it might be wise to assign "Doc" as his first name. In other words, follow the practice in use. For business and organization names, use the business letterhead or trademark as a guide.

Slavish adherence to any set of rules is not always the most efficient procedure. You must assess the rules in use frequently to determine if they are best suited for filing and retrieval efficiency.

Computer Filing

CBRMSs are used to enhance filing and retrieval of records. A CBRMS does not store the record itself; it stores information about the record, including the fields that classify the record. The software that is used to store and retrieve records uses the same field-by-field method that was described previously. One difference, however, is that most software uses the ASCII (pronounced "as-key") sequence for ordering fields character-by-character (see Rule 1.1a). Figure A.1 shows the ASCII sorting sequence. Note that roman numerals are not considered, and that the upper-case alphabet letters precede the lower-case letters.

Most computer software can be fairly easily instructed to ignore the differences between upper and lower case. This will aid the transition from a manual classification system to a CBRMS. But remember that the computer will follow only those rules in the software; it cannot make exceptions or guess a meaning. In normal operation, assume that the CBRMS should file and retrieve "as written" or, more appropriately, "as entered."

When a CBRMS is contemplated, determine what classification rules the software will support and then carefully review the proposed or existing filing to ensure compatibility.

Figure A.1 ASCII (American Standard Code for Information Interchange) Values and Characters

Value	*Character*	*Value*	*Character*	*Value*	*Character*
32	(space)	64	@	96	
33	!	65	A	97	a
34	"	66	B	98	b
35	#	67	C	99	c
36	$	68	D	100	d
37	%	69	E	101	e
38	&	70	F	102	f
39	'	71	G	103	g
40	(	72	H	104	h
41	)	73	I	105	i
42	*	74	J	106	j
43	+	75	K	107	k
44	,	76	L	108	l
45	–	77	M	109	m
46	.	78	N	110	n
47	/	79	O	111	o
48	0	80	P	112	p
49	1	81	Q	113	q
50	2	82	R	114	r
51	3	83	S	115	s
52	4	84	T	116	t
53	5	85	U	117	u
54	6	86	V	118	v
55	7	87	W	119	w
56	8	88	X	120	x
57	9	89	Y	121	y
58	:	90	Z	122	z
59	;	91	[	123	{
60	<	92	\	124	|
61	=	93	]	125	}
62	>	94	^	126	~
63	?	95	_		

Values less than 32 are not printable characters; typically, they are used as control codes for printer information, for example, ASCII value 10 is often a printer code for LINE FEED (move the paper up one line). Values from 127 and up are used similarly by printers for alternate symbols such as the Greek alphabet, mathematic symbols, etc.

References

Association of Records Managers and Administrators. *Alphabetic Filing Rules* (Prairie Village, Kan.: ARMA, Inc., 1986).

KARDEX, Indexing and Filing Rules. KARDEX Systems, Inc., Marietta, Ohio 44750, undated.

Ricks, Betty R. and Kay F. Gow. *Information Resource Management,* Appendix C—Filing Rules (Cincinnati: South-Western, 1984).

The World Almanac and Book of Facts (New York: Newspaper Enterprise Association, 1987).

Appendix B

Information / Records Management Publications

Administrative Management
Automated Office, Ltd.
1123 Broadway
New York, NY 10010

American Archivist
The Monumental Printing Company
3110 Elm Avenue
Baltimore, MD 21211

Form
National Business Forms Association
300 North Lee
Alexandria, VA 22314

Forms and Systems Professional
North American Publishing Company
401 North Broad Street
Philadelphia, PA 19108

IMC Journal
International Information Management Council
P.O. Box 34404
Bethesda, MD 20817

INFORM
Association for Information and Image Management
1100 Wayne Avenue, Suite 1100
Silver Spring, MD 20910

Journal of Data Management
Data Management Association
505 Busse Highway
Park Ridge, IL 60068

Management World
AMS
4622 Street Road
Trevose, PA 19047

Modern Office Technology
Penton Publishing Company
1100 Superior Avenue
P.O. Box 95795
Cleveland, OH 44114

The Office
Office Publications, Inc.
1600 Summer Street
Stamford, CT 06905

Office Systems
Office Systems, Inc.
941 Danbury Road
Georgetown, CT 06829

Records Management Quarterly
ARMA International, Inc.
4200 Somerset Drive, Suite 215
Prairie Village, KS 66208

The Records and Retrieval Report
88 Post Road West
P.O. Box 5007
Westport, CT 06881

Today's Office
Bob Byrne, Publisher
645 Stewart Avenue
Garden City, NY 11530-9854

Appendix C

Alphabetic Divisions

Alphabetic guides for last-name files have been determined empirically for different levels of division. For example, if you have 25 four-drawer units for standard paper last-name files, then use the 100-division set for preparing the labels for the drawer fronts. For 50 divisions, use every other division from the 100-division set; similarly, almost any level of division can be constructed from the sets.

The following guides have been constructed for standard, United States last-name files and may require adjustments for local differences. To determine appropriate divisions empirically for any set of alphabetic files, first obtain the total length in inches of the files. Suppose, then, that you want X divisions where X might represent the available file drawers. Divide the total inches by X and call this result the division length or DL. In this case, DL should not be less than 30 inches. Then start at the beginning of the actual files and note the name that starts each DL. At the end you will have listed all of your alphabetic divisions.

60 Last name divisions

A	Am	B	Be	Bi
Br	Bu	C	Ch	Co
Cr	D	De	Do	E
F	Fi	G	Gi	Gr
H	He	Ho	Hu	I
J	K	Ki	L	Le
Li	M	Mar	Mc	Me
Mo	Mu	N	O	P
Pe	Pi	Q	R	Ri
Ro	S	Sch	Se	Si
St	Su	T	To	U
V	W	We	Wi	XZY

100 Last name divisions

A	Al	Am	Ander	Ar
B	Bar	Be	Ber	Bi
Bo	Br	Bro	Bu	C
Car	Ch	Cl	Co	Con
Cor	Cr	Cu	D	De
Di	Do	Dow	E	El
Et	F	Fi	Fo	Fr
G	Ge	Go	Gro	H
Ham	Har	Hat	He	Hi
Ho	Hon	Hu	I	J
John	K	Ke	Ki	Kn
L	Le	Li	Lo	M
Man	McA	Me	Mi	Mo
Mu	N	Ni	O	P
Pe	Pi	Pr	QR	Ri
Ro	Ros	S	Sch	Se
Sh	Si	Smith	Sp	St
Sto	T	Tho	Ti	Tr
U	V	W	War	We
Wh	Wi	Wo	XYZ	

150 Last name divisions

A	Al	Am	Ander	Ar
At	B	Baker	Bar	Be
Ber	Bi	Bl	Bo	Bon
Br	Bro	Bu	Bur	C
Car	Cas	Ch	Che	Cl
Co	Con	Coo	Cor	Cr
Cu	D	Davis	De	Del
Di	Do	Dow	Du	E
El	Et	F	Fe	Fi
Fl	Fo	Fr	Fri	G
Gar	Ge	Gi	Go	Gr
Gre	Gro	H	Hal	Ham
Har	Harr	Hat	He	Hen
Her	Hi	Ho	Hol	Hon
Hu	Hun	I	J	John
Jones	K	Ke	Kel	Ki
Kn	Kr	L	Lar	Le
Lei	Li	Lo	Lu	M
Man	Mas	McA	McD	McK
Me	Mi	Miller	Mo	Mor
Mu	N	Ni	O	Or
P	Pe	Pet	Pi	Pr
Pu	QR	Re	Ri	Ro
Ros	Ru	S	Sch	Schm
Se	Sh	Si	Smith	Sn
Sp	St	Sto	Su	T
Te	Tho	Ti	Tr	U
V	Ve	W	Wall	War
We	Wei	Wh	Wi	Williams
Wilson	Wo	Wr	XY	Z

For some applications, it may be useful to have standard divisions for first names. For example, a two-color-code system of last name, first name is efficient for modest applications involving fewer than 100,000 names. The last name major divisions would be color coded into the twenty-six alphabetic intervals (A–Z). The minor or secondary divisions would be by first name and color coded. Because the first name divisions apply only to each of the twenty-six last name sections, they do not need to be extensive. Probably the highest division level would be tens, as given below.

10 First name divisions

AB	C	DEF	GHI	J
KL	MNO	PQR	ST	U–Z

Glossary

acquisitions Records that are acquired by a business, usually through the mail.

active maintenance phase Regular storage and retrieval of active records.

AIIM Association for Information and Image Management.

alphabetic classification system A method for arranging records in which the letters of the English alphabet are used for identifiers.

alphabetic color block An arrangement of colors on a file folder tab in which the colors represent letters.

alphabetic subject system A classification system in which topics are arranged in alphabetical order and subtopics within each category are arranged in alphabetical order.

analysis and design Analysis of a present system in order to establish the requirements for a new system followed by the design of the new system which should produce general and detailed plans.

aperture card A computer keypunch card into which microfilm is inserted.

archives A location for storing inactive, and usually historical, records.

ARMA Association of Records Managers and Administrators.

artificial intelligence The capability of a computer system to simulate human thinking.

audit A regular examination designed to verify that an activity is being carried out according to established procedures and policies.

audit trail Documents and procedures that verify that records functions are being carried out properly.

authoritative style An approach to management in which the manager relies entirely on his or her own judgment for making decisions.

bank-and-space numbering system A method of assigning space by banks (rows) of shelving. Each space is assigned a number according to its bank and shelf. It is similar to the numbering procedure used in the row-unit-shelf (RUS) system.

bar code An information code composed of thirteen to twenty-one bits or bars.

binary code A numeric image on microfilm.

blip coding A method of indexing microfilm, also referred to as image control, that associates each blip (mark) on the film image with a number.

box file Boxes used for storing letter-size or legal-size folders.

budget An estimated plan of operations for the future expressed in financial terms.

CARS *See* computer-assisted retrieval system.

cartridge microfilm A roll of microfilm permanently encased in a cartridge.

CBRMS *See* computer-based records management system.

CD-ROM Compact disk with read-only-memory.

central files A central files storage location, usually for active records.

centralization The placement of all items in one physical location.

Certified Records Manager A designation conferred by the Institute of Certified Records Managers (ICRM) to those who possess appropriate experience and a baccalaureate degree, and who have completed successfully the CRM examination.

chain of command The hierarchy of personnel in a department or business.

charge-back system A method of accounting for costs that charges the costs of using a records center back to the department or individuals that use it.

charge-out form The form used by records centers to keep track of records removed from the records center.

chief information officer (CIO) An information specialist in a corporation who is usually the head of the Information Systems division.

chronological file A classification system in which records are organized according to the date they are created.

CIM *See* computer input microfilm.

classification system A way in which records can be arranged.

client-based system When the primary and vital records of a business are client records. Client records always minimally contain the client name and address.

code dictionary A "dictionary" that defines the codes used in a CBRMS.

code line A method of indexing microfilm that associates lines on the film with lines that appear on a scale next to a computer screen.

coherence The two elements essential to a database are coherence and organization. Coherence means that the data are related to a specific activity or purpose.

color accenting A method of using color to decorate a filing system with different colors for folders, guides, and so forth with no meaning attached to the colors.

color coding The method of using color in a classification system to mean something such as a letter of the alphabet or a number.

color microimaging Filing in color (like color slides).

COM *See* computer output microfilm.

computer-assisted retrieval system A system of retrieving microfilm that integrates micrographics and computer technology.

computer-based records management system A system that involves computer hardware and software to track, report, and query records.

computer input microfilm The transfer of microfilm images to electronic data for input to a computer.

computer output microfilm Microfilm that is produced from computer digital data.

contract programming A system of programs that are custom developed for a particular business or business application.

controlling The management function in which the manager measures how well the objectives have been met and makes adjustments.

copyright The exclusive (and legal) right to publish, produce, or sell an original work.

Copyright Act The act that guarantees the owner of a copyrighted work the exclusive right to reproduce that work for public distribution.

correspondence arrangement The use of an alphabetic classification system for filing correspondence.

cost center A department or division in a business that does not contribute directly to the profits of that business.

CRM *See* Certified Records Manager.

cut The positioning of tabs on a file folder.

DASD *See* direct access storage device.

data Evidence that serves as a basis for decision making, measuring, calculating, or discussion.

database A base of data; a collection of data that forms the basis of an activity, such as names and addresses of customers, that is organized to permit access for multiple purposes.

database function A subset of information processing; the function that allows users to obtain information about records as a group.

database management The planning, controlling, and organizing of a database.

database management system The procedures and software for planning, controlling, management, and organizing of a database.

data processing center The business area that performs the regular processing operations that use computer facilities such as general ledger, accounts payable/receivable, and inventory.

data security and recovery The data component in disaster recovery that is concerned with ensuring the security of the data and recovery should disaster occur.

DBMS *See* database management system.

decentralization The placement of records or other items in two or more different physical locations, such as in different department or division offices.

definition phase The definition of a record for entry into the system.

delimiter A character, such as a space or a comma, that is used to signify the end of a computer filename, command, field, or item.

democratic, or participative, style An approach to management in which the manager encourages staff participation in decision making.

density In micrographics terminology, the degree of light transmission through a film image.

desktop publishing Microcomputer word-processing software that allows the use of fonts, various type sizes, graphics, and sophisticated formatting to produce copy that looks very much like it was typeset.

development and implementation A stage in the systems life cycle in which the hardware, software, and procedures are developed to meet the design requirements. During implementation, the switch is made to the new system within a planned time frame.

digital physical media Magnetic or optical disks and tapes used to store digital information.

direct access storage device A digital physical medium that allows data to be accessed directly.

directing The management function that involves training, supervision, and motivation of personnel.

directory The listing of filenames for files stored on magnetic media or in computer memory.

disaster Any event that removes records from normal accessibility.

disaster plan The policy and procedures to follow if a disaster occurs; specifies exactly what must be done to resume normal operations.

disaster recovery The process that a business goes through to recover its records after a disaster.

disaster stage The fourth and last phase in an organization's records management cycle in which problems with the records management system have become intolerable.

disk density The quality of the coating on a computer disk.

dispersal The practice of making duplicates of records and storing them away from the originals.

distributed records management The general process of integrating the records management of physically distinct locations.

division guide A guide used to divide and label sections in a drawer or of a shelf.

document assembly The process of combining standardized (prewritten) paragraphs into a finished document.

DP library The paper records of a data processing center.

drawer-type suspension file A suspension file that uses a metal frame from which folders hang.

dumb, or graphics, scanner A micrographics device that transfers an image to digital format with no knowledge of the contents of the document and no capacity to process (change) the digital information (text or picture).

duplexing The automatic copying of both sides of an original document without operator intervention.

duplicator In micrographics terminology, equipment capable of duplicating film images.

electronic editing The editing of an image electronically before the actual reprographic process.

emergency plan A plan for those times when a disaster is imminent; that is, when there is a warning of a disaster.

engraving and gravure Two processes that involve the creation of an image through materials removal via etching, carving, or cutting on a metal plate.

ergonomics The science of integrating the physical, physiological, and psychological factors involved in creating work to maximize productivity.

excess costs Those costs that would not be necessary if an efficient records management system were being used.

exit procedure The procedure for handling the records assigned to a particular practitioner who is leaving a firm.

expert system A computer system that allows a user to query a database and, if the answer is not in the database, to ask for and incorporate the answer into the database.

facsimile (fax) A reprographic process that combines a scanner, printer, and synchronous modem to send and receive special format bit-mapped images (graphics or text) over standard telephone lines.

fair use The provision of the Copyright Act that allows a copyrighted work to be copied if the intended use of the copy is for scientific, educational, research, or news reporting purposes and not for monetary gain.

feasibility study A study to determine if it is feasible to implement a system within reasonable resource limitations.

Federal Records Act An act passed in 1950 that focused on the retention, disposal, and storage of federal records.

fee-for-service cost system A method of charging costs generated in a records center.

filename The name given to a computer file, consisting of one or more nodes, that must conform to certain specifications.

file status The operations status of a file, usually based on frequency of use, such as active or inactive.

file type The category of record, such as payroll, or the physical type of record, such as folder or disk.

film record Data, pictures, or text stored on film.

final disposition phase The phase of the records life cycle in which records are defined as obsolete or of secondary value and are destroyed or archived.

firm-privileged records Those records that contain information specific to a particular firm and therefore should not leave the firm.

flash card A method of indexing microfilm similar to using guides in a file drawer.

flat drawer file A file in which records such as maps are filed flat in large, shallow drawers.

flexible disk Also called a floppy disk; a circular piece of pliant mylar plastic coated with a magnetic layer and encased in a jacket.

floor load The amount of weight per square foot that a floor can support without danger of collapsing.

follow-up procedure The process of finding out where records are located after they have passed their return date.

form A printed document on which some information stays the same and other variable information is inserted.

forms analysis The process of determining the purpose for a form and how the form can be improved.

forms analyst A person who analyzes existing and proposed forms.

fourth-generation language (4GL) A programming language that allows the user to structure questions in English language form and that seeks answers to vague or undefined parts of the question.

Freedom of Information Act This act requires federal agencies to release information on request by any person, institution, association, or corporate entity unless that information is exempted from disclosure.

from-this-point conversion A strategy for converting from a manual to a computer-based records management system in which the new system is installed, but the information about the records is entered only as needed and in small batches.

geographic arrangement A method of classifying records in which records are arranged and/or alphabetized by location.

gigabyte (GB) Approximately 1,000,000,000 (1 billion) bytes. (*See* Figure 16.H1.)

global filename character A character that can represent other characters in a computer filename, such as ? (question mark) or * (asterisk).

goals Long-term accomplishments.

growth stage The second phase in an organization's records management cycle, in which the business alters its characteristics and/or increases in size and the requirements for records management increase.

guide A heavy cardboard or plastic divider used to separate and identify sections of a classification system.

guide letter A standardized letter that a writer can use as a guide for composing correspondence.

guide paragraphs Paragraphs written for various situations and provided to writers to use in composing letters or reports.

high-rise unit A form of storage constructed of steel uprights with pressboard shelving that rises several tiers; used to store cartons of records.

Hoover Commission The commission established by President Harry Truman and chaired by former President Herbert Hoover, the purpose of which was to study the organization of the executive branch of the federal government.

identifier A record label; an identifier may be a word or number on a physical label or a computer filename.

image control A method of indexing microfilm, also referred to as blip coding, that associates each blip (mark) on film with a number.

image enhancement A process for making damaged records more readable by removing nonimage blemishes and improving image symbols.

image overlay A reprographics feature that allows multiple originals to be combined on the same copy image. Each additional image added to the original is called an "overlay."

image shift A reprographics feature that allows the user to shift the image that appears on the copy without moving the original.

inactive records Those records that are not accessed frequently; inactive status is defined by the individual business.

incident report The report dealing with a potential criminal incident.

incineration Burning; a method of destroying records.

incomplete information retrieval A problem situation that results from having insufficient information to retrieve a record.

index A listing of record names, labels, or identifiers that contains a pointer to records.

indexing capability In micrographics terminology, the capability of micrographics equipment to automatically number or code film as an image is created.

indexing units Parts of a label; for example, the first part of a person's or company name.

Industry Action Committee A committee comprised of records personnel in a particular field, such as insurance.

information Processed data or data that has been made more meaningful through analysis.

information processing Processing that transforms data into information.

information retrieval The acquisition of information from wherever it is stored.

in-service training Training provided within a department to improve the knowledge and skills of personnel.

intelligent copier A copier that combines data processing, photocopying, duplicating, and phototypesetting technologies.

interview The process of asking an individual to answer questions in a face-to-face situation; used in the process of conducting a records inventory.

inventory control system A system that provides information about inventory, such as quantity on hand, cost, and supplier. In a records management department, this term applies to forms management.

jacketed microfilm A plastic sheet or jacket with pockets or slots for microfilm.

jukebox hardware A device that stores and accesses optical disks in a manner similar to the way a jukebox stores and accesses phonograph records.

key accessory A method for controlling use of a copy machine. A device that must be inserted into the copy machine to activate it.

key word A nonunique word used to describe types of records; the key is used to efficiently search a database for similar categories of records.

lateral file Filing equipment in which folders are arranged across the width of the shelf or drawer.

layered tray file A file that has plastic jackets attached to a flat rack so that the jackets are layered. Records are inserted into the jackets.

Emmett J. Leahy The chairman of the 1947–1949 Paperwork Management Task Force, and the person considered the father of records management.

letterpress printing A printing process used for newspapers and similar printing jobs. It is distinguished by its direct printing operations in which the paper (letter) is pressed against an inked plate.

lexical electronic filing A system for managing word-oriented files in which the files are entered into a computer and accessed as computer files on magnetic or optical media.

library In data processing, a collection of similar modules.

machine downtime The amount of time that the machine is unavailable for use, usually due to malfunction.

magnetic media Data, pictures, or text stored and retrieved through magnetic encoding; typically associated with computers.

maintenance The second phase in the life cycle of a record, in which records are stored and retrieved; also the stage in the systems life cycle in which the system is operating but may need minor adjustments to keep it functioning efficiently.

maintenance stage The first stage in an organization's records management cycle, in which the records management system is adequate and operating with no serious problems.

management The planning, organizing, directing, controlling, and staffing of a process.

microfiche A sheet of film on which reduced images of records are arranged in a grid pattern.

microfilm A roll of film on which reduced images of records are stored.

microform Micrographic media such as microfilm or ultrafiche.

micrographic indexing The process of associating a film image with an identifiable marker for retrieval purposes.

micrographics A technology that records information as miniaturized images on film; also considered a particular field of knowledge.

micropublishing A technology that uses specially designed micrographic equipment to store and retrieve published and unpublished books and manuscripts on microfilm.

mobile shelf unit Shelf filing equipment that moves along tracks on the floor.

module Software that consists of one item, such as a program, table of data, or any single file.

multiple menu system A method for accessing information from a computer that proceeds through a series of menus.

NAGARA National Association of Government Archives and Records Administrators.

naming convention A consistent method for naming computer files within the hardware/software restrictions.

node One part of a computer filename; each node is separated by a "dot," or period, delimiter.

nonflexible disk A type of magnetic media; a disk in a rigid shell or jacket.

nonrecord Evidence that has not been stored or is unstorable.

notch-and-color system A method for coding microfilm jackets for storage and retrieval that uses placement of notches to represent an individual's last name and color strips to represent the first name.

notebook file A file that may be a single three-ring binder in which records are kept or an angled metal rack on which notebook pages are mounted. The latter may be several feet long.

numeric classification system A method of classifying records in which a number is used to identify the record and records are arranged by number.

numeric logbook A listing of numbers in sequential (numerical) order that shows the record name or topic assigned to each number; also called an accession book.

numeric subject system A classification system in which a number is assigned to each topic.

objectives Short-term accomplishments or steps taken to achieve goals.

OCR *See* optical character reader.

odometer A method of indexing microfilm based on the distance "traveled" to the required image.

offset printing A printing operation that prints from one roller, which is offset, to an image roller; quickly produces high volume, excellent quality output.

on-line index and retrieval system A micrographics system that allows both creation of an index for film images and creation of the film images simultaneously with the additional capability of also accessing the index and retrieving the image.

on/off-line index An index to micrographic images that can be accessed directly from the computer screen (on-line) or from printed copy (off-line).

optical character reader A scanner that captures the information content of an image and makes it available to a computer in a digital format.

optical disk document-image system A records management system that stores documents on high-density optical disks and then routes that information electronically to the appropriate people.

optical storage and retrieval The process of storing records on optical disks and retrieving them.

organizational records management cycle The sequence of events that societies, organizations, small businesses, and individuals go through in their attempts to manage records.

organizing The management function in which the manager arranges the tasks, people, and resources to accomplish the objectives set in the planning stage.

OSAR *See* optical storage and retrieval.

out guide A type of file guide that is inserted in place of a folder when the folder is removed.

paper media Any data or information on paper; often used in data processing to mean the hard copy listings of programs and their files.

paper record Data, pictures, or text stored on anything composed of the chemical composition of paper.

Paperwork Management Task Force The task force formed by the Hoover Commission to study the management of federal records.

Paperwork Reduction Act The act that changed the concept of information from a "free good" to a "management resource" to be managed as any other resource and that sought to regulate a wide range of information resources management activities in the federal government.

password A series of characters, numbers, or symbols that allows access to a computer system.

path name The complete file specification composed of the DIRECTORY\SUBDIRECTORY\. . .\filename.

performance evaluation The process of determining how well an individual is performing his or her job.

periodic audit An audit that is performed at a specific, scheduled time at regular intervals.

photo mode An option that adjusts the copy process to capture the tonal gradations (also called halftones), the grays between white and black.

physical inventory An actual hands-on records inventory that counts the physical items.

physical media The actual physical (and tangible) devices on which information is stored; for example, a floppy disk.

pigeonhole file Also called a roll file; these have many small square compartments in which rolled items are stored.

plain-paper reader-printer A type of micrographic reader that allows printing of a displayed image on regular plain paper.

planetary camera A type of camera that films documents on a flat surface.

planning The management function in which the manager establishes objectives and methods to achieve them.

primary guides File dividers made of heavy paper stock that have tabs in the first position.

primary value The original purpose for which a record is kept.

Privacy Act The act that protects the rights of individuals regarding the personal information collected and disseminated about them by federal agencies.

problem exploration Preliminary investigation to determine the scope and objectives of a system.

problem stage The third phase in an organization's records management cycle in which several serious problems in retrieval and disposal of records exist.

processing security Procedures that ensure that essential data processing could continue during disaster recovery.

programmable database A database management system that allows programming to customize storage and retrieval procedures.

professional office An office that provides medical, legal, or other professional services to clients.

Project ELF A program sponsored by ARMA to *e*liminate *l*egal-size *f*iles in government and industry and to establish letter-size paper as the standard for records.

project team A group of individuals who work together to put a computer-based system into operation.

public domain A classification for records and software that are not copyrighted or for which the copyright has expired.

pulverization The cutting or pounding of a document into minute particles; a method of destroying records.

purge A check of records and removal of those items, both record and nonrecord, that do not belong in a system.

query A request for information; often a question; an important element of a database.

random audit An audit that is scheduled to take place within a certain time period but on no particular date.

readability An attribute of written material determined by using a standardized formula to ascertain how much education a person must have to be able to read the written passage.

reader A type of micrographic equipment used for reading microfilm or microfiche.

reader-filler A type of micrographic equipment that allows reading of microfilm, selection and cutting of frames, and automatic insertion (filling) of the film sections into microfilm jackets.

record Evidence of an event that is in a tangible format that allows it to be stored and retrieved.

records analyst A person who assesses the value (or classification) of a record or the information in the record and who sometimes serves as liaison with other departments in a company regarding records needs.

records center A centralized facility for bulk long-term storage and retrieval of inactive records.

records clerk The person who files and retrieves records.

records information system An information flow that consists of specific stages related to the functions of records management.

records inventory The identification of records and equipment by type, location, quantity, and so forth.

records management The planning, staffing, organizing, directing, and controlling of records and those processes associated with records.

records management operation A process, such as micrographics, that is performed in a records management department.

records manager The manager of an entire records management operation.

records purge The checking of records and removal of records that do not belong in a system.

records retention schedule A listing of records or record series showing the status for their storage and/or destruction.

records security The process of controlling the access to records.

records technician A person who has a particular skill to operate records equipment.

reduction ratio The image size produced on microfilm in relation to the original size of a document.

relative index An alphabetical listing that shows the number assigned to a particular name or topic.

reprographics A records management operation that includes any type of reproduction function, such as photocopying or printing; also considered a particular field of knowledge that includes the management of personnel, equipment, and procedures used for reproduction processes.

request for proposal A proposal for bids submitted to a number of vendors. The proposal is a description of what the business wants the system to do.

resolution The amount of detail and contrast in microfilm images.

retention scheduling The process of determining how long records should be retained and the method to be used for their disposal.

retrieval handle In general, the name that is used to access an entity. In a CBRMS, the DESCRIPTION items (CODE, LINE, KEY WORDS) are the ways that the record can be retrieved.

rod-type suspension file A suspension file that uses a rod from which single records hang.

roll microfilm A roll of film on which reduced images of records are stored.

root directory The main directory in a tree-structured directory.

rotary camera A type of camera capable of feeding and filming documents at high speed.

rotary file Filing equipment in which the contents are accessed by turning the file.

rotational data Backup of computer data on tape (both business data and applications programs), which is rotated through secure off-site storage.

row-unit-space (RUS) system A system used for assigning numbers to the storage spaces available in a records center.

SAA The Society of American Archivists.

scanner A micrographics device that converts an image into digital format.

screen, or silk screen printing A printing process that can reproduce color and graphic images on a wide variety of surfaces such as metal, glass, cloth, and paper.

secondary guides File dividers made of heavy paper stock that have tabs in the second position.

secondary value The value of a record in addition to its original purpose (primary value) or after its primary value has expired.

sequential numbering A method of indexing microfilm based on the sequential number of the image starting from 0000.

service center A business that provides a particular records management service for an organization.

shared expertise The hiring of one records management expert by two or more cooperating organizations.

shelf file Filing equipment in which folders or other items are arranged on shelves.

shelving address system A method for assigning the spaces on shelving in a records center based on the row number and the number of boxes the shelving will hold.

shredding The cutting of a document into thin strips or pieces; a method of destroying records.

site license Permission to make sufficient copies of software to use at a particular site (location).

software piracy The practice of copying software illegally.

span of authority The areas or activities over which a manager has control.

span of control The number of employees supervised by a manager.

spindle file A thin, upright spike on which papers are impaled.

SQL *See* structured query language.

stacks-on-steel A type of shelving for storing records. Stacked cardboard drawers supported by a steel framework.

staffing The management function that involves selecting personnel to accomplish an activity.

standardization Uniformity in records management practices and equipment.

step-and-repeat camera A type of camera that films documents in a grid pattern to produce microfiche.

storage phase The phase in which records are defined as inactive, obsolete, or of secondary value and are moved to low-cost storage facilities.

straight numeric system A classification system in which records are arranged sequentially from the lowest number to the highest.

structured directory A computer directory that contains paths to other directories and subdirectories.

structured query language A nonprocedural language that specifies the desired results rather than how to get the results.

subdirectory A subgrouping in a directory that consists of a collection of files. Only the root directory cannot be a subdirectory.

survey questionnaire A method of doing research; used in records management for taking a records inventory.

suspension file A file on which items hang suspended from a frame or rod.

system enhancement A significant addition to a computer system that will improve the quality of operations.

system query A request for information from a database; often the query is phrased as a question.

system report A CBRMS report that describes the status of its records in terms of their location and characteristics.

system shell A CBRMS installed without the record information. The system operates as a shell with all of the processes but without all of the information.

systems life cycle The steps or stages in the development of a computer-based records management system.

telecommunications The transmission of information in visual, audio, or hard copy form via telephone lines.

telereprographics A combination of telecommunications and reprographics technologies (for example, facsimile).

terminal-digit system A classification system in which the last digit in a series designates the major storage division.

tickler file A classification system in which records are arranged according to the date on which some action must be taken on them.

transfer procedure The method for transferring records to a records center.

transient patient A patient who does not live in the area and who is unlikely to become a regular patient.

trashing The destruction of records by ordinary trash removal.

tree-structured directory A computer directory that branches to other directories and subdirectories.

turnkey system A computer equipment and software system that is so complete the user simply has to "turn the key" to get started.

ultrafiche Film that is physically similar to microfiche but with much smaller images.

ultrastrip A strip of film with extremely reduced images.

unity of command The number of superiors to which an individual employee reports.

vanilla system A minimal or least configuration of software or computer equipment for a particular purpose.

vertical file A filing method (also equipment) in which records are stored in an upright position (on edge).

videotext Displayed digital media; for example, the image on a computer screen display; also referred to as "vidtex" or "vidtext."

virtual central records The situation in which records are not centralized physically in one location but are accessible through telecommunications as if they were centralized.

vital processing The records processing that is absolutely essential to the operation of a business.

vital records Those records that are indispensable to the operation of a business. Vital records are very difficult to replace if lost.

vital records program A program for protecting vital records that includes equipment, personnel, and procedures.

weekend conversion The process of converting to a CBRMS in which everything is stopped in the old system and the new system is started up after all the information is entered; usually takes place over a weekend.

wild card character A character that is used in a filename to represent other characters. Computers usually recognize * (asterisk) and ? (question mark) as wild card characters.

window A space on a computer screen that "opens up" and overlays the text on the screen so that some data can be used while another file is being processed.

word processing The creation of text-based records, usually through a computer.

WORM *See* write-once-read-many.

write-once-read-many The capability of an optical disk to be written once and read many times.

Index